Don't Look Back 'Cause There's Nobody There

Seven Continents

Seven Marathons

One Runner

by

Ken Volk

Otter Bay Books
BALTIMORE, MD 2011

Please direct all correspondence and book orders to:
Ken Volk
10796 Grande Blvd.
West Palm Beach, FL 33412

Library of Congress Control Number 2010942587
ISBN 978-0-615-42964-9

Published for the author by
Otter Bay Books, LLC
3507 Newland Road
Baltimore, MD 21218-2513

Printed in the United States of America

Dedication

To my wife, Diane,
who has been at my side for 47 years.
My best friend, the love of my life.

To our children and their spouses:
Judd and Debbie; Derek and Amy;
Allison and Drew.

And to our grandchildren:
Dylan, Mariah, Ethan, Lilly, Emily, Brian,
Max, Serena, Amanda and Zachary,
for whom this memoir
was written.

I can't imagine
a person becoming a success
who doesn't give this game of life
everything he's got.

WALTER CRONKITE

Table of Contents

In The Beginning....

What in the world is a middle-aged man with asthma and a chronic lung condition doing running marathons all over the world? I'll tell you.

I had the luckiest and happiest of childhoods. World War II was in full bloom, and my dad – thanks to the classified contributions he was making on the Home Front – had been declared exempt from the draft. So for my first five years I was an only child . . . and then for the next five, I shared my parents with my younger brother, Roger. When Douglas was born in 1948, our family was complete.

Thankfully, the war ended in 1945 and everything was good. The economy flourished as the homecoming GI's sought housing for their new families. During these heady years, the GI Bill made it possible for our returning servicemen and women to attend college. Life seemed perfect, except for one disturbing fact: The Red Sox couldn't win a World Series!

But we loved them anyway. As a businessman with two partners in a fast-growing Boston-area corrugated box manufacturing company, my father insisted that the company purchase four Red Sox season tickets for every Sunday, night and holiday game. The highlight of the year for me was Patriots Day, on which the good citizens of Massachusetts commemorated Paul Revere's ride from Boston to Hopkinton to warn that the "Redcoats are coming!" Patriots Day meant two things: A Red Sox doubleheader with the hated New York Yankees and the running of the famous Boston Marathon, the nation's oldest.

It was quite a spectacle. Traditionally, Red Sox management would allow the fans to leave between games to walk the three blocks to Kenmore Square to watch as the marathoners plodded through Mile 24 of the race on their way to Copley Square. The elite runners had passed through long before the first game ended, of course, and the remaining participants (or at least those who were still erect and moving) could be better described as "reeling" than "running". Side to side they went, pitching and yawing dangerously, as the crowd cheered them on with encouragement. Even as an eight-year-old, I wondered why on earth anyone would ever do such an idiotic thing as run 26.2 miles!

It took me almost three decades to answer that question.

Some background: In 1968 my father and I launched a brand-new, startup corrugated box business in Biddeford, Maine. (His original box business had been sold to an integrated corrugated box manufacturer.) As his partner, I moved to Portland, Maine that same year – along with my wife Diane and our 18-month-old son, Judd. The new company was called Volk Packaging Corporation, and I was delighted with my role as the "inside guy" responsible for personnel and production. My father, the tireless and endlessly enthusiastic Ben Volk, was "Mr. Outside" – based on his terrific sales ability and his many contacts in the business world. His mantra, which he preached to me and our sales force constantly, was a simple one: "Our customers are our bread and butter!"

Establishing a new factory was a real challenge, and there were plenty of sleepless nights. We worked hard, however, and we were soon making good progress. But then one afternoon early in 1969, a shadow fell over my world. While sitting at my desk doing paperwork, I felt a sharp pain in my chest. It scared me and for good reason: In March of the previous year – and only three months before we were to commence operations at our new factory – my dad had experienced a severe heart attack and we almost lost him. On that occasion, Diane and I had returned home to our apartment in Swampscott, Massachusetts, whereupon Judd's baby sitter told us that my mother had just called and needed us right away.

My folks lived only a mile distant, so we sped across town to find my father writhing in pain with a black complexion, very little blood pressure and in the midst of a major coronary attack. He was next to death. But my mother had maintained her composure long enough to call a doctor who lived up the street, and he was already on the scene administering an injection to alleviate my father's pain. Luckily for my dad, as he was being rushed to the nearest hospital in Lynn, Massachusetts, a cardiologist who'd been called by the doctor attending him at home was following the ambulance as it arrived at the emergency entrance.

This fortunate sequence of events saved his life, since he received immediate attention from a board-certified cardiologist. But it was three months before he could resume daily activity and begin work. I think it important to mention here that this attack was almost entirely "stress-related". The pressures on my father had been enormous as he worked at securing the financing, locating a site, designing a building and ordering the equipment for the new facility. Psychologically, he was playing for some very high and very stressful stakes – because this enterprise was to be his dream come true, an arrangement whereby he and his three sons could be in business and work together toward a common goal.

As you might expect, I deeply admired my father's dedication to his family. As a youngster, I'd had no idea what particular career I might eventually choose. But I always knew the answer when people asked, "What are you going to do when you grow up?" It was always: "Whatever my father is doing!"

Given my strong emotional attachment to my father and my reaction to his heart attack, I was very attuned and sensitive to my own chest pains when they occurred. I headed to a cardiologist in Portland who ran all of the usual tests and proclaimed me healthy – in spite of the huge amounts of coffee I regularly ingested. He asked me what type of exercise I did, and when I told him I skied, played golf and bowled, he scoffed and asked me again: "What type of exercise do you do?"

Feeling more than a little insulted, I told him that I'd just answered his question. Then I asked him what *he* recommended in the way of exercise, and he promptly suggested that I should "go run."

Well, I went straight home, laced on a pair of sneakers . . . and loped along for exactly one block before running out of breath and stopping. But I loved it, and my running career had begun! Each night I would return home from work, lace up, and head out for a run. As my distances increased, however, I found it inconvenient to run in the evening – since my family would be waiting for me to return and shower before we sat down to dinner together each evening. So I began to run early in the morning before heading off to work.

There were very few runners in those days, which meant I was a real oddity whenever anyone saw me on the road. I persevered, though, and being the "Type A" personality that I am – as a man who's always been powerfully motivated to complete any self-assigned task – I soon became addicted to my runs and began to build up my distances and stamina, even though I was occasionally forced to take time off due to various injuries.

For the next few years I continued to run frequently, and then in 1976 the Y.M.C.A. and the Jewish Community Center of Portland banded together to create a running program called Lifeline. The program called for running one minute at first and building up to a ten-minute run after ten weeks. Then it continued through another ten-week stretch, until most participants were able to run for 20 minutes without effort. Ten individuals signed up for the program. While I was already running for more than 20 minutes per outing, I welcomed the program . . . since it seemed likely to prevent some of the injuries I'd been incurring. It also brought me some new friends with whom I could run.

As the months passed, the activity became increasingly popular, and within two years the "running craze" was in full bloom. Suddenly, there were runners all over the city at all hours of the day and evening. A running organization, The Maine Track Club, had been formed and I was a charter member. And most importantly of all, we were about to witness the inaugural year (1978) of The Casco Bay Marathon. That was a thrilling prospect, and as members of the club, many of us volunteered to serve as unpaid staffers who would help with the logistics.

It was an unforgettable event. Of course, the previous 30-plus years had brought many changes to the conditioning and quality of marathoners – and simply watching these hardy souls run past me got me so excited that I vowed to run in the 1979 Marathon. Nor was I alone in my determination to take part: When I returned to the gym for my run the next morning, I found myself surrounded by a platoon of fellow-runners who had decided the very same thing.

And thus began my Marathon Odyssey.

Casco Bay Marathon

NORTH AMERICA - OCTOBER 21, 1979

First, a disclaimer. If you're expecting to read a *Chariots of Fire* suspense story in which leads continually change hands and I eventually "break the tape" at the finish line, then please put this book down immediately. As you'll discover in the pages ahead, I never overtook anyone in any of my races . . . and I'm still not sure if I was passing that water buffalo on the cover of this volume, or if it was actually passing *me*!

Anyway, here's what happened. With a full year to prepare, I gradually began the build-up to a 26.2 mile run. First step: As soon as the applications were available, I applied so as to cement my commitment. I was so eager to run a marathon that my application was only the fifteenth to be received – as attested by my "singlet" number, 15. (Later, when I joked to several friends that I'd been "seeded 15th" in the event, a couple of them actually bought it!)

Next I went on a strict, no-martini diet, and as I slowly increased my daily training, the weight began to melt off. It certainly helped that I had ample company during the training period. Among marathoners in training, you see, a "herd mentality" usually prevails. Example: If someone were running long on a particular day, then all of us felt that we had to run long. (No one wanted to be the "shirker" or to fall behind in the training.)

Six days a week, rain or shine, we ran throughout the spring and summer. That's the type of commitment it takes if one is to complete a 26.2-mile run. The training involved a gradual increase in daily running time of about 10 minutes per week, and the full-time regimen officially started three months prior to Marathon Day . . . with a final 20-mile run two weeks prior to the event.

That was the formal schedule, anyway. But because we wanted to establish a good foundation from which to start our training, the conditioning build-up began in earnest right away. The plan was to complete two long runs during the week, with the lengthiest event set for one of the weekend days. The mid-week runs began at the University of Maine gymnasium in Portland and offered a multitude of routes. One of the most beautiful was called the "Prom to Prom" run.

To understand why, it helps to visualize the local geography. Portland is located on the Atlantic seaboard and provides shippers with the second deepest port on the east coast. Relying on that depth, large oil tankers often pull into the docks to offload their contents and then ship them directly to Canada via a pipeline. The Western Promenade section of the port (obviously facing west) is a residential area, and is dotted with aging, stately homes of brick and stone. Not many years ago, these increasingly decrepit homes were very difficult to sell; you couldn't even give them away. They lacked insulation, and the cost of heating them was prohibitive. Residents took to shutting off entire sections of these moldering domiciles, simply to cut costs.

So much for the western side of the port. But the Eastern Promenade hadn't fared much better; for many years, it had been considered the "low-rent district". The multi-storied homes, mostly constructed out of wood, were equally run-down and in great need of repair, and they faced the same problems that confronted the homes on the Western Promenade: worn-out insulation and high energy costs.

But the "bad old days" along the Portland harbor were now a part of history. In recent years, just before I began running through the neighborhoods, many of the homes on both the Eastern and Western Promenades had been beautifully rehabbed; now they were status symbols that spoke of gracious living in Portland.

As a runner, it was a real pleasure to make your way across this gorgeous landscape . . . especially if you set out before dawn for what we called the "sunrise run". When we ran along the Eastern Promenade, high above the city and overlooking the sparkling waters of Casco Bay, we tried to time our runs so that we would arrive at the top of the Eastern Prom just as the sun was making its first appearance over the land mass of the United States.

There it was – a huge yellow ball rising majestically above Portland and the rocky coast of Maine! Absolutely spectacular, and inspiring us to feel that anything was possible.

As the training progressed, my 10-year-old son Derek began to show a modicum of interest in my daily running. When I mentioned that a local restaurant was sponsoring a three-mile run in downtown Portland, he asked if we could run it together. You bet we could! The runners were to begin at the bottom of the Eastern Promenade, then zip up a hill and take off on a beautiful ramble along the Prom and then back to downtown Portland.

I jumped at the opportunity to be with my son, and we decided to run it together. Prior to the race I explained the value of pacing and how all the participants needed to run "within themselves". Derek appeared to understand, but as soon as the gun sounded he was off like a gazelle. (So much for pacing and running within one's capabilities!) At first he seemed to be running very well, as we made our way down Commercial Street (said to be the only street in America where one could get hit by a bus, boat, automobile or train!), but as we reached the bottom of the hill leading up to the

Promenade, I could see that his breathing was becoming labored.

No problem. We simply stopped and walked for a short stretch until he caught his breath . . . while I explained to him that walking *wasn't* a crime and that it was nothing to be ashamed of. (I also pointed out that he was entitled to some "slack" as the youngest entrant in the race.) Up the hill we went and he ran beautifully for the rest of the way.

As we neared the finish line and it came into view, Derek took off in a sprint to the cheers of the crowd. He barely nosed me out at the tape and finished in 134th place (out of a total of 138 runners), with a time of 30:41. He'd averaged not much more than 10 minutes per mile – and that was a time to be proud of. I clocked in nine seconds behind him but also finished with a big smile. And why not? It was a wonderful way to spend time with my son.

But then things became more difficult. When the pace of conditioning intensified and the weekly ten-mile runs every Tuesday and Thursday were combined with increased mileage on the weekends, I found myself growing short-tempered and edgy. The training was really wearing me down, but the peer pressure from my fellow runners and the intense desire to accomplish my goal kept me on track. My conditioning was improving by the day; my weight was dropping into the low 180s, and my running times had improved from about a nine-minute average mile to the low eight-minute range. Increasingly, I felt capable of conquering anything that came my way.

Wrong, again! What I didn't realize, of course, was that my stern conditioning regimen had begun to take its toll on my psyche. The grind was slowly wearing me out – and it was also beginning to put some major wear and tear on Diane and the kids.

Diane and I had been married for 16 years, and we'd always done very well together. In all that time, I don't think we'd had more than five arguments. These disagreements had been fairly mild – more like animated "discussions" than actual fights – and looking back, I think it's quite likely that I was wrong in all five!

EVERYBODY LOVES
BOXES
PACKAGING CORP.
MAINE
VOLK

Suddenly our disagreements were becoming more frequent, however, due to the marathon pressure that was weighing me down. On one occasion, for example, we got into a brief squabble over our son Judd's rapidly approaching Bar Mitzvah. That momentous event was set for November, only a few weeks after the marathon, and I found that I simply couldn't focus on it. One evening when Diane wanted to discuss making arrangements for a photographer, I lost my patience for the discussion and told her in no uncertain terms that whatever she wanted to do was fine. "Just tell me what time to show up!"

I was totally unreasonable, and once I had come to my senses, I apologized. All at once I realized that the words coming out of my mouth were those of a very tired and irrational individual . . . and I decided to rectify the situation by cutting my training regimen back from six to five days per week. I would continue to run the two mid-long runs during the week and the long one over the weekend – but I would also make the time to recharge my batteries by scheduling a couple of "down" days.

Soon after beginning our training period, my running partners and I decided to enter the Bowdoin 10 Mile Run to the Coast and Back. It was to be a good example of coupling training with competition in a mid-level mileage run – and also a chance to enjoy what seemed on its surface to be an appealing trek across a pretty landscape. However, with the daybreak came stifling heat. I'd hoped to finish the run in 85 minutes and considered any time over 100 minutes a disaster.

But at the five-mile mark my legs were like jelly, so I went into what I refer to as my "survival shuffle". The runners had taken off at the Bowdoin College football field and then sped out of Brunswick toward the ocean. There was absolutely no shade to protect us from the boiling sun. Nonetheless, I was preoccupied with achieving the time I wanted and got caught up in the idea of running eight-minute-plus miles. Big mistake! It was "one leg in front of the other" for the final five miles with the local observers hosing runners down as they passed. (Anything to try to keep cool.) My official time was 1:40:01, only a tenth of a second over the 100-minute mark.

Sitting in the middle of the Bowdoin football field with a hose gushing ice-cold water on my head, I felt as if I'd undergone an amputation of my lower body. To make matters worse, if that were possible, I was also suffering from "runner's nipples". This affliction is caused by the friction of the singlet against the sweating body. It sounds trivial at first, but a runner's nipples can become sensitive to the point of actually bleeding. It's very painful, but I considered it another lesson learned. From then on I would put Vaseline on my nipples prior to every run, and the problem was permanently eliminated.

Make no mistake: I was really hurting after this demanding run. Describing my condition, Diane pointed out that I made little sense in our post-event discussion. I was zombie-like and I can't remember ever feeling so bad after a run. It was my first experience with dehydration and a good learning tool for the future. (Lesson: Remember to take water whenever it's offered!)

When they handed me my certificate, I immediately passed it on to Diane, telling her that it was "too heavy to hold." Then I slept for the entire afternoon and awoke feeling refreshed, if not very confident about my running ability. It doesn't take much to shatter a runner's confidence, and I dreaded the thought of having to return to the gym on Monday for another run. But the following morning I arrived there at 5:30 a.m. for a short, three-mile lope which brought that old confidence back. I was quite relieved.

During the training for the Casco Bay Marathon, I kept a daily diary. I would dictate my thoughts into a tape recorder and one of the secretaries in my office would then transcribe them for me. Later, while working on this book, I came upon my entry of September 24, which struck me as an apt metaphor for my life and my outlook in general. I had written: "This morning I think that my brother Doug summed up my feelings about this training grind and my general outlook by asking me one simple question.

"As we started running this morning, everyone was commenting about how they ached after yesterday's run, and Doug asked me how my legs felt, whereupon I told him that they felt just fine. He then looked at me and said, 'Don't you ever complain about anything?' I am just so happy to be able to run like I am and to have lost all of the weight that I have that I really don't feel that I have anything to complain about. I think that I am on a perpetual high."

To this day, I think that diary entry perfectly describes my general attitude. I feel like I'm the luckiest guy in the world, with a wonderful wife, three great children and, as I write this, ten grandchildren! My glass is always half-full.

The White House

OCTOBER 4, 1979

As my company grew and prospered, I became involved – albeit in a peripheral way – in the State of Maine's industrial development program.

In addition to being very interesting, my participation gave me some insight into what was happening regarding companies moving into or out of the state or relocating within Maine itself. (Let's face it: A little advance knowledge also helped at times in our company's securing a new account!) Serving as a volunteer in this program allowed me to "do some good for Maine," while also benefiting personally – so it was a "win-win situation" for everyone involved.

Here's what happened: Governor James Longley had appointed me as one of the founding members of The Maine Capital Corporation, and I was elected its Treasurer. Maine often has a difficult time convincing companies, both large and small, to relocate in the state. Its energy costs are high, for one thing, and its transportation costs when shipping nationally are prohibitive – since every shipment can move in only one basic direction: west.

In addition, the state has traditionally been run by a very labor-friendly Democratic legislature which to this day doesn't have a clue about what it takes to operate a successful business. Both the state House and Senate are dominated by individuals whose business experience is limited to, say, running a variety store on the Canadian border . . . while employing only a wife and/or a daughter as its only full-time workers. In this commonly observed scenario, the politico's primary income comes mostly from his job at the Statehouse.

Not exactly a scintillating recipe for industrial development, you must admit.

Recognizing that unhappy fact, the governor pushed to have legislation passed that would create The Maine Capital Corporation and the task of choosing its members fell to the governor. Six businessmen from across the state were appointed, and our charge was to raise $1 million from Maine businesses, individuals, banks and insurance companies. These funds would then be lent as "seed money" – an enticement for a firm to move to Maine.

The system actually worked rather well. We proved to be quite successful and contrary to generally established norms for venture capital lending, we were actually instrumental in funding six very successful Maine companies – two of which eventually became *public* companies. We had leveraged the $1 million with $4 million more from the federal government's Small Business Administration, and we paid it all back with a profit to the investors when we liquidated the company. Understandably enough, we were all very proud of ourselves!

So far, so good. And then things got really interesting. During the course of one of the Maine Capital meetings, one of my partners mentioned that he'd been invited to The White House to meet with Jimmy Carter. He explained that President Carter was conducting a series of town hall meetings with business and civic leaders from across the nation, in order to help build momentum for the implementation of the proposed SALT II Treaty between the United States and the Soviet Union.

Carter hoped that by influencing prominent individuals at the various local levels and having them return home to expound on his message (along with contacting their representatives in Congress), he could create a groundswell of support. That sounded good to me, and with nothing to lose, I returned to my office and sent a nice letter to President Carter asking if I could attend one of his meetings.

The answer was a resounding "yes." On September 18th I received a letter from the Secretary of State, Cyrus Vance, inviting me to participate "along with a consortium of distinguished Maine business, civic, and world affairs organizations, in a conference on 'U.S. Security and the Soviet Challenge.'"

This was quite thrilling, of course, but I was a bit disappointed to learn that the conference had been scheduled for The Red Coach Grill in Portland. For some time, I'd been imagining myself sitting in the Lincoln Room in the White House and offering wise counsel to a grateful president.

Somehow, The Red Coach Grill seemed like a step down from 1600 Pennsylvania Avenue! Still, after eventually overcoming my disappointment, I did manage to make the all-day conference. And indeed, the event turned out to be extremely interesting . . . especially when we discovered that the day's activities were to be capped by a speech by The Honorable Paul C. Warnke, the former Director of the U.S. Arms Control and Disarmament Agency and the former Chief U.S. Negotiator for the Strategic Arms Limitations Talks.

Soon after the conference in Portland, I received the following Western Union Mailgram, dated September 26:

> *On behalf of the President, I am pleased to invite you to a briefing regarding the Strategic Arms Limitation Agreement (SALT II). The briefing will be held on Thursday, October 4, 1979 in the East Room of the White House. The briefing will begin promptly at*

2:00 p.m. A reception will follow in the State Dining Room of the White House.

The briefing will be conducted by the President and by Dr. Harold Brown, the Secretary of Defense.

Please respond to The White House Social Secretary at (202) 456-7787. If you will be attending, the Social Secretary will need your Social Security number and date of birth.

You will enter The White House via the southwest gate. We look forward to seeing you on October 4.

–Anne Wexler, Assistant to the President

Needless to say, it didn't take me long to respond affirmatively to her invitation.

I was eager to attend, and not only for reasons of state. As it turned out, the day following the White House conference (October 5) was the thirteenth birthday of our oldest son, Judd. His Bar Mitzvah was scheduled for the following month . . . and the more I thought about that salient fact, the more interested I became in trying to see if I could somehow involve the White House in Judd's once-in-a-lifetime spiritual celebration as a young man who was at last coming of age!

As I meditated on how I might include Judd in the White House conference, I was also thinking about photos. I doubted that picture-taking would be allowed, due to security concerns. (Diane, meanwhile, was hoping photos would be permitted . . . and she was also just a tad miffed that I hadn't asked if *she* could attend, immediately after being invited to the Presidential powwow!)

Not to worry, however. From Portland City Manager John Menario, I soon learned that he *had* been allowed to take photos during his own recent Presidential encounter – and that he'd gotten some vivid images of President Carter. That sounded very promising . . . maybe I could get a shot of Judd's dad shaking hands with the leader of the free world. Regardless, it was a very nice "bonding moment" for me and my son, when I kissed him goodnight (a daily ritual with all our kids) and told him that I'd be meeting with the President the next day. During our exchange, I also asked if it would "be okay to invite Mr. Carter to your Bar Mitzvah."

Of course, I also warned Judd that he would undoubtedly be "upstaged" at the service and the later celebration, if the President decided to attend. Really, he could hardly expect to be "the star of the show" with Jimmy Carter among the well-wishers. Ever the pragmatist, Judd replied with characteristic humility: "It's okay, dad. If the President comes, I won't mind taking second place!"

The next morning, October 4th, I awoke at 4:30 and took off on an abbreviated run of only four miles. (I was still in training, and I hated to miss even a single day.) Then it was off to the airport for the first flight to Washington, D.C. with my trusty camera in hand.

It was an exciting adventure, to be sure. For starters, I was very pleased to be meeting up with an old pal – John Goshko, who'd been my best friend's brother during my high school days in Swampscott. John was a reporter at the Washington *Post,* and by now was serving as the paper's Pentagon correspondent. He'd led a very interesting life after graduating from the University of Pennsylvania (where he'd also helped me to become a member of the undergraduate student body, since he was a high-ranking editor on the student-run *Daily Pennsylvanian* and had some clout with the Dean of Admissions).

John was a terrific journalist, and I'd watched his career unfold with a great deal of interest. Example: During one high-profile reporting stint in South America, he'd been given exactly 24 hours to vacate Peru by that country's angry government, after penning a series of unflattering articles that criticized the ruling dictatorship.

He'd also traveled across South America with Pope John XXIII . . . before returning home to cover the State Department and the Department of Defense.

John was a walking encyclopedia on the ways of the federal government, and it was a real treat to be able to join him for lunch at the Sans Souci, one of the capital's most popular restaurants. It was quite a heady experience, to be exploring the huge working mechanism of one of the country's finest newspapers, and also the one that had been credited with uncovering the story of the Watergate break-in. That famous *exposé* had led to the resignation of President Richard M. Nixon and it had earned high praise for the reporters who'd broken the story. David Broder, the nationally renowned columnist and ubiquitous television guest, was at the next desk; the executive editor, Ben Bradlee, was very visible in his office behind glass walls, and Bob Woodward and Carl Bernstein even stopped by to say hello. We were joined at lunch by Bob Kaiser, the current Moscow correspondent, who would also be attending the White House Conference. Schooled by these top journalistic pros, I was soon armed with the cutting-edge background information I needed to understand the policymaking nuances that were sure to be addressed at the White House.

With lunch concluded, I took a leisurely but somewhat anxious walk to 1600 Pennsylvania Avenue and its Southwest Gate. I was still nervous about being able to bring a camera along, but after the White House security people asked me to confirm the information they'd previously requested, I was admitted to a large foyer. Here a circular stairway led upstairs to what I guessed was the East Room. My hosts were very gracious, and when they asked if there was anything they could do for me, I requested directions to the nearest restroom. No problem: I was sent to a nearby room in which the well-known Presidential "fireside chats" and photo ops with foreign dignitaries are held. Behind the fireplace which is so visible in these photo ops was a hidden bathroom – a discovery that made me feel like a real "insider," since I now knew a secret place in the most famous house in the world!

After doing my business, I rushed back to the foyer, hoping that the group had not yet been allowed upstairs. And my wish was granted; the visitors were still milling about. I moved in close to the staircase, and was in good position to lead the way upstairs and then hopefully secure a front-row seat. And that's exactly what happened. I wound up sitting just to the right of the lectern, and right beside the mayor of Solon, Ohio. After shaking his hand, I told him that I hoped to ask the President a question. If I succeeded in that quest, would he take a picture with my camera? The mayor was very gracious – while pointing out that he, too, wanted to ask a question. If he did, would I please take *his* photo? You bet! (One hand washes the other, as my dad used to say.)

I was happy to agree to this arrangement, of course. But then I found myself wondering: Would the two of us be competing against one another in a battle to get the President's attention first? It's a terrible thing to admit . . . but the truth is that the mayor was afflicted with a noticeable limp, and I couldn't help thinking: *Okay, I'm in "marathon shape," and he's been slowed down – and if I have to, I'm sure I can jump out front to get the President's attention faster than he can!*

(Pretty shameless, eh? But one way or another, I was determined to get that photo!)

The conference was opened by Dr. Harold Brown, the Secretary of Defense, who also served as moderator. After a short speech by Secretary Brown and a question-and-answer session, we heard the familiar words, "Ladies and Gentlemen, the President of the United States." I had been in the White House for tours on a couple of previous visits to the capital, but the thought of standing in the East Room in the presence of the leader of the free world gives me goose bumps even to this day. I'd also met President Kennedy when he was a senator and I owned an autographed photo of him with my mother and my brother Roger, but this was really special!

President Carter spoke for about 20 minutes. He outlined the reasons why he supported the ratification of SALT II and told the gathering at the outset that he'd be taking questions at the conclusion of his talk. All at once I understood what it was like to be a White House correspondent at a Presidential press conference. To say that I was an eager questioner is putting it mildly. At every pause, uncertain as to whether the President had concluded his remarks, I launched what I came to call my "presidential jump-up." Like a human jack-in-the-box, I kept springing upward and then just as quickly retreating. President Carter did notice me on a couple of occasions, but there was no acknowledgement on his part. At last he finished his prepared speech and took his first couple of questions – from the center and the left side of the room.

Fully energized now, I kept on jumping . . . until he finally motioned to me and intoned: "I'll get you next." I didn't have a heart monitor with me, but I can assure you that my pulse had leapfrogged from a normal resting rate of 58 beats per minute to the mid-100's. Why was I so tense? It was simple: Along with asking the President of the United States a question about national security, I was going to offer him an invitation to a Bar Mitzvah! (My fear was that the President might think I was making a mockery of the proceedings, but that was of course the farthest thing from my intent.)

Minute by minute, the suspense mounted. The mayor, gracious as ever, had taken my camera in hand; now he was standing by to snap the photo. I was next in line, and true to his word, the President nodded and pointed to me as the next questioner. My presentation went as follows:

"Mr. President: As I understand it, SALT II does not have any binding effect on countries such as Pakistan, who with the financial backing of Libya is allegedly developing a nuclear capability. This possibility has me worried considerably more than the threat from the Soviet Union or China. My two-part question is this: What can be done and what is being done about such countries; and, secondly, in a less serious nature, I have an invitation from my son, who is being Bar Mitzvah'd next month, for you and Mrs. Carter, and he asked me to ask you if you could attend."

Having concluded my question, I proceeded to the podium and handed the President the invitation – to applause from the crowd and smiles from the President, Secretary Brown and Ms. Wexler. Now I breathed a huge sigh of relief. (At that moment, I didn't realize how prescient my question actually was – in light of the nuclear-development threats that would later emerge in several Third World Countries.)

After I returned to my seat, the President gave me a very long answer, which he began by saying, "Now you have me confused between Libya, Pakistan, nuclear bombs and Bar Mitzvahs. I shall respond to your son personally." As he spoke, his eyes were

focused directly on me. I could hardly wait for him to finish and concentrate on someone else, and so I remembered little of his response . . . other than his candid admission that the proposed treaty did not in fact cover such eventualities.

After the briefing was concluded we were ushered into the State Dining Room, where a musical trio played and Marine Corps enlisted men passed out *hors d'oeuvres*. Many of the attendees approached me to ask about the Bar Mitzvah and when it would occur. I was also interviewed by the Toledo Blade and the Cleveland Plain Dealer. But I had a plane to catch back to Maine and left shortly afterwards.

Outside the White House the national television cameras were set up on the lawn and they were corralling individuals for interviews as they left. I wasn't chosen to be interviewed, however. I wasn't so lucky in my flight home, either, since flights were being cancelled due to weather and I missed my connection from Boston to Portland. I did manage to join forces with five other strandees, though, and together we rented a car (at Delta's expense) to make the drive back. I arrived in Portland at 1:30 in the morning, but the long day had pumped me full of adrenaline and I was unable to sleep.

The following morning I brought the film from the conference to a local developer. I sent the finished photos directly to President Carter for his signature. About three weeks passed, and then one afternoon Diane received a call from the White House telling her that the President was heading to Camp David for the weekend and was taking the photos with him for signing. The spokesperson asked how we wanted the President to sign the two photos I'd sent him, and Diane suggested that he sign one to "The Volk Family" and the other one to Judd personally.

The President did so. Today one of those photos hangs on the wall in my office and the other one can be found in Judd's home in New York. (We will probably never visit Camp David in our lifetimes, but at least our photos have been there!)

I shall now flash forward (and past Marathon Day) to the first Sunday in January of 1980. President Carter was in the fight of his life. Seeking re-nomination, he was struggling to fend off a potential challenge by an upstart from within his own party, Senator Ted Kennedy, who was threatening to run. Politically, the embattled Carter was being "held hostage" at the White House – due to the negative impact of the Iranian Hostage crisis. (If you recall, the 52 U.S. hostages were ultimately released after being held for 444 days. They were set free as President Reagan took the Oath of Office in January 1981 . . . in what amounted to a humiliating slap in the face to President Carter.)

Unfortunately for the incumbent, the Carter campaign was poorly managed, and the bungling began early in the process, when his team chose to begin running major television ads at 7 p.m. on that first Sunday . . . right at the start of the National Football League playoff games. My guess is that the President had an audience of about two – probably the same two people who'd been watching the Jimmy Carter ads and then immediately called me on the phone. "Kenny," they shouted into my startled ear, "did the President come to the Bar Mitzvah?" (It was a couple who'd moved to New Jersey from Portland and who were obviously not football fans – since they'd chosen to watch a 30-minute promo on "A Day in the Life of the President.")

Believe it or not, the day that was portrayed in the promo was the same one on which I'd visited the White House . . . and the Carter extravaganza ended with me asking the President my question and presenting him with the invitation to Judd's special day! The campaign also featured his answer to me, and then his walking down the hall to the Oval Office with his Marine aide and slapping the invitation into his hand . . . while cheerfully announcing: "Well, at least I got me an invitation to a Bar Mitzvah!"

At last I'd been granted my "15 minutes of fame!" The next morning I called the local ABC affiliate to secure a copy of the program but was referred to the local Washington station. They were unable to help or provide me with a copy, however, since the tape was controlled by the Democratic National Committee. After some effort, I finally was put in touch with Gerry Rafshoon, the President's media advisor and a member of his inner circle of Atlanta friends. Somewhat cool at first, he warmed up after I told him we had mutual Atlanta friends – my good buddy Ron Balser, an Atlanta native whose wife Rafshoon had previously dated.

In the end, Gerry proved to be most obliging and sent me a videotape of the program, after which I gratefully sent the Committee a $100 donation.

A satisfying outcome, all around. But now that my brief fling with media fame was over, it was time to get back to work . . . and back to thinking about whether I was going to run any more marathons. For some time, I'd been dreaming about making the world-renowned Paris run. What a thrill that would be, if I could actually pull it off. But was I really willing to commit the time and energy to make it happen?

During the next few years, I would wrestle frequently with that question . . . before finally deciding: Yes, I'm going to do it!

Casco Bay Marathon

MARATHON DAY - OCTOBER 21, 1979

In order to paint a clear picture of my first marathon, I'm going to rely on several passages from the daily training diary I kept in the fall of 1979. That document is very helpful because it contains entries I made immediately before and after the race, when the euphoria was at its peak and my memory freshest. In this chapter I'll quote some of it verbatim.

"Oct. 21, 1979. BEFORE THE RACE: Today is the day! It's 8:30 a.m. and we've just arrived at the Expo Building in downtown Portland, Maine for the start of the race. The place is bustling and it was difficult to find a parking space. The weather is overcast and cool – about 60 degrees – and great for running. I'm sure it will be quite a bit warmer by the time we finish, but there doesn't seem to be any problem with the weather for our start. (Hopefully the cool breeze will alleviate some of the expected humidity.)

"I find myself becoming more nervous and apprehensive about my ability to finish as the 9 a.m. starting time approaches. I hope that my body can withstand the pressures and pain which I am certain are to follow. I am, however, looking forward to the challenge and find myself wishing the time would pass more quickly. I did my stretching exercises, limited as they were, and tied and re-tied my New Balance shoes three or four times. In my nervousness, I somehow forgot how tightly I like my shoes tied. Every little thing, even something as simple as tying one's shoes, seemed to magnify itself into a problem or worry!

"All of my training partners had already arrived, including my brother Douglas, who had also done the training with me. Since we have been running at about the same pace in recent days, we were hoping to run together. All the participants were in a state of suspended anxiety. I made one final stop at the Men's Room, took some water, and headed to the starting line . . . where the runners self-seeded themselves according to the time in which they expected to finish the race. I slotted myself at the 4:00 hour sign next to Doug and Paul Trusiani, the owner of two local grocery stores and one of my regular training partners. My honest hope was to break the four-hour mark, but I didn't want to get run over by faster runners slotted behind me by seeding myself at a too early time. At exactly 9 a.m. the gun sounded and we were on our way.

"THE RACE: The Expo is located at the crest of a hill, so down that hill we plodded, all bunched up like a school of sardines. Gradually the runners created some distance between one another, as we crossed the Back Bay region of Casco Bay onto Route One in Falmouth and then took Route 88 on our way to Yarmouth. Just as we made the turn onto Route 88, we reached the five-mile marker and a water stop. Doug, Paul and I had completed the first five miles in 43 minutes – faster than anticipated – and we realized that we'd started too quickly.

"We were likely to pay the price later on in the race, but we weren't too concerned at this point. (The classic mistake of the rookie marathoner. Poor pacing is the bane of all marathoners and we were its 'poster boys!')

"The three of us continued along the rolling hills of Route 88, trying to concentrate on our pace while at the same time enjoying the run and the beautiful homes situated along the route. I consider Route 88 the nicest road for running in the area. Dotted with lovely homes – each seemed grander than the next – the area featured houses on lots that sloped directly down to the ocean; these delightful properties flanked us on the right as we ran. This route offers shade, rolling hills, scenic views of the ocean and no opportunity to become bored with the run.

"Running smoothly, we continued on to the eight-mile mark, where Paul (who was feeling the best among the three of us) decided he wanted to pick up the pace and move away from Doug and me. We wished him well, while at the same time admonishing him to watch his pace. As we entered the Town of Yarmouth, we faced a very short but very steep hill into the town center. It would be our first walk of the day. We had taken this route many times during the official 13-week training and found that we accomplished nothing by trying to run up this hill. We could walk it just as fast and not expend the energy required for running.

"The idea was to finish the marathon – not to have to stop in mid-race due to ego or stupidity! Diane and the kids were waiting for me at the top of the hill, and Derek and Allison both joined me in running to the water stop. The crowd got a big kick out of seeing the two of them running with me and it really picked me up. (Judd also wanted to run but he was coming down with some sort of 'bug,' so he was relegated to taking pictures.)

"At the Yarmouth water stop, Doug told me he was going to slow down, so I continued on alone down Main Street to West Elm and the back side of the marathon. This section of the race is rural. We passed many farms as we continued to climb more hills – and we also faced long, boring stretches of nothingness. The pretty section of the marathon was behind me, and now it was a matter of simply surviving the final 14 miles. Luckily, I eventually joined a runner from New Hampshire who ran at my pace.

"We hung together for about five miles until he too decided I was a bit too slow for him and took off. He'd never run the route before, so he appreciated my 'advance information' as to what to expect. I didn't see him again until I was rounding the track to the finish line and he came running up to me to wish me luck and root me in. (This was a typical case of one runner encouraging another.)

"It was about this time, somewhere around the 13-15 mile mark, that the humidity began to rise and my legs began to tighten. The temperature had risen to 75 degrees – too hot to enjoy a pleasant 26.2 mile run. I decided that 'positive thinking' was the only answer, and that I simply wasn't going to pay any attention to the weather. This was the day the good Lord had deigned for us to run this race, and I was going to finish it!

"Easier said than done, however. By this time I was walking up every hill that presented itself. The balls of my feet were burning up, and I could feel the blisters forming, but there was no way I was going to quit. From time to time my knees ached. Then my hips ached. Then my toes. My head. I became nauseous. What next? Derek and Allison joined me to run for about a mile at the 20-mile marker and I was then joined by my dear friends Jerry Goldberg and Matt Goldfarb, who had volunteered to meet me and run with me for encouragement.

"Then Derek and Allison peeled off to meet Diane and Judd, so they could see me at the finish line in Fitzpatrick Stadium in Portland. By this time I was unable to run continuously, even on level stretches, so I would run some, walk some, and keep repeating the process by putting one leg in front of the other in my 'survival shuffle.' Had I been running alone, my problems would have been multiplied, since I'd have had no one to speak with and nothing to think about except how awful I felt.

"When we reached Baxter Boulevard in Portland, the final three miles of the race, I began to have difficulty breathing. The problems with my legs, hips and feet were nothing compared to the asthma attack I was having. Gasping my way to the finish, I caught sight of The Oaks, a local city park, looming just ahead. Now it was only a short hop through the park, then another two blocks or so, and I'd be entering the stadium for a victory lap and the finish line.

"Derek and Allison joined me for part of that final lap and then went to the infield to be with Diane and Judd as I continued. Like the rest of the runners in my time bracket, all of whom were feeling the same fiery mixture of pain and euphoria that I felt, I did my best to put on what was for me a 'burst of speed.' A moment later, I had forgotten about the hurts and the asthma and was crossing the finish line with a big smile and a big cry, as the joyful tears flowed."

"POST MARATHON: My asthma attack continued. While standing I was unable to breathe, so I sat down and put my head between my legs, just as I had seen Judd do in the past. (Our son is a severe asthmatic whom we've had to hospitalize on two separate occasions.) When seated and completely at rest, I felt better. However, as soon as I stood up it was a return to gasping for breath. Diane kept insisting that I remain seated, but I was so keyed up, I just wasn't listening to her. Then Diane sent Brian Goldberg – Jerry's son, who was there with his bicycle – to our car to retrieve the cortisone spray we always keep handy for Judd.

"After taking the prescribed three whiffs, I began to feel better. I still had to remain seated, but feelings of normalcy were slowly returning. Soon the asthma vanished and I was able to join the cheering for our training partners as they arrived at the stadium. I was very pleased when I saw my brother Doug enter the arena and finish about five minutes after me.

"Each time I arose to cheer someone on, though, it was with great effort, since it was difficult to switch from a sitting to a standing position. The problem lay mainly in my quadriceps and was exacerbated when I tried to walk downstairs or even on the slightest of down-hills.

"My running partner, Paul Trusiani, whom I mentioned earlier, just missed breaking the four-hour mark by 14 seconds. Good for him! After about 50 minutes of recuperation, I felt strong enough to enter the Expo building to pick up my cherished 'Finisher' t-shirt and a couple of granola bars, and we headed home for a good hot shower and a power nap."

AFTERTHOUGHTS DICTATED AFTER THE NAP: I will quote from the diary almost verbatim here, since the entries convey my feelings clearly during the hours immediately following the race, as I began to contemplate my accomplishment.

"As I sat on my front steps watching the kids play in the driveway and enjoying the beautiful October day, I could hardly help thinking about the incredible stress and pain the human body can withstand. I'm certain that our bodies were not originally conceived to run 26.2 miles in the heat. In spite of the discomfort, however, I'd like to do it again. But I'm very torn at this time as to whether I would want to run the Casco Bay event again, since I would like to run different marathons.

"However, there is something to be said for running with friends, and I do expect that I will return next year. New York or Chicago would be very glamorous, but nothing can replace the comradeship and genuine feeling of closeness that develops between those training together with the same goal. Running alone at a strange marathon, especially when you know that all your friends are running in Portland, would be very lonely.

"At Casco Bay, the spectators along the route were just fantastic. The gentleman from New Hampshire I mentioned earlier couldn't get over the number of people who were calling out to me by name. Yes, it's a wonderful 'high.' These loyal fans make a big, big difference in the quality of your running. It's as if you don't want to let them down. They are rooting for you so hard, it's as if you're running just for them. You just cannot quit; you must keep going. Such wonderful support would surely be missing when running in a foreign marathon. I do want to continue, though, and hope to run two marathons each year, with one taking place in Paris next year. I think that would be very exciting, and I understand that it's not a hilly or difficult route. The Paris Marathon route is so beautiful that they say it's a shame to run it fast. Well, that's something I won't have to worry about!

"Tonight we are heading to a post-marathon celebration, and I'm glad I ordered a specially designed t-shirt for Diane – a shirt that says: 'I survived my husband's marathon training.' I also purchased one for me which reads: 'I put my wife through my marathon training.' We plan to wear them to the party.

"Regarding my finishing time, I had hoped to break the four-hour mark, but due to the extreme heat and humidity, it became readily apparent very early on that this was a rather unrealistic goal. Still, I harbored at least a small hope of clocking that time, after reaching the 20-mile marker in 3:01. At that point, I could have achieved my goal by running the final 6.2 miles at just a shade under a ten-minute pace. But I never envisioned the pain which was to haunt me for that final six miles. My time for that stretch was actually 12 minutes per mile. But that was just as well; I managed to complete the run, and I have no regrets. I trained as hard and as diligently as I could, and that was my best effort. End of story!

"One more word about Doug: I kept looking back for him when I was running with Jerry Goldberg and Matt Goldfarb because I was hoping that he'd catch up with me. Had I been able to spot him, I would have slowed down so that we could've finished together. We had both trained so hard together that I wanted to be able to run into the stadium side by side with him in a dead heat. Unfortunately, he was more affected by the heat than I was and couldn't close the gap. I knew he was somewhere behind me but I never knew how *far* behind, and I was so tired that I was afraid to stop and wait. I feared not being able to re-start my engine. But once I realized that I couldn't break that magical four-hour mark, my time became inconsequential . . . and if I'd seen him, I'd have tried to wait. But he never came into sight and the opportunity to run in together passed.

"CONCLUSION: All in all it was a super day and one which I will remember for the rest of my life. I'm proud to have competed; I'm proud to have trained so diligently, and I'm proud to have finished! Most of all, I'm proud of my family – Diane, Judd, Derek and Allison – for their patience and understanding when I was so tired during much of the training period.

"I could never have done it without them and their total, 100-percent support and love, and I consider myself the luckiest guy in the world."

Interlude

1979 -1989

I think the Rolling Stones probably said it best, with their classic rock n' roll hit of 1968: "You Can't Always Get What You Want."

After having survived the Casco Bay run, what I wanted most – as noted in my post-race diary – was to be able to successfully complete two marathons a year.

It wasn't to be, however. Let's face it: Running 26-plus miles without stopping might not be so difficult for a guy who weighs 140 pounds. But for a Clydesdale like me, it would prove to be an immensely difficult challenge.

What happened was that soon after my successful run at Casco Bay, Diane and I bundled up the kids at Christmas break and left for Florida. This was an annual tradition for us; each year around December 15th, we drove down to the Sunshine State and enjoyed the (usually) mellow ocean breezes until the week after New Year's. (All three children were good students, and so we figured they could afford to miss a few days in the classroom – an assumption that would be regarded as highly dubious today!)

At any rate, we took off for Florida in good spirits. And although I'd resumed my five-day-a-week training schedule about a week after the marathon in Maine, I really hadn't given any thought to when (or where) my next marathon attempt might take place. Imagine my surprise, then, when I returned from Boynton Beach and environs to discover that all of my running partners at the gym were already neck-deep in preparing for their next agreed-upon challenge: the Lowell Marathon (held near Boston each year), which was set to take place at the end of March.

The event was only three months away . . . which left me just barely enough time to prepare. So I went to work immediately. Having been raised in the pretty North Shore town of Swampscott, Massachusetts (and having visited Lowell on many occasions on business), my question to my running pals was: "Have you ever *been* to Lowell?" When most of them shook their heads, I told them bluntly: "It's ugly. It's depressed. Why Lowell?"

Actually, they had some pretty good reasons for the choice they'd made. The city of Lowell (population: about 100,000) was convenient (only 34 miles from Boston, in fact), and the date of the event seemed to fit in nicely with everyone's schedule. Getting to the marathon would be easy and inexpensive, as well.

Their arguments made sense, I had to admit. Still, I wasn't exactly thrilled by the choice. Sure, I wanted to run another marathon, and the sooner the better – but Lowell wasn't exactly at the top of my "Glamorous and Exotic Cities of America" list. And what about my family? If I were going to put forth the enormous effort required to complete a marathon, I wanted it to be in a place that Diane and the kids could fully enjoy.

So I asked myself: Could I find a better marathon venue, if I sat down and did a little research?

Hoping to answer that question, I got busy . . . and it didn't take me long to come up with a terrific alternative: the Virginia Beach Marathon, which was set to unfold during the very same weekend, on the lovely coast of southern Virginia. It was perfect . . . and the best part was that I could continue to prepare with my running partners, whose training schedule would still match mine!

Considerably heartened by this switch in locales, I went back to work with renewed vigor. Soon I was grinding through two long runs during the week . . . followed by increasingly lengthy runs over the weekend. My training progressed nicely, until an event that took place on a nice day in early March (and only two weeks before we were to leave for Virginia Beach). On that particular afternoon, I was engaged in the longest run of my training regimen – a 20-mile ramble along the Casco Bay Marathon route.

As I neared the 15-mile mark that day, I got an unpleasant surprise. All at once I was experiencing a severe ache in my right femur, or thigh bone. The femur is the largest bone in the body, and it extends from the hip to the knee. What could the matter be? This wasn't excruciating pain . . . more like a persistent ache. It was bearable, but very uncomfortable . . . which caused me to adjust my gait in order to continue running.

I soon developed a pronounced limp – a hitch in my stride so noticeable that Sandy Utterstrom (the wife of my running partner, Al Utterstrom), who was following the run in her car and providing drink and nourishment) implored me to quit running and climb into her car. My response was, "How can I quit? If I can't run 20 miles, how am I going to be able to run 26.2 miles in two weeks?"

It just wasn't in my nature to quit – on *anything*. So I limped along and finished my scheduled run. Big mistake! Unbeknownst to me, I had incurred a stress fracture of the right femur, and in order to run through the pain I'd altered my stride so much that I'd also injured my left hip. Ouch! During the following week – the last one before our scheduled departure – I tried without success to run pain-free.

No such luck. Much to my dismay (and to the disappointment of our kids), I now faced the prospect of having to tell them at dinner one evening that I simply couldn't make it to Virginia Beach, and that I was canceling my entry. I wasn't surprised when they gave me their full support, in spite of their disappointment . . . and I decided that I'd take a hiatus from running until the hip (which hurt more than the thigh) was completely and thoroughly healed.

Little did I realize that this "hiatus" would last ten years! Eventually I reached a point where it was difficult to stand after getting out of a chair. I tried everything in the hope of getting better. Rest. Acupuncture. Cortisone. More rest. Ultrasound. Physical therapy. But nothing worked – not until I finally implored my orthopedist, Dr. Doug Brown, to operate and see if I could benefit from having him take a look inside. He scheduled the surgery for a weekday morning at Mercy Hospital in Portland. Then he proceeded to open the hip and remove what he called "scar tissue."

The surgery wasn't terribly complicated, since I could pinpoint with my finger exactly where it hurt. I walked out of Mercy Hospital totally pain free and a new man. Let freedom ring! But my euphoria was tempered by the fact that I had to drive from Mercy directly across town to the *other* hospital in Portland – the Maine Medical Center – where our son Judd was at that very hour being treated for a severe asthma attack.

Fortunately, both of us recovered . . . although the courageous Judd still suffers to this day with asthma. His chronic condition requires careful management, but the good news is that he now has the ailment under firm control with medications and inhalers.

I healed well enough . . . but the "Interlude" period of my running career had begun in earnest – and I soon came to the conclusion that completing two marathons per year wasn't a realistic goal. Instead, I came up with a strategy that seemed to make better sense: "A marathon every ten years, whether I need it or not."

Having accepted the physical limitations that I faced, I resigned myself to waiting out the ten-year period and told my friends that the next target-date would be "Paris in '89." With that ringing phrase as my mantra, I had thrown down the gauntlet – while also buying some time before it would be necessary to resume a grueling training regimen.

Instead of running day in and day out, it was time for me to do some international traveling, accompanied by Diane and the kids.

The context: In the early years of our marriage, Diane and I had decided that when our children were Bar/Bat Mitzvah'd, we'd use the money that ordinarily would have been spent on a dinner dance and party to celebrate with a meaningful family trip. The first such post-Bar Mitzvah event, Judd's in the summer of 1980, began in Paris (*all* trips to Europe had to include Paris!) . . . and we also traveled north to the Normandy Beaches for some World War II history. After that, our itinerary took us to Brittany and the Riviera, followed by the beautiful Aosta Valley in northern Italy, where from our hotel room we had a magnificent view of Mt. Blanc. From the base of the Valley we were able to take a cable car to the top of Mt. Blanc and over into Courmayeur, Italy. Then we headed off to Switzerland and Germany, before ending our European sojourn in London. (All the trips were about six weeks long.)

The second such journey, Derek's in 1982, took us to the west coast of the United States, where we traveled in leisurely fashion from San Francisco to San Diego. We stopped to play golf at Pebble Beach and then from San Diego flew on to Las Vegas . . . after which we took a bus to Lees Ferry, Utah for a nine-day trip down the Colorado River in a raft. That adventure took us back to Las Vegas, from which it was an easy drive east to Colorado for the return flight home.

The final "Bat Mitzvah Trip," Allison's in 1984, carried us back to Paris and then on to several areas that had been deeply touched by the First World War. We visited lovely Venice, then drifted south to what was then Yugoslavia and down its Adriatic Coast to Dubrovnik – a beautiful walled city which was later shelled and partially destroyed during the Serbo-Croatian War of 1991-1995. Then we traveled by boat from Bar, Yugoslavia to Bari, Italy and up the west coast of Italy to Pompei and Rome. There is nothing I could write about Rome that hasn't already been written. As many travelers have noted, it's a majestic city full of history and magnificent buildings. We visited St. Peter's Square and toured the Vatican – and this latter experience became very memorable for our family because of two remarkable experiences.

The first incident occurred as we were visiting the Sistine Chapel – the location of the Papal Enclave, in which the Cardinals of the Church periodically gather to elect a new Pope (and where the crowning artistic achievement of Michelangelo's Sistine Chapel ceiling provides an internationally renowned artistic landmark). The Chapel contains 12,000 square feet of magnificent artwork, all of which took the great artist four years (1508-1512) to complete. In spite of the Chapel's grand reputation, however, our youthful Allison didn't seem terribly impressed. While the tourists around us "oohed and aahed" over the world-famous layout, Allison could be heard asking in a loud voice: "What's so *big* about it?" The words of a 13-year-old!

Our second unforgettable incident involved the Pope himself.

While touring the Vatican, we'd been told that Pope John Paul II held an audience in St. Peter's Square every Wednesday. Tickets were required for entry from the Vatican office. The following morning, I went out for an early run – a jaunt that had been strategically designed to end at the Vatican . . . and just in time for me to join the line for tickets for the following day's papal audience.

Everything went smoothly – until the moment I was to be allowed entry into the Vatican to retrieve my five tickets. Just as I was about to enter, I was told that since I was wearing shorts rather than long pants, I could not be granted entry. What to do? Reacting quickly, I asked the three young girls standing next to me to please secure the tickets I needed. They did . . . and I breathed a bit easier when they returned with the precious tickets.

So much for the "pants problem." Now it was time to meet the pontiff. We'd scouted out the entry-point the day before . . . and we'd also done some sleuthing that told us we should arrive there about two hours early, if we hoped to obtain good seats.

Fair enough. On the day of the big event, we woke the kids early, fed them breakfast, and then arrived with them at the heavy wooden entry doors by 7:30 a.m.

We looked to see which way the doors opened and stationed all three children at the exact opening point. Their instructions were to run as quickly as possible to secure front-row seats in the first section open to the public. (The immediate section in front of the altar was reserved for clergy.)

At last the hour arrived. The big doors swung open precisely at 10 a.m., and the kids were masterful in pinpointing and then reserving five seats, just as we'd hoped. And we didn't have long to wait. Within a few minutes we heard the burst of fanfare that introduced the white vehicle – affectionately called "The Popemobile" – which traditionally carried the Holy Father in a circuit around the entire Square. As we were expecting, the Pope soon materialized directly in front of our area – and all five of us reached out excitedly to shake his hand. We aren't Catholics, of course . . . but I must say that shaking the hand of the Pope – the spiritual leader of millions of Catholics throughout the world – was a very moving experience and one which none of us will ever forget.

It was time to resume our journey. Right after the service, we left Rome for Pisa and Florence. Then it was on to the Riviera for a few days, followed by the flight back home. Content in the knowledge that we'd "seen what we came to see," we made our way back to Maine in high spirits. Our three trips were very memorable for all of us, and they've now become a family tradition – since our three children and their spouses have all taken their own kids on similar visits to far-off destinations in recent years.

All things considered, the "Interlude" period was a very good one for our fast-growing family. During my long break from heavy training, Diane and I got in a lot of travel. We skied in Vail, Colorado, and we spent some quality time at our condo in Boynton Beach. I was still jogging along happily every morning, five days a week, but I was spared the pressure that accompanies intense marathon training.

As the months turned into years, however, I continued to repeat my twin mantras: "Every ten years, whether I need it or not," and "Paris in '89."

And then, almost before I knew it, the calendar suddenly said "1989." All at once it was time to stop the idle chatter – and to get down to the serious business of marathon training again.

The Paris Marathon

EUROPE - APRIL 30, 1989

For the past ten years I had been telling my friends, "Paris in '89." A bold statement! I knew I was capable of completing a marathon; I'd proved that at Casco Bay. But there was no denying that my time there hadn't earned me any medals . . . not at a turtle-slow four hours and 12 minutes. To compensate for my lumbering pace (and get my finishing-time down into the more respectable "three hours-plus" range), I'd told dozens of people over the years: "Oh, yes, I really zoomed along . . . I finished in only three hours and 72 minutes!"

Interestingly enough, very few people had noticed my defective math; most had responded by congratulating me on my blazing speed!

It was an amusing way to make fun of my slow-footed pace at Casco Bay . . . but it also left me wondering: "What will happen the *next* time I attempt to run 26 miles?" And my uncertainty about the answer to that question made it quite easy to keep postponing my long-dreamed-of attempt at the Paris Marathon.

As we approached New Year's Day 1989, in fact, I still had no idea when the Paris event would be held or how to enter. I'd checked all of the national running magazines, looking for information, but to no avail. (Actually, I wasn't even certain that there was a Paris Marathon.)

But then Diane stepped in and helped straighten everything out.

Luckily for me, Diane had spent her college years at Simmons College, and had participated through the college in the Hamilton College Junior Year Abroad Program. Her year of foreign study had taken her to the Sorbonne, and she'd had the good fortune to live with a wonderful family that included her "French Parents," Egli and Daniel Jung and their four daughters: Joelle, Bernadette, France and Dominique. (The latter two were still living at home while Diane was in Paris. Could these wonderful friends help us in the quest for information about marathon-running in France?)

Diane felt certain that they could. After watching me come up empty for a while, she got on the phone in December of 1988 and asked her French "sister" (the beautifully named France) to give us a hand. France instantly agreed to do her best to pinpoint the exact time and place of the 1989 Paris marathon.

While she dug for information in Paris, I started working on my physical conditioning. And that would be no easy task – because at this point in the late 1980s, I knew I was in no condition to compete in a marathon anytime soon. (It was winter, after all, and for a long time I'd been running only sporadically.)

Fortunately, it didn't take long for our dear French friends to get the job done. What happened was that Diane and I traveled to Vail, Colorado each February to meet with a group of ten other corrugated box manufacturers to talk business and ski. Our group, affectionately known as "SPOOC" (the Sheet Plant Owners and Operators Conference), consisted of ten company owners from all over the country. (I'd been invited to join in 1985, when a vacancy occurred.) Anyway, while we were in Vail we received a call from home informing us that "someone from France" had called with information regarding the Paris Marathon. Instantly excited, we placed a call to Paris and were told that the date of the Marathon was April 30, 1989. All at once, my bold statements of the past ten years were coming home to roost!

It was time to get down to brass tacks. Upon returning to Maine in mid-February and realizing that I had only ten weeks to race day, I immediately began a crash training program. Since I was badly out of shape, I found that I could only run about 30 minutes before the gas tank read "empty" and I had to walk. What to do? My plan was to increase my average daily running time by ten additional minutes per week – and also to pray a lot! It wouldn't be easy . . . and since I knew no one else who might be interested in training with me, I would have to run alone for the entire time.

Of course, I was still active in my business and had to work each day, so my training would have to take place in the morning before I headed off to the factory. To say it was lonely work would be a gross understatement. But train I did, six days a week, and by the time April rolled around I felt ready to run.

Nervous, yes. But ready.

Diane and I had a good arrangement, whenever we took a vacation. She planned the trip, made the reservations, took the photos and did the homework regarding whatever we were to see or visit during our stay . . . while also cheering me on during my training and the race. I was in charge of training for and running the marathon, paying for the trip and *schlepping* the luggage. Then I kept my mouth shut – since she had done all the legwork and made all the phone calls.

This arrangement worked well for us on trips we took during the marathon years, and on many that followed them. Over time, Diane had become an expert on using Frequent Flyer miles, so she booked us on Air France in First Class.

After arriving in Paris, we checked in at the Hertz counter and were asked if we would be happy with a Mercedes instead of the

Fiat she had reserved. Not a very difficult question to answer! I had never driven a Mercedes so I was most happy to accommodate the Hertz agent. We found our car without a hitch, and as we were leaving the garage, I looked at the gas gauge and saw that the indicator was sitting right on the "R" at the bottom. Since I was used to "F" and "E," I asked Diane to check with the attendant. After all, she spoke fluent French and wrestling with the native lingo wasn't in my job description. No problem. After a couple of minutes, she emerged from the Hertz office and told me that all was okay. That "R" meant *rempli,* or "full" in French. Of course, it never occurred to us that we were driving a German-made Mercedes and not one manufactured in France. Nor did it occur to either of us that the needle was at the bottom and not at the top of the gauge! (I have to give Diane a "pass" on this one, since I was the driver and thus the only one with a clear and unobstructed view of the instrument panel. However, the real truth eventually came out . . . when Diane confessed that she hadn't actually asked anyone at the Hertz desk about the meaning of the "R" on the gas gauge – the line of customers had simply been too long!)

Ah, well. Ignorance is bliss, as they say, and so we headed off to our small hotel on the *Île de la Cité* without a care in the world. Our home away from home was located right near the Notre Dame Cathedral, and parking spaces are at a premium in Paris . . . but I was lucky to find one about a block from the hotel.

And there the car stayed until we departed the following Monday after the race.

Our first order of business after checking in at our hotel was to locate the marathon office. At that point, I still hadn't been able to enter officially or receive any paperwork, so I was somewhat nervous that I might be denied entry. The offices turned out to be located in a third-floor walk-up near the original Picasso Museum – which meant they were conveniently within walking distance of our hotel. So far, so good. But the secretary at the office told us we had to go to their bureau at the Place de la Concorde to obtain the official entry.

Not a problem. We hurried over and found it to be a very popular place; when we reached the bureau (at the lower end of the Avenue des Champs-Élysées), we found hundreds of people milling about. But our registration went smoothly, and we had no problem paying our $20 for the entry. Interestingly enough, the fee also bought us a commemorative t-shirt – and I definitely wanted to bring home t-shirts for everyone in the family. Being used to American running events, I expected to find vendors everywhere on race day selling the shirts – but there wasn't a single one to be found. The only way to get a shirt was through the entry process; in hindsight, it never occurred to me to simply sign up each of my kids and get them a shirt *that* way. As a result, Paris became the only marathon in which I wound up with only one shirt to bring home.

Before I knew it, race day was upon us. On the eve of the marathon, Diane's "French sister," Joelle, trained into Paris to make me a spaghetti dinner at her apartment so I could "carbo load". Joelle is an anesthesiologist in Le Mans and she traveled in specifically to make me dinner and then accompany Diane the next day, when they planned to chase me around the city's marathon route via the Metro. It took some real effort on Joelle's part to journey in from Le Mans, and both Diane and I really appreciated her efforts.

A little background on Diane's "French Family": As I mentioned earlier, it consisted of the two parents and four daughters. Daniel, the father, was a wine merchant; his wife, Egli, had immigrated to France during the Russian Revolution by escaping over the mountains of her native country with her governess and family. They were oil barons and according to Daniel would have been one of the wealthiest families in the world, had they been able to retain their oil fields. Bernadette, the second-oldest daughter, now lived in London; Joelle, as noted earlier, was a resident of Le Mans and practiced medicine with her then-husband in a clinic they owned.

France was an accomplished artist and painter who'd already had works purchased by the French Museum of Modern Art and taught at the most prestigious art school in France, Beaux Arts. Dominique, meanwhile, worked for the government.

Diane had always felt blessed to have been the house guest of this highly accomplished family. She and her roommate had been treated like members of the clan, and their well-being had been looked after to a surprisingly generous extent. Example: Many of their classmates were only allowed to shower once a week by their French hosts – and some were even limited in the amount of toilet paper they could use! But Diane's French Parents were very generous in the treatment of their youthful American guests. Since Daniel was a wine merchant, that heady beverage was served with each dinner, and it wasn't in short supply. (Diane soon discovered that wine at dinner on evenings prior to an exam was not a good recipe so she abstained on those evenings.)

Understandably enough, Diane very much appreciated being included in all family functions and even attended the wedding of France and her architect-husband, Vladimir, in a Russian Orthodox wedding ceremony. (Over the years we've become close to France and Vladimir and always visit with them during our Paris trips. Diane had always felt that I wouldn't really understand her feelings for this family until I'd met them personally, so in 1973 – as a way to celebrate our 10th wedding anniversary – we had traveled to France for a three-week sojourn. I especially enjoyed that adventure, because it was the first time I'd ever traveled abroad.

We booked our anniversary trip through a travel agent who advised us to splurge in Paris, and he made reservations for us at The Grande Hotel at the astronomical rate of $50 per night. Our room overlooked the building housing the French Opera and was the largest hotel room I'd ever been in. (At $50 a night it was hard to enjoy, however, since my budget was really stretched.) When we checked in, we found a message from Daniel saying that he would pick us up at the hotel and take us back to his apartment for dinner . . . and that a student currently living with them would meet us and help us get acclimated to Paris.

While walking around the city, Diane asked the young student about the family. He told us what each of the girls was doing and that Dominique had married an industrialist who ran a big company. (Since I was also a "big industrialist" in Biddeford, Maine who employed about 15 people in my 22,000-square-foot factory, I wasn't really too impressed!) Two nights later we were invited to dinner at Dominique and Noel's apartment. Noel didn't arrive home until about 8:30 and he and I sat down for a drink.

During the course of the discussion I asked him how many people he employed. He thought for a minute, scratched his chin, and replied, "I'm not sure. I think it's about 25,000-30,000." Recovering, I asked how many factories it took to house all those workers. "About 35" was his reply. It seems he was the Managing Director of a division of a public company, Schlumberger, which made instruments used in the oil industry to measure the heat of the earth so that drill bits won't melt or disintegrate as they penetrate deep into the soil.

A bit ruefully, I concluded that the "big industrialist" from Biddeford wasn't so big after all.

After a week of visiting tourist attractions in Paris, Diane and I headed off into the French countryside. We traveled north to Normandy and the World War II battle sites of Caen and St. Lo – and we also stopped to explore the impressive military cemeteries on the northern coast of France. From there we made a beeline south to Le Mans, where we planned to stay at Joelle's home. (She and her husband were away but had offered their lovely house to us.) It was a beautiful place with an outdoor swimming pool accessible from the inside, which meant that it could be used year-round. Envisioning the luxurious layout, we felt very pampered . . . and also very grateful.

As we traveled through the countryside, we weren't always sure we were on the correct route. Our approach was a simple one, but effective: while I drove, Diane navigated. When unsure, we stopped so that she could ask directions. Always the reply was, "*Tout droit*," or "straight ahead." We were never really lost, but I soon came to the conclusion that *tout droit* meant "up yours" – so as we pulled away I would always smile and quietly reply, "Up *yours*!"

We had a great time traveling from the northernmost region of France to the Riviera. We also visited the Loire Valley and Biarritz, where Diane had spent the first six weeks of her foreign-study year taking a French language immersion course. Eventually, our wanderings brought us to the Dijon region, famous for its magnificent yellow mustard fields. It was here – in the French wine country near historic Beaune – that Daniel's wine company produced its excellent products. We toured his winery, the highlight of which came at the end of the tour. (No, the highlight didn't involve any wine-bibbing!) For me, the most exciting moment of the tour came when we reached the location where the wine is packed in cartons for shipment. As you might imagine, given my profession, I was quite interested in where the corrugated packaging was made.

As we left the winery, Diane gave me my driving instructions and I promptly headed in the opposite direction. Fired up by our quick visit to the wine-packaging facility, I was now determined to visit a corrugated box plant. We drove about 50 miles in the opposite direction from my driving instructions . . . and we arrived just in time for lunch. We were greeted by a gentleman who introduced himself as the Managing Director, but he explained that, unfortunately, he had little time to serve as our guide – because his wife happened to be waiting for him in their car.

Nonetheless, he couldn't resist the urge to show off his plant. In spite of the time constraints he faced, he couldn't have been more cordial. In the end he gave us ninety minutes of his time, while his wife waited patiently outside. Fortunately, Diane knew enough "corrugated terminology" and enough about the box-making process to translate, since he spoke only French.

An hour and a half after meeting our gracious host, we were on our way south to our next destination. And what a treat it was each day to drop by a local food shop for the items that would allow us to picnic beside the road: a bottle of high-voltage wine, a baguette and a thick stack of ham slices and pungent local cheese. (Our odyssey took place well before the concerns about drunken driving became paramount . . . and I must say that as a parent, I'm now rather mortified by the fact that we were willing to drink an entire bottle of wine at lunch and then drive!)

But it was great fun. And it also brought us closer together – literally. After more than one of our wine-fueled picnics, we discovered that our inhibitions had vanished . . . and we didn't hesitate to pull the car over for a quick "matinee" in the woods abutting the highway. Ah, the joys of foreign travel!

Our earlier French travels had been delightful, but they'd taken place back in 1973, long before I'd committed to running the Paris Marathon. Now it was late April of 1989 – and the day of the race had finally arrived. I'd been training hard, and I felt that I was in pretty good shape. Deep down, I was hoping that I could better my time at the Casco Bay Marathon, even though I was ten years older. My weight was down to 180 pounds and the training had gone well, but even the best marathoners are nervous during the hours leading up to the event.

Diane and I woke early that day and had a light breakfast. Then we headed back to the Place de la Concorde. The race organizers had placed signs along the starting route so that the runners could seed themselves according to their expected finishing times. I positioned myself just beyond the four-hour sign, which was located about 300 yards from the Place de la Concorde, the largest of the squares in the French Capital. This famous landmark is dominated by a giant Egyptian obelisk in the center of the square which Napoleon had brought back to Paris after his Egyptian conquest. The monument is decorated with hieroglyphics exalting the reign of Pharaoh Ramses II.

Designed in 1755 and originally named "Place Louis XV," the square has a remarkable history. The statue of Louis XV, originally located here, was removed during the French Revolution . . . after which it was replaced by a guillotine! The square then got a new name: "Place de la Revolution." The first great French aristocrat to be executed there was King Louis XVI, and his fate was soon shared by Queen Marie Antionette, Princess Elizabeth of France and Maximilien Robespierre. During the "Reign of Terror" in the summer of 1794, more than 1,300 people were executed in a single month, during what had to have been one of the most frightening epochs in the history of Paris.

At first glance, the marathon route seemed rather formidable. The opening stretch, from the Place de la Concorde to the Arc de Triomphe – partly along the slightly uphill Avenue des Champs-Élysées – would make for an energy-draining start. Let's face it: Although walking that gentle incline isn't difficult, running it at the start of a 26.2-mile endurance test seemed guaranteed to take the wind out of your sails.

But there was no getting around it. Approaching the starting point, it was easy to feel nervous . . . especially since the race organizers had fenced off the street for the run and sequestered the ranks of observers behind a low picket fence. There was a lot of nervous energy on the loose, and some of the men, including me, found that a bladder emptying was in order. With no facilities in sight, many of us just found the nearest tree and took care of the "problem."

Nobody seemed to mind . . . and I overcame my own squeamishness by remembering that this was France, after all. Why fret, when the sophisticated local populace didn't seem to object – or even to *notice* our last-minute, pre-race ritual? No doubt they'd seen a lot more risqué behaviors (and a lot more impressive anat-

omy) than we were presenting to their cosmopolitan eyes, in the moments before the marathon got underway!

In a marathon as large as the one in Paris, it takes a while after the gun goes off for a back-of-the-pack runner like me to reach the starting line. But I hung in there and finally my turn came. I was off! I ran uphill to the Arc de Triomphe and then downhill along one of the fanciest streets in Paris, Avenue Foch. It led me to an inner city park, the Bois de Boulogne. Those runners who hadn't had the benefit of a tree on the Avenue des Champs-Élysées now took full advantage of the woods, and both men and women could be seen from the road doing the same thing I'd just done to a tree.

But everyone was far too busy to take notice and you could almost hear them thinking: *C'est la vie!*

The run through the Bois went on for approximately 13 miles before we exited and then suddenly confronted the Seine River and the Eiffel Tower. What a sight!

Somewhere in the Bois I had an epiphany. One of our dearest friends from Portland, Maine, Madeline Cohen, had passed away a couple of years before from a brain tumor. Madeline and her husband Gene were Portland natives and very active in the general community. They were two of the first people we'd met after moving to Maine. Two years after her passing, Gene was diagnosed with the same disease and also died, leaving behind their two sons.

Touched by their plight, I began to reflect on the fact that when children from Portland were diagnosed with cancer, they often had to travel two hours to Boston for treatment. To help rectify that situation, the Maine Children's Cancer Program (MCCP) was founded to treat children from all over Maine, and Diane now served on its Board. How could I help? All at once an idea occurred to me. Why not scrap the idea of "running a marathon every ten years whether I needed it or not" and instead run a marathon on each of the seven continents of the world as a way to help raise money for the organization? Life is unpredictable, after all, and far too short . . . and I suddenly realized that I wanted to be able to say that I had "given back."

As an aside, I should point out that even as I'm writing this memoir, I'm recuperating from a melanoma that was recently removed from my chest. The growth was "in situ," meaning that it was self-contained and didn't require radiation or chemotherapy. Maybe, if you believe in "fate," or in "providence," you could say that I've been repaid for my fund-raising efforts by this positive outcome in my own experience with cancer? Maybe! And maybe this book would never have been written, otherwise. I'd been talking about the project since 1996, while endlessly postponing the process.

Perhaps the sudden melanoma had finally given me the impetus to proceed? Life is fragile, after all; if I waited too long, I might never get the book on the shelf!

At any rate, I knew immediately that my spontaneous idea of running marathons worldwide in order to raise funds for pediatric cancer patients was a winner. Of course, I had no idea what would be required of me, if I really hoped to accomplish this challenging goal. How does one run a marathon in Antarctica? In my naïveté, I imagined taking a boat to the Antarctic, then jumping off and running around some town for what I thought was 26.2 miles. The fact that there are no "towns" in the Antarctic never occurred to me. Nor did I have any idea about how I was going to raise money for the program. Oh, well . . . all good things in good time!

What really mattered at that moment was that I knew I wanted to help, in whatever way I could manage.

As I exited the Bois and ran along the Seine, I passed large crowds of enthusiastic onlookers, many of whom were shouting "Bravo" and other words of encouragement. In many cases, they were also offering oranges, water and fruit to the runners. In addition, there were bands strategically placed along the route which played marches and other lively tunes. Both the people and the bands did a wonderful job of boosting the morale of the runners, and it was a thrill to hear them cheering us on.

Since Diane and I had been to Paris on numerous occasions prior to the run, I was somewhat familiar with the city. Most of the time, I knew exactly where I was and where I was headed. Our route took me past the huge Renault factory that we had passed in 1980 on our way to Versailles with our children, then past the Eiffel Tower, the building housing the French Congress and the Notre Dame Cathedral. After that, we left the city behind. Diane's "French sister," France, had her studio along the route and we'd been there many times.

All things considered, I was in great shape at that point. Being familiar with the route helped a lot, and the crowds and the bands were pumping me up. All in all, I was feeling very good as I trudged along the Seine and began counting down the miles to the finish. My original hope had been to improve on my Casco Bay time in 1979 . . . and I was on target until I came to a hill on mile 25. During miles one through ten, that hill would not have fazed me – but at mile 25 it suddenly loomed like Mt. Everest.

Within a matter of seconds, all of the remaining steam and strength drained from my legs. From that point on, I would be in "survival mode." Desperately, I put one foot in front of the other, knowing that with each shuffling step I was one step closer to the finish. It was brutal . . . but at last the end was in sight, and I put on whatever little burst of speed I had left to cross the line. I also looked around for Diane and Joelle, but they were nowhere to be seen. Why? It was simple: The finish line was at the Chateau de Vincennes – and there was no subway stop within a mile. And that was a shame, because all during the race, Diane and Joelle had been following me via the Metro – from which they would periodically emerge to greet me on the marathon route.

Since it was a Sunday and not a workday, however, the subway schedule had been curtailed, and it was difficult to catch me at some of the spots where my "projected time" would permit me to appear. But we learned a good lesson, and I soon realized that I should have hired a driver – a possibility that had never occurred to either of us. Anyway, due to the relatively long distance from the finish line to the nearest Metro stop, Diane and Joelle didn't make it to the finish line before I arrived. Indeed, it was a wonder that we even managed to find each other! After doing so, the three of us embraced in a flood of unembarrassed tears, such was our joy and relief.

I finished the Marathon in four hours, 25 minutes, 26 seconds (13 minutes behind my pace in my previous marathon). That glittering time was good enough to win me 6595th place!

It was over . . . and all at once, I began to feel better. Somehow, the act of completing a marathon produces a wave of euphoria. The adrenaline kicks in and you feel rejuvenated, in spite of the fatigue. And that describes how I felt to a tee, as Diane, Joelle and I took a leisurely stroll back to the Metro stop. Joelle was headed for the rail station and a return to Le Mans; Diane and I were returning to our hotel.

That curious hostelry could best be described as "quaint." For one thing, the amenities were so crowded together that all of your bodily functions (shower, shave, sleep and s _ _ t) could be completed without having to move a step. Not only that, it was also as if our neighbors were rooming with us. (There wasn't much in the way of insulation or sound barriers, either.) I took a very leisurely shower . . . and then indulged in the most wonderful sex with the love of my life. I don't have any idea where I got the strength, but the two of us were terrific, if I may say so myself. All at once, a brand-new running tradition had been born: a delightful ritual that we would henceforth refer to as our "Post-Marathon Exercise."

Please allow me to backtrack for a minute. In 1975 I surprised Diane with a trip to Paris to attend the opening of a one-woman art exhibit of paintings by France, her French sister. We'd received an invitation to the show, and through American Express I was able to secure plane tickets, a hotel, a token gift at the Galleries Lafayette, a trip down the Seine aboard one of the famous *Bateaux Mouches* (tour boats) and transfers to and from the airport . . . all for less money than the plane tickets alone would have cost.

The hotel, the InterContinental, was located at the bottom of the Avenue de la Grande Armée and was one of those large, "touristy" places that don't seem to have much personal charm. But it served our purpose well – since all we really needed right then was a bed and a bathroom. Once outfitted with these essential amenities, we were content and could live happily without the kinds of luxury services (such as touring and restaurant reservations) that are usually provided to guests by American Express.

On our first night there, while heading to a restaurant near the hotel, we passed another one that had a long line outside. Every night as we left our hotel, we noticed the same backup of patient diners waiting outside this particular dining spot. So one night we decided to join them and eat there. Known as "L' Entrecôte-Le Relais de Venise," the eatery features a surprisingly limited menu, and the service also seems a bit unusual.

Here the waitresses serve steaks and *pommes frites*, period. The waitress comes over and asks how you would like your steak; then she writes your order on the paper table covering. Before long the steak arrives, drenched in a delicious mustard sauce made with a closely guarded secret recipe, along with a mound of the most delicious *pommes frites* available on Planet Earth. I really can't explain why the fries are so tasty; my theory is that the Parisian restaurants use the same grease when making them that was used during the Napoleonic era. The grease and oil have never been changed, and their flavor (and thus the flavor of the fries) has been wonderfully enhanced over time

The dinner, coupled with a bottle or two of house wine, is then topped off with a choice of positively orgasmic desserts, our favorite being *La Tulipe,* which consists of a flower-shaped cone filled with vanilla ice cream, luscious strawberries and whipped cream. Le Relais had become our favorite Parisian restaurant and one which we would visit at least once during each of our stays in Paris.

So why am I wasting precious ink here, in order to focus on the delicious fare at Le Relais? Good question. And the answer is quite simple: All during the Paris Marathon, I had been dreaming of having dinner there. But this was Sunday afternoon, and I was terribly afraid that the place might be closed. Imagine my euphoria when the deskman called and found they were open!

Bon appetit! As soon as we'd finished our afternoon sojourn in the hay, we began strolling toward the restaurant. But this wasn't like walking across the street; it took us a full hour to reach the restaurant. The walk was worth it, however – and we fully enjoyed our steaks. But when the waitress stopped by to ask if we'd like dessert, she got a major shock.

Because Diane does all the talking when we need to converse in French, I asked her to let the waitress know that I wanted another meal. She did so . . . to the consternation of the French-speakers at the nearby tables, most of whom then looked at us as if we'd just descended from outer space. Not to worry, however: Diane quickly explained that I'd just completed the Paris Marathon – whereupon I received a wonderful round of applause from our fellow diners.

(Famous at last!) After consuming a second *entrée* and two bottles of wine, we walked all the way back to our hotel, arriving about midnight.

At 2:00 a.m. I was awakened by our next-door neighbors, who obviously had just enjoyed a night on the town. And it must have been a *fine* night . . . since they provided me with an audio show for the next 45 minutes – an extravaganza that included screaming, laughing and exhortations by the female reveler that her partner should "keep on going!" (I translate very loosely.)

Fireworks *à la Française*! I was tempted to awaken the slumbering Diane, who missed the show entirely, but I didn't have the heart. (Later, I wondered if that had been a tactical error – had we both participated in this unavoidable eavesdropping, we might have wound up echoing their amorous hullabaloo!)

The next day, our departure day (May 1), was the French "Labor Day." As in the United States, everything was shut down and the populace was on holiday. The traffic leaving the city was very light and as a result, we were able to find our way to the countryside with ease. We were on our way to Heidelberg, Germany.

We were also moving along quite swiftly. Knowing that no one pays attention to speed limits in Europe, I was zooming along at about 90 mph – and cars were passing me like I was standing still. I was also noticing something else, however: the curious behavior of our gas gauge. With every mile, the indicator appeared to be moving closer to the "R" – which supposedly stood for "*rempli,*" or "full."

The thought came to mind that the Germans must be very clever, indeed – since the farther I drove, the fuller the gas tank got! And then it happened: Just as we were heading up a slight incline, the car began to buck and jerk. Diane asked me what was wrong, and remembering my teen years (when I'd had a fuel pump or two die on me while presenting the same symptoms), I explained: "It must be the fuel pump."

Eventually, I was able to pull over to the side, open the hood, and take a look. Being the savvy mechanic that I am, I soon announced that "everything looks okay in here!" And then we sat. And sat. And sat . . .as cars barreled by at 100 mph. Finally a bus stopped and the driver asked if he could help – and at that moment it occurred to me that we were out of gas. What else could it be?

The driver nodded, but then told me that he didn't have any fuel to offer us, since his vehicle was diesel-powered. Once again the crack mechanic in me spoke up: Why not use diesel in our Mercedes? It would burn, wouldn't it? The driver gave me a pitying look, then assured us that he would summon help for us as soon as he could. We thanked him and he was soon on his way.

Shortly thereafter a repair vehicle pulled up, put a couple of liters in the tank and we were off to a station to fill 'er up. But that station turned out to be only about 200 yards distant, just on the other side of a steep incline. We'd sat there for more than two hours . . . not knowing we were only a three-minute walk away from a gas station. Hey, as a guy who'd managed to run 26 miles the previous day, I'm pretty sure I could have managed that 200 yards!

Live and learn, right? If there was a silver lining in this cloud of errors, it was probably that we were reimbursed in full for the road service and the gas. Looking back, I felt pretty foolish about the blunder . . . but at least we'd been made "whole."

By the time we reached West Germany on our whirlwind European tour, I was feeling pretty good about having survived the Paris run. To celebrate, I decided to call Larry Glick in Boston.

A bit of background: Mr. Glick was a very skilled talk show host whose weeknight shows ran in the early hours, from 1-5 a.m. on WBZ Radio. One of his clever gimmicks was to award a "Glick University" t-shirt to anyone calling in with a good suggestion for an interview. I'd already sent him an "Everybody Loves Boxes" t-shirt from Volk Packaging, and I'd also called him with the suggestion that he interview me after I ran the Paris Marathon. He thought it a good idea and sent me a "Glick University" shirt to wear during the race. I didn't actually wear it during the event, but donned it soon afterwards for a post-race photo. Then, after we reached Heidelberg, I phoned him (his show was by then running in the daytime) and we did the interview.

We talked via a hookup run through our factory loudspeakers at Volk Packaging, and it was a thrill to be taking part in my first-ever radio interview . . . even if nobody offered me a chance to host my own show after hearing me rhapsodize about my adventures in Paris.

So much for my showbiz career. Soon after I'd signed off at WBZ, Diane and I completed our tour of beautiful Heidelberg and set sail for West Berlin. Since this was April 1989, the Berlin Wall was still up and the city was still divided. As we were driving on the autobahn toward Berlin (we were on the East German side coming from Heidelberg), we noticed a sign for Potsdam. This was the city where the conference had been held among Roosevelt, Churchill and Stalin in which they'd divided Germany into four sections controlled by the United States, England, France and Russia. That arrangement had also included dividing Berlin into East and West sectors. East Berlin and the rest of East Germany were now controlled by the Soviet Union and West Berlin by the democratic powers.

In order to reach West Berlin from Heidelberg, we had to drive through the East German sector. No one had told us that we were not to get off the autobahn under any circumstances, and that we were to proceed directly to West Berlin. In addition, our pass to enter West Berlin required entry at a specific gate. Diane knew all of this, but she figured (incorrectly, as it turned out) that we wouldn't have a problem getting back on the autobahn toward West Berlin. So without a care in the world, we detoured into Potsdam to tour the home where the conference was held.

We were able to locate the site of the historic meeting place without much difficulty, although we had to maneuver around a number of rotaries. Like Hansel and Gretel with their breadcrumbs, I tried to hang onto a geographical memory of our route, but soon lost my bearings. We arrived at the conference site about 30 minutes before they were scheduled to close, but we were able to pass quickly through the building and grounds. With that mission accomplished, we now had to find our way out of Potsdam and get back onto the autobahn. Not so easy! Soon we were hopelessly lost and traveling along a route which took us near an air force base. (We may have been piloting the only Mercedes within the entire East German sector!)

Looking around, we felt increasingly uneasy. All the other vehicles were tiny tin cans, and all were painted in what Diane affectionately called "puke green." We stood out in our black Mercedes 190 like the proverbial sore thumb. I was getting a bit nervous, since we weren't where we were supposed to be – and the East Germans weren't known for their staunch support of due process. Nor did driving past an East German Air Force base give me a warm and fuzzy feeling. All I could picture was the two of us being arrested with no consul nearby and no right to make a phone call. After all, these guys were shooting their *own* citizens (or at least those who tried to breach the wall and escape to a better life in the West).

Finally, after some terrific navigation by Diane, we were able to locate the autobahn. But there was a hitch: we couldn't tell if we were heading to the East or the West Berlin entry point. After consulting the map for what seemed an eternity, Diane arrived at the conclusion that we were, indeed, heading in the *wrong* direction and that we would reach the Berlin entry at the Eastern Sector. Not good. There was no way they'd allow us through there . . . nor were we interested in trying to drive through East Berlin and then exit into West Berlin, even if that were possible (which it was not). Scary? You bet. By now I was drenched in perspiration.

Was there a way out? Maybe. All we really needed to do was to make a u-turn on this major highway and then head in the other direction. Fortunately for us, there was a rest stop on the other side of the road – and after we'd lurched daringly across the median strip, Diane was able to communicate with the locals well enough to ascertain that we were now headed to *East* Berlin! (We'd been driving on the correct route after all!) Back over the median strip we went, and soon we were on our way, with high hopes that our understanding of these new German directions was correct.

I breathed a temporary sigh of relief. It's hard to explain the helplessness one feels when traveling in a country not friendly to the United States (and also a country under virtual martial law). Dotting the highway were lookout towers with armed guards. Barbed wire loomed everywhere, and the landscape seemed gray and dismal. In addition, many of the people we passed were walking with their heads pointed toward the ground, frowning and grimacing with gloomy anxiety. Not a happy camp!

We reached West Berlin with great sighs of relief. At least now we were among friendly faces ruled by a friendly government. Yes, the comparison between East and West had truly been startling. West Berlin with its main shopping and pedestrian street, the Kurfurstendamm, was a beehive of activity. There were discos, hotels, and ice cream parlors, and you had to "stand in line to walk" even at midnight. As a former "WWII baby," I found it fascinating to be visiting the homeland of our former adversaries and viewing the exact spot where Hitler and his wife, Eva Braun, had committed suicide.

The Berlin Wall was also a remarkable sight. Erected in August 1961, it was 96 miles long and 11.8 feet high on average. Topped off with barbed wire and broken glass, it was a significant deterrent to East Germans who wanted to escape. In addition, the 830-mile border between East and West on the Eastern side contained a steel mesh fence running along a "death strip." That formidable barrier was flanked by bands of ploughed earth; their purpose was to slow down would-be escapees and also reveal their footprints.

Minefields also abounded in this grim region.

To view Hitler's Bunker, one had to mount a platform on the Western side and look over the wall at a mound of dirt which indicated the site of the bunker entrance. There was no marker and no stone – just a pile of dirt. All he deserved.

We paid a visit to the Reichstag, the home of the German Parliament. Opened in 1894 after more than 23 years of construction, it was almost destroyed by fire under very suspicious circumstances in 1933. The ensuing allegations of politically motivated arson gave the National Socialist Party (the Nazis) a reason to suspend civil rights and declare martial law. The resulting propaganda also provided a great impetus to Hitler's rise to power. Interestingly enough, the building's rear façade now served as the dividing line between East and West Berlin. Directly behind the building was a narrow stream which had been crossed by those who'd succeeded in escaping the tyranny of East Germany. And on the East German side were buildings whose windows had been cemented over to prevent the citizenry from jumping into the stream and swimming to freedom.

During our visit we were told that the East Germans had placed sharp poles in the water just beneath the surface to prevent anyone from swimming to safety. Those foolish enough to make the attempt would have been instantly impaled on the poles. And behind the Reichstag was a metal fence on which crosses were mounted; they bore the names of those who'd died in search of a better life in the West. On the Western side of the wall, graffiti had been painted and covered the barrier as far as the eye could see. Directly behind the Reichstag and painted on the Wall was a moving epigram: "The wall will fall. Beliefs become reality." Guard towers were strategically placed along the top of the structure, as well, with armed soldiers more than ready to shoot anyone foolhardy enough to attempt the escape.

On our second day in West Berlin we took the train across

Checkpoint Charlie into the Soviet Sector of East Berlin. On the short trip across the border, we spoke with a Protestant minister from Denmark; he explained that he traveled on a Diplomatic Passport because he conducted services at a small church on the Soviet side. We also noticed that he was bringing copies of *Time* and *Newsweek* with him, along with some other western magazines. When we questioned him as to how he was able to do this, he explained that his Diplomatic Passport gave him immunity. Apparently, he couldn't be searched or detained. He told us that East Berlin was in turmoil and that people were meeting in basements, church cellars and wherever else they could, in order to protest their government and its treatment of its citizens. These brave souls were fomenting change, said the minister.

Fascinated, we hung on every word. And yet we found it hard to believe that an "uprising" against the Soviets could ever occur – especially after having witnessed the intimidating presence of armed soldiers endlessly patrolling the eastern side of the border. Remember, this was May, 1989 – only two years after U.S. President Ronald Reagan had stood at the Brandenburg Gate (June 12, 1987) to commemorate the 750th anniversary of the founding of Berlin. Reagan had made one of his most famous speeches at the Gate and had concluded it by saying: "General Secretary Gorbachev, if you seek peace, if you seek prosperity for the Soviet Union and Eastern Europe, if you seek liberalization: Come here to this gate! Mr. Gorbachev, open this gate! Mr. Gorbachev, tear down this wall!"

As we listened to the minister predict an "uprising" in the days ahead, the possibility seemed remote and unreal. Imagine our astonishment – only seven months after we'd visited the Brandenburg Gate – when the Wall actually did come crashing down and the Soviet oppression of the East Germans came to an end.

In a small but very real way, we'd been witnesses to living history.

In order to enter East Berlin, you must purchase the equivalent of $20 U.S. in East German marks. (Of course, it's virtually impossible to *spend* $20 in East Berlin . . . but East Germany needed the hard currency that the U.S. dollar provided.) We tried to ask an East German guard where to purchase the currency we needed, but he wanted no part of us. No problem: Diane, in her own way, was able to figure out what we were expected to do. We entered East Berlin at a huge train station, while watching the silhouettes of armed soldiers patrolling the parapets above. The scene reminded me of World War II war movies I'd seen as a young boy. It was a totally depressing environment.

But we soldiered on. Try as we might, Diane and I found it impossible to spend our $20 in marks. In the end, we bought sausage sandwiches from a street vendor and simply gave him the entire amount. The contrast between East and West was truly glaring. While walking through the main shopping districts of West Berlin, we'd noticed that the shops exhibited stylish clothing and that the travel agencies advertised trips to exotic spots such as the French Riviera, Spain and the United States. In contrast, the East Berlin agencies advertised trips to wonderful spots such as Algeria, Bulgaria, Albania and Libya. Those lucky East Berliners! Everything here – the people, the buildings and the atmosphere – had a gray tinge. People walked silently, their heads down. There was no joy. No laughing. It was total depression, and we couldn't wait to depart.

On our return before we left the station, the train's undercarriage was thoroughly searched with dogs and mirrored poles to ensure that no stowaways were hanging onto the bottom. We disembarked at Checkpoint Charlie, the most famous checkpoint from the American point of view – since it contained a museum consisting of artifacts from the occupation and automobiles that had been used in smuggling East Berliners out, along with other symbols of the Cold War. This was the single crossing point to the East for foreigners and Allied forces.

We were back on *terra firma* at last. Diane and I loved being in West Berlin with its lively night life and the *joie de vivre* of its residents. How happy we felt to be back in the West!

One afternoon, after touring Berlin on foot for the entire morning and into the early afternoon, we headed toward Wannsee Lake. Wannsee is a recreation area for the local populace, but it's best known worldwide as the site of the Wannsee Conference in January 1942. This was a meeting among notorious senior German officials who were intent on designing a procedure for achieving the "final solution to the Jewish question." Reinhard Heydrich was the chairman, and he would present the plan to Adolf Hitler for his approval. There were 15 in attendance. During the proceedings, Adolf Eichmann was given the responsibility for implementing the plan. Fortunately, he wasn't 100 percent successful in carrying it out . . . since the original blueprint targeted not six million Jews for extermination, but 11 million!

One fact was especially hard to contemplate: The fact that the entire meeting took only 90 minutes. Ninety minutes to reach a decision that would have eliminated an entire group of people from the face of the earth! The Wannsee scheme called for the deportation of the Jewish population of Europe to German-occupied areas, and for the eventual use of that Jewish population in road-building and other projects. During the course of this slave labor, of course, it was expected that most of the slaves would eventually die.

But as the Germans were pushed back by the Soviet onslaught, the Jews instead were sent to concentration camps for extermination. The villa in which the conference had been held was dedicated as a Holocaust Memorial and Museum in 1992. For his part, Reinhard Heydrich died in Prague on June 4, 1942, as a result of injuries suffered during an attack by Czech and Slovak resistance fighters who'd parachuted in from England. Eichmann escaped to Argentina after the war and lived there in anonymity until captured by Israeli agents and spirited out of the country to Israel. There he was tried, found guilty of "crimes against humanity" and executed in May, 1962.

During our visit, we learned that you could take a boat around the lake and then down a neighboring stream. On one side, marked by very noticeable stakes jutting above the water line, we were in West Germany; the opposite side belonged to the East Germans. Nowhere was the stark difference between the two cultures and their standards of living so evident. The Western side had beautiful homes, boats and manicured lawns and gardens. The eastern side was walled off and thoroughly depressing.

The next morning we left Berlin for Munich. While checking out of our hotel, we were warned by the *concierge* to watch our speed heading to Munich, since we would once again be passing through East Germany. This time I knew enough not to exit the road for any reason but found it difficult to believe that anyone actually paid attention to speed limits. As we were driving directly behind one of the aforementioned "puke-green" cars and coming over a small hill, however, a policeman appeared out of nowhere. After letting the East German car pass, he waved me over. How could I be the guilty party – when I was following a car directly in front of me and he had allowed it to pass?

The black Mercedes was the tip-off, of course. With growing anxiety, I watched the officer approach and demand my papers. He was speaking German and the moment I opened my mouth, he knew I was an American. And since I spoke no German at all, he became quite exasperated at my inability to produce exactly what he was looking for. It took him several minutes to get across the idea that I had been "speeding" and that he wanted to see my license. When I finally gave it to him, he spent an inordinate number of minutes sitting in his car behind us.

The longer he took, the more nervous we became. We were back in the region of no due process, after all, and no American representation. But he finally returned with a ticket in hand and a demand for $50 in American currency. He didn't leave us a lot of choice in the matter . . . and I certainly had no desire to return to fight it out in court, so I paid the money grudgingly and we were on our way. I deemed it unlikely that East Germany would have reciprocity with Maine regarding traffic tickets, so I jokingly told Diane that this "sham ticket" probably wouldn't affect my license or insurance.

Sadder but wiser, we headed toward the East-West German border and back to being with freedom-loving people. (But wait, not so fast!) When we arrived at the border crossing, we had a long wait to reach the customs booth. All of the cars in front of us had been routinely waved through with little wait. Not us, however. We were stopped and our passports were taken . . . and then we were left to wait for 30 minutes while they carried them into an office and did their "make an American miserable" thing.

As the clock ticked on and on, we became increasingly nervous. But in the end our passports were returned to us and we were sent – quite happily – on our way.

On to Munich, home of the famous Beer Garden in which Hitler held court prior to assuming power. Munich is a pretty city with a charming pedestrian mall at its center, but with a dark history. It is the home of the infamous Dachau Concentration Camp, a prime vehicle for the implementation of Hitler's Final Solution.

In the center of the pedestrian mall is the city hall, which houses an unusual clock. Each hour, colorful figures emerge from the clock face and dance in a circular motion. It's a big thing for the tourists, and they seem to materialize in large numbers just before the hour is struck, in order to watch this clock. Diane had done some research and said this was a "must see" . . . so we arrived at the square in plenty of time. I thought it hysterical that so many people would interrupt their day to watch this silly scene, but there we were. Why? Because it was the "thing to do," that's why!

Picture hundreds of people with their necks craned upwards to watch a series of cartoon-like figures in historical costumes emerge from a clock, dance around, and then re-enter the big timepiece. Aren't tourists just a bit *daffy* at times? But just as I got ready to blast them for their foolishness, I realized that I was one of them!

Next we took a train to the outskirts of Munich to visit Dachau. Neither of us had ever visited a concentration camp; we'd only seen photos dating back to World War II. From the train station we walked through some very nice residential areas with well-manicured homes. (It seemed like a strangely incongruous location for such heinous crimes against humanity.) These residences weren't large, but they were nicely maintained – and you had to wonder how so many people in busy neighborhoods such as these could have missed seeing the smoke and smelling the odor of burning flesh as they cooked their own dinners or sent their children off to school in the morning. But that was the claim, all too often, in later years: "We knew nothing."

Dachau was the first of the concentration camps built by the Nazis. Its smokestacks were visible to all of the neighboring areas. Most of the buildings had been razed but the footprints of the barracks were still evident, so that one could discern the make-up of the camp. The building housing the ovens and "cleansing showers" was still erect. One or two at a time, the bodies had been fed into the ovens. The "poor workers" in the camp must have had a difficult time keeping up with the output from the showers. Looking at all of this horror, I couldn't help wondering: Was the continuous supply of bodies at Dachau one of the first examples of achieving a continuous supply of "raw materials" in order to maintain "job security in the workplace?"

In the days that followed our Dachau visit, Diane and I felt so lucky that our grandparents had had the wisdom to emigrate to the United States. We also felt a great deal of compassion for the trials our forebears had endured, along with an eagerness to get safely home. Of course I was also eager to begin planning for my marathon runs on all seven continents . . . while also trying to put together an effective mechanism to raise money for pediatric cancer patients. Perhaps it was just as well that I had plenty of other things to think about, as we bid farewell to the horrifying nightmare that was the Dachau Concentration Camp.

After three days in Munich we boarded our plane for home. We were $50 poorer after the East German "speeding ticket" – but were we ever happy to be heading back to beautiful Maine and the freedom of the United States of America!

Lake Kawaguchi Marathon

ASIA - NOVEMBER 24, 1991

Now that I was safely back on U.S. soil, I found myself eager to begin working on the problem of raising funds for the Maine Children's Cancer Program (MCCP). In the days since my "epiphany" during the Paris Marathon, I'd become more convinced than ever that I wanted to give back to the community – along with helping those who'd been struck by this terrible childhood disease.

But how to proceed?

While I scratched my head and wracked my brain, a sudden thought occurred: As the owner of a successful (and very visible) corrugated box factory in Maine, I would probably be able to tap into our "supplier base" for donations. And of course I also intended to lobby my friends and acquaintances.

A good start. For a while, I also thought about contacting our customers . . . but I soon backed away from that possible strategy out of fear of alienating them. (We needed our customers for economic survival, and I certainly didn't want them to feel they were being "put on the spot!")

After a few days of mulling several different fundraising approaches, I got down to business. As a first step, I started compiling a list of suppliers and friends . . . and I added to it each time a new name came to me. Nor did I fret over asking these sources for help. How could they say no to helping out in the struggle to defend kids against cancer?

I worked almost daily on the project, and soon I had a long list of possible donors. Then the real work began, as I set out to present each one with a heartfelt request for funds. This was well before the arrival of the "computer age," remember. No one had ever heard of "email," and the concept of soliciting thousands of recipients with a single electronic message hadn't been dreamed up yet.

It seems very primitive now, but in that long-vanished pre-Internet era, my company's most advanced communications tool was an electronic typewriter that could be programmed to type the same letter again and again – provided that you inserted each new blank page by hand into the machine's cumbersome platen. It was a slow, laborious process by today's standards . . . and yet it was much easier than manually typing each letter individually.

Armed with my now-antique "automatic letter writer," I went to work. By the middle of March, I was sending out a few solicitation letters almost every day. And within a couple of weeks, I actually began to receive donations in the mail.

I was very careful about the donation procedure. For one thing, I asked all contributors to make their checks out directly to MCCP, so there would be no question as to where the money was going. (This step also guaranteed that the donors would be able to receive tax deductions for their gifts.) I also told all potential contributors that in the event I didn't enter or complete any future marathons – regardless of the reasons why – their donations would *not* be returned.

My point here was an important one: I wanted every donor to understand that I had completed only two marathons so far, and that my quest to become the first person in history to run the 26-mile event on all seven continents represented an enormous personal challenge.

As my letter made clear – even though I didn't say it directly – success was by no means guaranteed, and the outcome was highly uncertain.

I wrote the letter in an effort to be completely honest with potential donors . . . but I must admit that I also had a second motive. By letting potential contributors know that I faced a huge challenge as a runner, I hoped to inspire them to challenge *themselves* . . . by digging a little deeper into their pockets for kids with cancer!

Right from the start, raising funds for sick children was a thrilling experience.

As people heard about what I was attempting, total strangers would approach me to ask if they could be put on my mailing list. Of course I was happy to accommodate them. And it wasn't long before the checks started rolling in. None were very large; most amounted to no more than $25. But one day I received a $100 donation, and I felt a powerful surge of excitement and energy. My approach was working!

It wasn't long before I established a regular routine. About once a week, I would bundle the checks and deliver them personally to the MCCP office. To enter the waiting room was like entering another world. Children who'd lost their hair to chemotherapy would be playing together and laughing in the corner. Mothers would be huddled together, talking softly among themselves about their difficult lives and the ordeals they faced in watching their loved ones undergo brutally difficult treatments.

On one particular day that I'll never forget, I hurried into the office with an unusually large batch of checks, and I felt very happy to be the bearer of lots of money for children with cancer. But then I spotted a young mother in the corner, sobbing inconsolably. I could only imagine the angst and turmoil she must have been suffering – and it brought me back to earth in a hurry. All at once, I felt a new urgency and a new sense of dedication as a fundraiser for this group of struggling parents and kids.

Responding to the powerful emotion of watching that mother suffer, I redoubled my efforts And by the time I was ready to leave for Japan, I had raised more than $5,000 in small donations for MCCP. I was very pleased to have been part of the process – and I was deeply touched by the outpouring of support that had helped me to raise the funds.

Interestingly enough, Japan had actually been my second choice as the setting for my Asian marathon. My original plan had been to compete in the Beijing Marathon . . . but dealing with the Chinese government and its mountains of red tape was nearly impossible, 20 years ago.

And that was a real shame, as far as I was concerned. For a couple of very good reasons, I'd long been dreaming of running in Beijing. First, Diane had read a great deal about China, and I knew she'd be avidly interested in seeing the country "up close and personal." And second, I owed her big-time for giving me so much love and support during my earlier training sessions and marathons. Diane was the glue that held our family together, and a trip to China was the perfect way to say, "Thanks for sticking with me through thick and thin!"

Of course, I also had my own reason for wanting to run the Asian leg of my marathon-challenge in the Middle Kingdom. Twenty years ago, far-off China was still thought of as an exotic, mysterious destination by most Westerners – and running a marathon there sounded a lot "sexier" than running it in Burma or South Korea or the Philippines!

Intent on treating Diane and myself to a Chinese adventure, I'd earlier contacted the country's Tourist Bureau in New York City. The staffers there were polite and friendly, but they couldn't tell me anything about marathons in Beijing. Frustrated, I then called the

Chinese Embassy in Washington. But once again, I got nowhere; nobody seemed to know anything about marathon-running in the great capital city of China.

After a great deal of fumbling around, I finally reached a Chinese official with whom I could clearly communicate. This helpful functionary assured me she would "do some research" on the question. And she was as good as her word: Only two days later, I got a phone call in which my new Chinese friend assured me that there was indeed a Beijing marathon. And she even had the date!

Success at last. But my jubilation was short-lived; after reading me the schedule, she went on to point out that all of the participants in Beijing are required to complete the 26-mile distance in no more than two hours and 50 minutes. Why this draconian demand? It was simple; because of the huge volume of traffic in Beijing, the authorities didn't dare close off the marathon route through the city for more than three hours!

Crestfallen, I thanked the lady and told her that I could easily run in the required 2:50 . . . but that I'd probably be at the 14-mile mark when the time expired!

So much for my dreams of Beijing. Suddenly, I faced a difficult challenge: I needed to find a running location in Asia, and the marathon would have to take place in late fall. Because my asthma made it impossible to train during the summer months, when the humidity soared, I was limited to late-fall marathons or to those that took place in the winter months. Of course, training in Maine from December to March wasn't a walk in the park, either, due to the extreme temperatures. But training in the cold was at least *possible.*

Feeling frustrated and confused, I started doing some serious research on Asian marathons. But I didn't learn much. I read through *Runner's World* magazine, along with several other running publications, and got nowhere fast. What I needed was an expert – so I contacted Joan Benoit Samuelson, the first woman to win an Olympic Marathon, who lived in Freeport, Maine. I'd met her previously at some of the short road races I'd taken part in . . . and I also knew her husband Scott through my business.

As I expected, Joan was most helpful and put me in touch with Amby Burfoot, a former winner of the Boston Marathon who at that time worked for *Runner's World*. Yes, I was in some very heady company! After I explained my predicament, Amby promised he'd go right to work helping me. He called back promptly and gave me a list of Asian marathons – one of which was the Lake Kawaguchi Nikkan Sports Marathon, held yearly at the foot of Mt. Fuji.

The event was scheduled for November 24, 1991. Perfect!

Every February Diane and I traveled to Vail, Colorado for a week of skiing, along with a group of ten corrugated-box factory owners from all over the country. Affectionately known as "SPOOC" (the Sheet Plant Owners and Operators Conference), our annual get-together had originally been designed as a skiing vacation combined with some business discussions . . . an arrangement that would allow the government to pay for part of the action via a tax write-off. Over the years, however – as the members aged – it gradually became more about business and less about skiing. I'd been invited to join in 1985, when a vacancy occurred.

It was a good time for all of us. After the week of skiing and eating, Diane and I would visit the magnificent Cordillera Spa in the adjacent mountains, before I headed back to Maine and the daily grind of selling corrugated boxes.

While relaxing one afternoon in the hot tub at the pool, I happened to overhear a woman who was planning a visit to her son in Japan. Her trip was being organized by a travel agent in Denver. When I asked her about her upcoming journey, she happily gave me the agent's name and phone number.

Diane called him as soon as we returned home. Dennis Briel owned The Travel Society, Inc. in Denver, and he was an accomplished world traveler. He'd visited Japan many times and was very excited about helping us plan our trip – especially when Diane told him that we'd set aside three weeks for the journey. (You'll soon notice – if you haven't already – that Diane doesn't do "short trips.") Her attitude is that if we've decided to go somewhere, let's do it right and spend enough time to really get to *know* the country we're visiting.

A wise strategy, don't you think? Dennis went straight to work.

While Diane worked on planning the Japan trip, my marathon training continued. Week by week, I slowly increased my mileage and did my best to avoid injury. Even though I had ample time, I felt pressure to maintain my five-day-a-week schedule for fear of losing conditioning. At the same time, I was doing my best to balance my business life and my married life . . . while also spending quality time with Judd, Derek and Allison.

At that point, I was running on a regular basis with two different groups. One group, which included Bob Delaney, Bob Rodman and Tracey Mezzanotte, ran the short days; the other group was content to run long, even though its members weren't training for a marathon. My three long-run partners – Al Mack, Bill Davenny and Kim Konieczny – were all faster runners than I was, but they never balked at slowing down to accommodate my pace.

Since we all had to be at work each morning, we sometimes left the gym in Portland as early as 3:00 a.m. in order to be able to complete a 15- or 18-mile run. I would often leave even earlier so I could set out water on the route every five miles or so; then I'd meet them at the gym at the prescribed time. Never did they fail to show up or choose sleep over a 15-mile run in the middle of winter. I'm indebted to each of them, since they made my quest both possible and doable.

Things were going well, but then I took a tumble. Somehow during this training period, I had hurt the rotator cuff in my right shoulder and had been undergoing physical therapy to curtail the discomfort . . . since lifting my arm out to the side was exceedingly painful. One early morning in pitch darkness, as the four of us were in the middle of one of our 10-mile runs, my foot hit a small pipe protruding from the street. I went airborne and landed directly on my right shoulder.

The pain was incredible. I was a couple of paces behind my partners when I fell, and when they couldn't hear the "swish" of my nylon running suit any longer, they looked back to see me lying prostrate on the asphalt. They rushed back, hoisted me to my feet and debated whether or not to call an ambulance. I assured them that I could complete the run and deal with the pain later. As I continued running, I noticed that the pain was subsiding and that I could move my arm in all directions, pain-free.

Maybe the worst was over? Back to the orthopedist I went to find out. Imagine my surprise when he informed me that I'd accomplished what he defined as a "self-manipulation" of my injured shoulder on the run! Somehow, I'd managed to knock my shoulder back into its proper position. What a fluke! Until then, I'd always thought that for "self-manipulation" you simply needed some privacy, a bathroom and a copy of Playboy or Penthouse!

From this point on, my training was uneventful and proceeded as in the past, with me increasing my mileage each week by about ten minutes. "Uneventful" may not be the correct terminology, however, since my running regimen had begun to take a major toll on the family. I felt wonderful and as if I could "conquer the world" – but I was also fatigued much of the time and not very good company when at home.

Diane and the children were very patient with me, however. Meanwhile, work on my mailing list for MCCP was continuing, and donations were arriving in the mail each day. At the same time, I had begun to realize just how satisfying and meaningful my fundraising was to me. Bringing the weekly checks to MCCP was very gratifying – but the satisfaction produced by delivering the money couldn't match the excitement I felt when raising it. In truth I was getting a lot more out of my efforts than I was putting into them . . . and the feeling I had about this volunteer work could best be described as "euphoric." But even that powerful word can't fully describe the joy I experienced as I worked to help these struggling Maine children.

Two weeks prior to our departure for Japan, I was at the gym and set to begin an easy three-mile warm-up run.

The street on which the University of Southern Maine gym is located contains a slight uphill incline, and it was here that we would begin our usual training runs. Now, you might assume that after 11 weeks of strenuous marathon training, a slight uphill run of less than two-tenths of a mile would be no problem. And yet, on this particular morning, I quickly found myself out of breath and struggling mightily. What to do? Amazed and disappointed, I cut the run short. Then I returned to the gym – thoroughly dismayed at my inability to complete something as simple as a three-mile jog.

I needed answers, and fast. So my first piece of business after reaching my office was to place a call to my allergist of many years, Dr. Bob Sigler. For the record: I've been a known asthma-sufferer since 1968, and I recently was diagnosed as having a chronic lung disease. Known as "COPD," or "chronic obstructive pulmonary disease," this progressive ailment can sometimes make it difficult to breathe. And according to the U.S. Department of Health and Human Services, "progressive" means the disease gets worse over time.

Not very comforting, when you think about it. But there it was – a diagnosis that couldn't be avoided after Bob gave me a breathing test in his office and I flunked it with flying colors.

He wasn't surprised by the outcome, however. And when he looked at the test results, he couldn't understand how I'd ever been able to run 26.2 miles in the first place. Nor was he able to tell me when the illness had begun. Since we had no "base-line" of past lung evaluations to work with, there was simply no way of knowing whether my lung deficiency had begun at birth or had developed later in my life. Bob's findings were troubling, of course, but not for long – because my attitude about such matters has always been to pay no attention to them. And I was now determined to live my life to the fullest, lung disease or no lung disease!

Still, it was an interesting – and unsettling – medical exchange. Bob is a barrel-chested guy with an ever present one-liter bottle of Coca-Cola on his desk and a pack of cigarettes tucked into his shirt pocket. He's also become a good friend over the years. How could I not laugh when he leaned back in his chair with his hands tucked behind his head and calmly said to me: "I hate to tell you this, but you're fucked!"

I looked him in the eye. "I know, but it's your job to un-fuck me! I'm leaving in two weeks for Japan, and I'm gonna run a marathon there."

Poor Bob just shook his head. But then he immediately put me on a high dosage of prednisone, a powerful steroid designed to combat a multitude of maladies. Within a week I was feeling better, breathing better, and ready for the trip to Japan – although not exactly brimming with confidence.

Our travel agent, Dennis, had outfitted us with a detailed, 25-page typewritten itinerary with guides provided all along the route. We flew First Class from Portland, Maine to Portland, Oregon, where we spent the evening at the airport prior to our departure. Upon our arrival in Nagoya, Japan, we were met by a guide and directed to the bus that would take us to the train station for the 43-minute trip on the Bullet Train to the ancient capital of Japan, Kyoto.

The change in scenery was fascinating, but it wasn't easy making ourselves understood. On previous trips abroad, Diane's French had been powerfully effective – but there was no correlation between Japanese and any language we knew. To prepare for the communications gap, we'd arrived at the Kyoto Rail Station armed with a map in English of the location of our hotel for the week, the Uemura Ryokan. Our game plan was to first secure a taxi, then show the driver our map and hope he could tell where we were headed.

That part of the strategy worked very well; the driver was able to drop us about a block from the *ryokan* (transliterated Japanese for "bed & breakfast"). But the tiny, ancient street on which the hotel stood was too narrow to allow for automobiles. To help us in such situations, Dennis had also given us a card which listed phonetic phrases such as "Doe chee ra hoe des ka?" (What's that, reader? Are you saying you don't understand a simple Japanese question such as: "Which direction is it?")

Somehow, we got where we needed to go. Here's how: We would ask, people would point, we would walk a block or so and then we'd repeat the process until we finally arrived at our ultimate destination. Unlike in the United States, most streets in Japan don't provide signage... so this is the method by which even the Japanese find their way around. Fortunately, they are a very friendly people and were most helpful in guiding two greenhorns from the States.

Soon after arriving in Kyoto, we met our Japanese hostess – a warm and friendly woman who loves Americans and speaks better English than we will ever speak Japanese. Right away, our savvy guide explained that there's a long-established "procedure" for entering a *ryokan*. It calls for visitors to enter the premises on a stone floor and then immediately don house slippers that are stationed near the entry. (Stepping onto a wooden floor in street shoes is strictly taboo.)

At Uemura Ryokan, we followed this procedure carefully and were delighted to discover that ours was the largest of the six guest rooms. It looked out on a tiny garden and featured the traditional *tatami*-matted floor. The hostess preferred that we remove our slippers and step on the *tatami* mat in our stocking feet as we entered our bedroom, and we were happy to oblige. There we quickly underwent a second "slipper routine."

All of this seemed a bit strange at first, and we were also startled to learn that when we required a visit to the W.C. (toilet), we would have to go down the hall, since none of the rooms contained their own toilets. When entering the stall, we were advised to leave our slippers outside the door; this strategy would tip off other visitors that the stall was now occupied. We then donned rubber slippers that were provided inside the stall. Interestingly, there were two distinct types of stalls: eastern and western. The latter contained a toilet, while the former consisted simply of a hole in the floor, over which the ladies squatted and did their business. It amazed me that the Asians found it more convenient to squat than sit, but traditional habits are difficult to break.

Of course, a similar ritual was required when visiting the *ofuro*, or bathing room. This vitally important enclosure contained a large tub and shower (for the Americans, I presume), and I found the experience very sexy. The bathroom was tiled and immaculately clean . . . and although it was small, we found that we had more than enough room in which to splash around and enjoy each other's company. Here the ritual called for sudsing yourself down and rinsing off under the shower, before climbing into the tub.

Dennis had earlier pointed out that the tub was large enough for only one . . . although two people could use it together if they were willing to be "very creative." And he was correct! We thoroughly enjoyed our "tub time," even if we eventually decided that the floor mat in our room was the best place for romance . . . after learning that the gymnastics required for *amore* in the tub were daunting in the extreme!

Another interesting ritual occurred daily at breakfast, which is traditionally provided at a Japanese *ryokan*. At the Uemura, a choice of traditional Japanese- or American-style fare consisting of toast, coffee and eggs was offered to guests each morning. Our attitude was, "When in Japan, do as the Japanese," so Diane and I both opted for the indigenous cuisine. Dennis had advised us to sample each – so we could decide which we liked better – but we wound up disregarding his advice. Japanese breakfasts are very flavorful – if you're a devotee of seaweed, pickled vegetables and raw eggs, that is! (You're supposed to pour the eggs over steaming hot rice, which supposedly cooks them a bit.)

Let's face it: a traditional breakfast in Kyoto isn't about Rice Krispies or Corn Flakes, and the pickled vegetables can be a bit strong in the early morning, to put it mildly. Their aroma reminded me of the mass halitosis that can overwhelm a New York City subway car when rush-hour passengers are sitting skin to skin and heart to heart. Not pleasant!

After breakfast, we headed off to meet our guide, Naoko Koizumi, otherwise known as "Rocky," who was waiting outside the front door of the *roan* (short for *ryokan*). The area in which it was located can be found in Kyoto's oldest neighborhood, called the "Goon." Behind the vertical slats of wood that front each building are some of Kyoto's most famous old wooden homes. It's a very understated neighborhood – intentionally so – and the headquarters for some of Kyoto's most famous *geisha* houses. In the evenings after dinner, Diane and I would often watch the *geishas,* dressed in their magnificent robes and sashes, as they walked along the streets. Arthur Golden hadn't yet written his bestselling *Memoirs of a Geisha,* which was unfortunate; that keenly observant book could have provided us with some helpful insights about their position and purpose in Japanese society.

Expertly guided by Rocky, we went first to the Old Imperial Palace in the very center of Kyoto. Even today when an emperor is crowned, the ceremony takes place here and not in Tokyo. Once again, it was off with the shoes and on with the slippers. Early in our visit, we briefly wondered if our discarded shoes would be safe, but we needn't have worried: There was no risk of footwear thievery in these tradition-minded precincts. (But *finding* your shoes later wasn't always easy – not when there were hundreds of pairs to choose from!)

Like the proliferating shoes, relics and statues of the Buddha are also ubiquitous in Japan. Almost every site that Rocky showed us either displayed vivid images of the great Asian religious symbol or proudly declared that some of the holy figure's ashes were buried on the grounds. We visited the Sanjusangendo Shrine (the name refers to the 33 bays containing "One Thousand and One" Buddhas located at the site) and also the Kiyomizu Temple, which is built on stilts and overlooks the city of Kyoto.

Then we went on to the Heian Shinto Shrine – an exact replica of the first Imperial Palace – and the Todai-ji Temple, which houses Japan's largest figure of Buddha. The great sculpture is 48.9 feet high, and its face alone measures 17.5 feet across. The eyes are more than three feet long and the ears extend more than eight feet. This temple is the largest wooden structure in the world, and it was indeed an impressive sight.

As we toured the various shrines and temples, Diane and I were constantly on the lookout for water. Our thirst was nearly unbearable . . . and it took us a while to realize that the culprit was our exceedingly salty breakfast. Apparently, the pickled vegetables and the pungent seaweed had taken their revenge!

We survived, however, and soon it was lunchtime. Once again, Rocky led the way (we'd hired him for the entire day). This time we enjoyed a simple, quiet meal . . . which left us quite hungry by the time the dinner-hour finally rolled around. Our guide had departed by then, so the two of us simply walked around our Kyoto neighborhood and chose a restaurant at random.

Ordering the meal turned out to be a comically difficult task. Since we had no idea what to order – or even what we would be eating – we were grateful that the Japanese in their infinite wisdom had placed plastic replicas of the various meals in the windows of their restaurants. Thank heavens! Both of us are reasonably quick learners, and it didn't take us long to establish our dining procedure. First step: Diane and I would enter the establishment where we intended to eat and then either find our own table or be led to one.

Next step: order a Kirin Beer. Then we'd scan the menu, quickly conclude that we had no clue what it said . . . and then take the nearest waiter by the hand and walk him right out of the restaurant – so that we could point out the "plastic version" of the meals we wanted.

That first evening in Kyoto, we chose something like "shrimp tempura." It was okay, if rather bland and ordinary-seeming . . . but when the bill arrived, I nearly fell out of my chair. Apparently, we'd ordered a very expensive delicacy! From then on, we limited ourselves to less exotic noodle dishes that were tasty and filling . . . and far less costly. This "point to the plastic" restaurant ritual continued throughout our entire stay.

One of the things we soon discovered in Japan was the importance of food in our daily travel – and how much we enjoyed looking forward to our next meal. (Eating was less fun when you didn't know what you were consuming, however . . . and we *did* grow weary of the non-stop noodles!)

On our second day with Rocky (we'd only contracted for a one-half day tour, and the balance of the afternoon would be spent exploring by ourselves), he dropped us off around noon. As he left in his taxi, Diane asked me what I'd like to do for lunch. I had been thirsty for two complete days by then (yes, we'd made the same "breakfast mistake" on Day No. 2), and my exact words to her were, "I don't know about you but I spotted a McDonalds about a block back – and that's where I'm heading!"

Up until the Japan trip, I don't think I'd eaten at McDonald's more than once or twice in my entire life. But there we were in Japan, nearly 6,000 miles from the U.S., and shamelessly enjoying the most delicious hamburger and fries I'd ever eaten!

Kyoto is a wonderful introduction to Japan and certainly one of its most beautiful and historic cities. But I still had a marathon to run – so each day we were in Japan, I needed to engage in some sort of training run, as short as it might be. During these sessions, I was always very nervous about finding my way back to our *ryokan* . . . so I made a practice of running straight down a main street and then back, with no turns or side streets allowed.

Looking back today, I still wish I'd been able to schedule the run at the start of the Japan trip, rather than at the end. Such an approach would have made the tour of the country more relaxed. As it was, however, I felt the pressure of knowing that 26.2 miles were still facing me, throughout our journey. As a result, I was conscious of every twinge or ache. In addition, I was thinking a lot about my fundraising for MCCP. Having raised nearly $10,000 for the kids, I was determined not to let my donors down by failing to complete the marathon.

Pressure! And it continued to mount, as we traveled for several weeks throughout the magnificent landscape of Japan.

Since Japan is deservedly famous for its shrines, temples and Buddhas, I won't attempt to describe every one we visited. Suffice it to say that the highlights of our amazing journey included the famed Kofuku-ji Temple, which houses the oldest pagoda in the world and which dates back to around 700 A.D. Two other highlights were a classic fishing village near the city of Onomichi, located on the Inland Sea and reachable only by boat . . . and of course, tragic Hiroshima.

Visiting the major shrines and temples of Japan was a memorable experience – but as a child of World War II, I was most interested in seeing Hiroshima. The largest city in the Chugoku region of western Honshu, it was the first urban metropolis to have been destroyed by an atomic bomb. It happened on August 6, 1945, when a nuclear weapon of unheard-of destructive power was detonated over the city.

Ironically named "Little Boy," the bomb wiped out huge areas of Hiroshima and helped bring a rapid end to the war. By this time, of course, the ultimate defeat of Japan was a foregone conclusion. Because Japanese Emperor Hirohito had refused to accept the Potsdam Declaration and surrender unconditionally, the Western world faced the grim prospect of being forced to attack the Japanese mainland with ground forces.

Some background: The historic Potsdam Declaration had stated that the Allies would invade Japan unless that nation surrendered unconditionally. But the invasion seemed certain, in the words of the Declaration, to result in "the inevitable and complete destruction of the Japanese armed forces and just as inevitably in the utter devastation of the Japanese homeland."

The ominously worded Declaration spoke for itself – but nowhere did it mention the option of dropping atomic weapons on Japan. Two days after it was issued, the Japanese rejected it outright – while announcing that it amounted to nothing more than a rehash of previous demands. Quite simply, they intended to ignore it. As it later became clear, they recognized the fact that defeat now loomed, but they were secretly negotiating with the Soviets to make peace on terms they imagined would be more favorable. (It should be noted that the Soviets had not yet declared war on Japan, even at this late date. Ever the opportunists, the Russians would ultimately wait until August 8, and just before the atomic bombing of Nagasaki, to declare war on Japan and then invade the Japanese puppet-state of Manchuria.)

U.S. President Harry Truman now faced the dilemma of choosing either to invade the Japanese mainland – a step that seemed certain to result in the loss of an estimated 1 million American lives – or to drop an unproven weapon of mass destruction on the stubborn Japanese. It was a brutal choice to have to make. The Allies had been firebombing the mainland on a nightly basis for months in an effort to convince the Japanese that there was no alternative to the unconditional surrender they demanded, but to no avail. Sixty-seven Japanese cities had been virtually leveled, triggering hundreds of thousands of fiery deaths.

Meanwhile, three cities had been selected as possible atomic targets: Hiroshima, Yokohama and Kyoto. Kyoto was a backup choice, due to the historical significance attached to the city as the country's ancient capital, and Hiroshima had become the primary target because it contained an important military depot, was the home of Japan's Second Army and also included a major communications center.

Early on the morning of August 6, 1945, a U.S. B-29 Superfortress bomber nicknamed the "Enola Gay" and piloted by Col. Paul Tibbets set out to make the fatal run over the city. Accompanied by two other B-29s, the bomb-carrying plane left the tiny island airfield of Tinian in the West Pacific for the six-hour flight to Hiroshima. As the planes approached Hiroshima, the clouds miraculously lifted to provide an open view of the city. Little Boy was then released for detonation at 1,900 feet above the city. When it exploded, nearly 80,000 people were incinerated immediately, with another 70,000 badly injured. Nearly 90 percent of the doctors and nurses in Hiroshima were killed or injured.

The carnage was overwhelming, but when the Japanese still refused to surrender, a second bomb was dropped on Nagasaki, killing another 80,000 and destroying the city.

Six days later the Japanese accepted the Allied terms of unconditional surrender.

It was with this history in mind that Diane and I arrived in Hiroshima for our visit to Ground Zero and the Hiroshima Memorial. The Hiroshima Peace Park is dominated by the Memorial Cenotaph, an arch-shaped structure shaped like the roof of an ancient Japanese house and symbolizing the concept of a comforting shelter for the souls of the victims. Beneath the arch is a chest containing the names of more than 140,000 people who died in the blast.

On the Cenotaph a powerful epigram declares in Japanese: "Let all the souls here rest in peace, for we shall not repeat the evil."

When Diane and I had our picture taken in front of the sculpture, the Flame of Peace and the Atomic Bomb Dome were visible in the background. We walked the circumference of the Peace Park, while sadly recalling the devastation and terror the natives must have felt during the nanoseconds before they were obliterated. In a somber mood, we then made our way to the Museum exhibits, where we also watched a film about the dropping of the bomb.

The museum isn't large, but the exhibits are very moving. As we soon learned, the schools of Hiroshima had been closed for sometime in August of 1945, while all able-bodied residents were being recruited for the war effort. Children were instructed to pick up bricks for re-use and at the time of the blast, 8:15 a.m., most were outside and at work. As we walked through the glassed-in exhibit area, we couldn't help but be moved by what we saw. A child's shoe or a child's shirt was the only item left behind that could identify its wearer. The bodies were unrecognizable. We looked at shattered eyeglasses and at briefcases which had somehow survived the searing heat of the blast.

It was very emotional. Imagine yourself as a parent summoned to identify your child by the shirt he or she had been wearing. Or by a shoe. Soon we were called to watch a brief documentary film . . . but it was at this point that I lost my feelings of sympathy and wanted to scream: "You started it!" Had these people forgotten the Bataan Death March and the documented beheading of American prisoners of war? The film portrayed the devastation in great detail and included gruesome pictures of scorched bodies. It was totally one-sided and cast the Japanese as victims and the Allies as ogres.

As sad as I felt about the young children killed and maimed, I still left the film angry. In spite of feeling irked at this rewriting of history, however, both Diane and I were pleased that we'd been able to make the journey to this remote area of Japan, since we're both enthusiastic history buffs.

On we went to the cosmopolitan city of Nagoya and a dinner with an illustrious gentleman-industrialist named Mr. Osawa. Throughout most of the trip, we had subsisted primarily on noodles . . . but tonight would be very different. Here's why: My company, Volk Packaging, had invested in a very expensive machine in order to manufacture its own corrugated sheets, and we'd bought that high-end item from Mr. Osawa. We'd had five partners in on the project – five packaging companies from four New England states who rarely competed with each other, but all of whom badly needed a dependable source of raw materials for our box-making.

Unfortunately, however, the giant machine needed to manufacture those materials – mainly sheets of corrugated cardboard – was cost-prohibitive. To solve our supply problems, our six companies had banded together and contracted to purchase 100 percent of our needs from our mutually created enterprise. We'd also collectively purchased the jumbo-sized sheet-manufacturing machine we needed – a $6.7 million beauty made by the Osawa Company of Nagoya, Japan.

Now, thank our lucky stars, it was Mr. Osawa himself who was going to take Diane and me out for dinner. I guess for $6.7 million, he could afford to spring for some Kobe beef! And so he did. The meal turned out to be amazingly delicious and featured an elaborate presentation, as the meat was cooked right at our table.

We could hardly wait. And we had prepared carefully for our meeting, because we knew that in Japan, making gifts to friends and associates is very important. When you're invited to someone's home, for example, a gift is always necessary. At weddings the invitees are expected to give the bridal couple a gift – and the happy newlyweds must *also* make a gift to each one of the guests. The present doesn't have to be something expensive; in Japan it's the thought that counts!

Having learned a great deal about this ancient Japanese custom, we'd brought along numerous souvenirs such as Maine-produced blueberry jam and Maine calendars galore. These goodies were already wrapped and ready to be presented to Mr. Osawa and anybody else we needed to impress. In return, the Japanese industrialist had brought us a clock and a small ceremonial knife with his company's name embossed on it.

It's a pleasing tradition, no doubt . . . but in all honesty, I suspect that none of these gifts made it past the nearest trash can!

We had now reached "crunch time," and the pressure on me was building faster than the volcano pressure at Pompeii in 79 A.D. I could feel my stomach churning and my temper becoming shorter by the minute, although my turmoil had nothing to do with Diane or anything she had done. The truth is that I was simply feeling the normal internal pressure associated with running 26.2 miles and becoming totally exhausted and depleted in the process.

While I did my best to fend off the heebie-jeebies, we trained to the Mishima rail station and were met by a driver for the ride to Kawaguchiko ("ko" means lake) and our stay at the Fuji View Hotel. From our window we had a magnificent view of the holy Mt. Fuji with its snow-capped, volcano-shaped peak. Upon checking in, we asked about the marathon and where we should sign in. The desk clerk had no idea about the sign-in location for the race; as a matter of fact, he had no idea that a marathon was even to be run in his city in two days.

His lack of knowledge about such a major event momentarily froze my blood, as I remembered an incident some years before in which one of my running partners – Kim Konieczny – had trained for months to run the Hamburg, Germany Marathon . . . only to discover on her arrival in the German city that the marathon had been cancelled! Recalling her trauma, I felt beads of perspiration forming and nausea rising in my gut. What if there was no marathon, and all my work had been for naught!

Yikes! Fortunately, however, we soon found a gentleman on the hotel desk who spoke passable English. He quickly made a call to the local police department and confirmed that there was indeed to be a marathon. Happily, the police officials even directed us to the starting line – which turned out to be located right down the street from our hotel!

Remarkably enough, the marathon had been mapped out so that it ran directly behind our lodgings. I'm not certain what our deskman was smoking, but it must have been powerful stuff!

After dinner in the hotel, Diane and I took a leisurely stroll to the starting point of the race. As we walked along, I couldn't help but notice that each of the electric poles had a very nice marathon banner hanging low enough to be easily reached. Thank you very much! With a cheerful smile, I instructed Diane to remove one of the pennants as soon as the gun went off to start the race. And why not? I figured the Japanese were too polite to question anyone about the pilfered banners . . . and also that they'd probably assume Diane had authorization to remove one. What could go wrong? Strangely enough, however, Diane didn't seem terribly interested in meeting my request.

Compared to the suspenseful Paris event, the Lake Kawaguchi Marathon was one big bore! Before the race, I'd had this romantic notion of running around the base of Mt. Fuji with magnificent scenery looming in every direction. No such luck. The route simply looped around the lake for two and a half revolutions, and I wound up looking at the same unchanging scenery throughout the entire run.

The only saving grace: the route was at least *flat*. But that didn't save me from the monotony of running for nearly five hours while feeling totally bored.

Still, the takeoff was interesting. Diane and I arrived at the starting point and milled around for a bit, just taking in the holiday atmosphere of a multitude of nationalities and American servicemen and women who were all eagerly anticipating the start. The two of us had been kidding each other that I would likely be the tallest person in the race. Not true. But I did earn another kind of distinction: Looking around at my fellow runners, I quickly realized that while I might not be the tallest, I was certainly among the heaviest!

A whistle sounded and without any verbal instruction at all, everyone around me began doing calisthenics. I joined the five-minute warm-up and then headed to the starting line for my Marathon Number Three. The roads around the lake were very narrow, so with 13,000 runners on hand, it was quite crowded and difficult to find ample running room. On two different occasions I had to come to a complete stop and wait for the road to clear itself of packed-in runners.

But it was really quite exciting, at first. The takeoff seemed extremely festive – given that the Japanese are very vocal and demonstrative – but as we headed away from the starting point and into the rural areas around the lake, it was rare to find anyone watching or cheering. There were no bands, as in Paris. There were no spectators handing out chocolates or fruit, either, and there was no crowd noise. Just the constant plodding of my feet against the pavement, one foot at a time, in the hope of finally arriving at the 26.2 mile mark and saying goodbye to my Asian marathon!

Diane was unable to follow me along the route, since there was no public transportation . . . and even if there had been, the enormous throng of runners would have made it impossible for vehicles to travel along these jammed roadways. There *was* a local water taxi for hire – but this strategy didn't seem practical to us, so Diane simply busied herself by having tea in one of the hotels along the route. As she waited for me to complete my first revolution of the lake, she noticed a number of Japanese runners stopping to eat or have a cigarette and gab with their families. Enjoying a cigarette in the middle of running a marathon, were they? My throat constricts and I find myself battling back a gag reflex at the very thought of inhaling a cloud of tobacco smoke under such conditions!

With the first third of the run concluded, I approached the starting point for the second time and all at once I saw Diane waiting for me. I also noticed that the marathon banners were still hanging from the poles. I asked her about our earlier discussion as I hobbled to a brief stop, and she confirmed that she had not yet complied with my request. Once again, I pointed out that the Japanese authorities weren't very likely to try and stop her, if she could find the nerve to go ahead and nab one. She sent me one of her famous "knowing nods" – her way of showing that she'd heard me, but didn't fully *agree* with me. Too bad! I wanted to argue with her, of course . . . but how do you quarrel with your mate when you're gasping along in the middle of a 26-mile endurance contest?

Back out I went for lake-lap number two. After completing my second go-round of the water-circuit, I looked up to discover a remarkable fact: At least eight of the roadside poles were now without banners. Once again, my wonderful wife had come through! She'd not only filched the single pennant that I'd requested – she'd also managed to swipe banners for our three children and one for the Maine Children's Cancer Program as a memento of my efforts on their behalf.

Suddenly, I felt terrific. And so what if by now my breathing had become labored and I was working very hard just to put one foot in front of the next? Actually, I think that much of my physical difficulty was simply due to the fact that you can only look at the same scenery for so long without starting to become comatose. Mt. Fuji is a magnificent spectacle, of course, but it was so distant as to be nearly invisible to those of us who were running ourselves into the ground that day.

Sooner or later, all things must pass, and the marathon eventually came to an end. Don't ask me how I did it, but I managed to plod along until the finish line was within plain view. It took me exactly four hours, 37 minutes and 40 seconds to cross that line, and when the gun finally sounded I was happy to have at last finished one of the most tedious runs of my life. As Diane and I returned to our hotel, weighed down by eight contraband banners which I was careful to keep concealed, several exhausted runners labored past us on the way to the finish line.

Let freedom ring throughout this land, I thought: I wasn't going to finish last in Japan!

The next morning we boarded our express train to the Narita Airport and began our voyage home. The marathon had been partially sponsored by a Tokyo newspaper, so while we were at the airport, we snapped up a special edition of a major newspaper that had printed the names of all of the marathon finishers. And as we

leafed through the eight-page extra, written in Japanese, I suddenly came upon my picture! The paper had run photos of only 36 of the 13,000 runners . . . and there was No. 12196 – the kid from Maine who'd battled his way to a thrilling 1066th-place finish – among his age group of 1,235 runners, that is. At least I hadn't come in last!

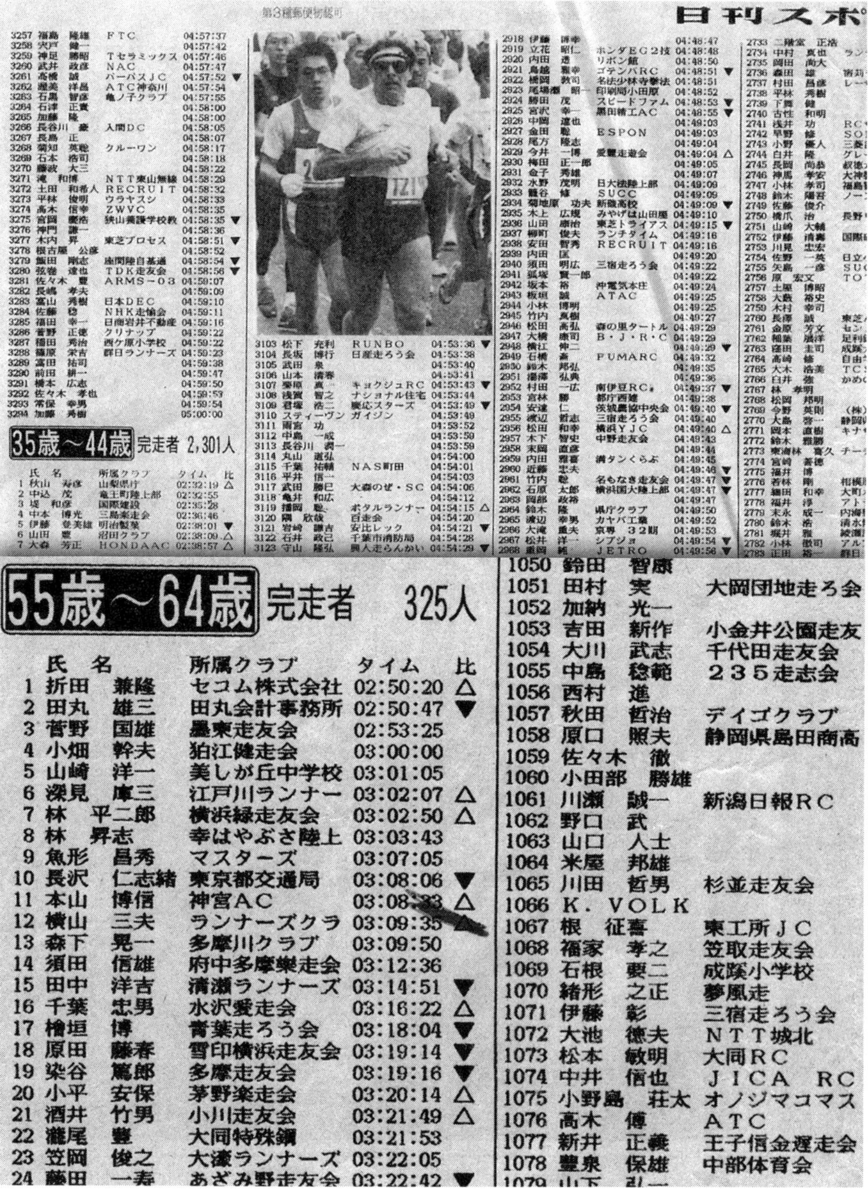

第3種郵便物認可

日刊スポ

	氏名	所属クラブ	タイム	比
3257	福島 隆雄	FTC	04:57:37	
3258	宍戸 健一		04:57:42	
3259	神足 勝昭	Tセラミックス	04:57:46	
3260	武井 政彦	NAC	04:57:47	
3261	高橋 誠	パーパスJC	04:57:52	▼
3262	渥美 洋昌	ATC神奈川	04:57:54	
3263	石黒 智彦	亀ノ子クラブ	04:57:55	
3264	石津 正貴		04:58:00	
3265	加藤 隆		04:58:00	
3266	長谷川 豪	入間DC	04:58:05	
3267	長島 正		04:58:07	
3268	菊知 英聡	クルーワン	04:58:17	
3269	石本 浩司		04:58:18	
3270	藤波 大三		04:58:22	
3271	滝 和博	NTT東山無線	04:58:29	
3272	土田 和希人	RECRUIT	04:58:32	
3273	平林 俊明	ウラヤスシ	04:58:33	
3274	高木 信幸	ZWVC	04:58:35	
3275	宮岡 慶浩	狭山養護学校教	04:58:35	▼
3276	神門 謙一		04:58:36	
3277	木内 昇	東芝プロセス	04:58:51	▼
3278	根古屋 公彦		04:58:52	
3279	飯田 剛志	座間陸自基通	04:58:54	▼
3280	弦巻 達也	TDK走友会	04:58:56	▼
3281	佐々木 豊	ARMS−03	04:59:07	
3282	長嶋 孝夫		04:59:09	
3283	富山 秀樹	日本DEC	04:59:10	
3284	佐藤 稔	NHK走愉会	04:59:11	
3285	福田 幸一	日商岩井不動産	04:59:16	
3286	菅野 正徳	クリナップ	04:59:22	
3287	稲田 秀治	西ケ原小学校	04:59:22	
3288	篠原 栄吉	群日ランナーズ	04:59:23	
3289	露田 祐司		04:59:38	
3290	前田 耕一		04:59:47	
3291	橋本 広志		04:59:50	
3292	佐々木 孝也		04:59:53	
3293	常保 幸男		04:59:54	
3294	加藤 秀樹		05:00:00	

35歳〜44歳 完走者 2,301人

	氏名	所属クラブ	タイム	比
1	秋山 寿彦	山梨県庁	02:32:19	△
2	中込 茂	竜王町陸上部	02:32:55	
3	堤 和彦	国際建設	02:35:28	
4	中本 博光	三島楽走会	02:36:46	
5	伊藤 登美雄	明治製菓	02:38:01	▼
6	山田 豊	沼田クラブ	02:38:09	△
7	大森 芳正	HONDAAC	02:38:57	△

	氏名	所属クラブ	タイム	比
3103	松下 充利	RUNBO	04:53:36	▼
3104	長坂 博行	日産走ろう会	04:53:38	
3105	武田 泉		04:53:40	
3106	山本 清春		04:53:41	
3107	栗原 真一	キョクジュRC	04:53:43	▼
3108	浅賀 智之	ナショナル住宅	04:53:44	
3109	君塚 浩二	慶応スターズ	04:53:49	▼
3110	スティーヴン ガイジン		04:53:49	
3111	雨宮 功		04:53:52	
3112	中島 一成		04:53:59	
3113	長谷川 潤一		04:53:59	
3114	丸山 道弘		04:54:00	
3115	千葉 祐輔	NAS町田	04:54:01	
3116	平井 信一		04:54:03	
3117	武田 勝巳	大森のぜ・SC	04:54:06	
3118	亀井 和広		04:54:12	
3119	播岡 聡	ポタルランナー	04:54:15	△
3120	隅 欣哉	百走会	04:54:20	
3121	岩崎 謙吉	安比レック	04:54:21	▼
3122	石井 政己	千葉市消防局	04:54:28	
3123	守山 隆弘	興人走らんかい	04:54:29	▼

	氏名	所属クラブ	タイム	比
2918	伊藤 洋幸		04:48:47	
2919	立花 昭仁	ホンダEG2技	04:48:48	
2920	内田 透	リボン館	04:48:50	
2921	鳥越 雅幸	ゴテンバRC	04:48:51	▼
2922	横岡 教司	名法少林寺拳法	04:48:51	
2923	尾場瀬 昭一	印刷局小田原	04:48:52	
2924	勝田 茂	スピードファム	04:48:53	▼
2925	宮沢 幸一	黒田精工AC	04:48:55	▼
2926	中岡 達也		04:49:03	
2927	金田 聡	ESPON	04:49:03	
2928	尾方 隆志		04:49:04	
2929	今井 一博	愛贋走遊会	04:49:04	△
2930	梅田 正一郎		04:49:05	
2931	金子 秀雄		04:49:07	
2932	水野 茂明	日大法陸上部	04:49:09	
2933	鶴谷 修	SUCC	04:49:09	
2934	菊地原 功夫	新磯高校	04:49:09	▼
2935	木上 広規	みやげは山田屋	04:49:10	
2936	山田 康治	東芝トライアス	04:49:15	▼
2937	柳町 俊夫	ランチタイム	04:49:16	
2938	安田 智秀	RECRUIT	04:49:16	
2939	内田 匡		04:49:20	
2940	須田 明広	三宿走ろう会	04:49:22	
2941	狐塚 賢一郎		04:49:22	
2942	坂本 裕	沖電気本庄	04:49:24	
2943	板垣 誠	ATAC	04:49:25	
2944	小林 博明		04:49:25	
2945	竹内 真樹		04:49:27	
2946	松田 高弘	森の里タートル	04:49:29	
2947	大橋 康司	B・J・R・C	04:49:29	
2948	横江 伸二		04:49:29	▼
2949	石橋 斎	PUMARC	04:49:32	
2950	鈴木 邦弘		04:49:35	
2951	播澤 弘典		04:49:36	
2952	村田 一広	南伊豆RC	04:49:37	▼
2953	宮林 勝	都庁西建	04:49:38	
2954	安達 仁	茨城農協中央会	04:49:40	▼
2955	渡辺 哲志	三宿走ろう会	04:49:40	
2956	松田 和幸	横浜YJC	04:49:40	△
2957	木下 智史	中野走友会	04:49:43	
2958	末岡 直彦		04:49:44	
2959	内田 雅喜	満タンくらぶ	04:49:45	
2960	近藤 忠夫		04:49:46	▼
2961	竹内 聡	名もなき走友会	04:49:47	▼
2962	石原 太郎	横浜国大陸上部	04:49:47	▼
2963	岡部 政裕		04:49:47	
2964	鈴木 隆	県庁クラブ	04:49:50	
2965	渡辺 幸男	カヤバ工業	04:49:52	
2966	大滝 盛夫	京専 32期	04:49:53	
2967	松井 洋一	シブジョ	04:49:54	▼
2968	鶴岡 純	JETRO	04:49:56	▼

	氏名
2733	二階堂 正浩
2734	中村 真也
2735	岡田 尚大
2736	森田 雄
2737	村田 昌彦
2738	平林 秀樹
2739	下舞 健
2740	古性 和明
2741	浅井 功
2742	早野 修
2743	小野 優人
2744	白井 隆
2745	長岡 [illegible]
2746	神馬 孝安
2747	小林 孝司
2748	鈴木 陽哲
2749	佐藤 俊介
2750	横爪 治
2751	山崎 大輔
2752	伊藤 清美
2753	川見 忠宏
2754	佐野 一英
2755	矢島 一彦
2756	原 宏文
2757	土屋 博昭
2758	大數 裕史
2759	木村 幸司
2760	長澤 誠
2761	金原 芳文
2762	桐島 勝洋
2763	窪田 圭司
2764	高崎 修
2765	大木 浩美
2766	白井 強
2767	林 孝明
2768	松岡 邦明
2769	今野 英則
2770	大島 啓一
2771	岡本 直樹
2772	鈴木 雅勝
2773	東海林 寛久
2774	宮崎 善徳
2775	福井 博
2776	若林 剛
2777	細田 和幸
2778	福井 淳
2779	末永 成一
2780	鈴木 浩
2781	堀井 強
2782	小林 徹司
2783	正田 裕一

55歳〜64歳 完走者 325人

	氏名	所属クラブ	タイム	比
1	折田 兼隆	セコム株式会社	02:50:20	△
2	田丸 雄三	田丸会計事務所	02:50:47	▼
3	菅野 国雄	墨東走友会	02:53:25	
4	小畑 幹夫	狛江健走会	03:00:00	
5	山崎 洋一	美しが丘中学校	03:01:05	
6	深見 庫三	江戸川ランナー	03:02:07	△
7	林 平二郎	横浜緑走友会	03:02:50	△
8	林 昇志	幸はやぶさ陸上	03:03:43	
9	魚形 昌秀	マスターズ	03:07:05	
10	長沢 仁志緒	東京都交通局	03:08:06	▼
11	本山 博信	神宮AC	03:08:33	△
12	横山 三夫	ランナーズクラ	03:09:35	△
13	森下 晃一	多摩川クラブ	03:09:50	
14	須田 信雄	府中多摩楽走会	03:12:36	
15	田中 洋吉	清瀬ランナーズ	03:14:51	▼
16	千葉 忠男	水沢愛走会	03:16:22	△
17	檜垣 博	青葉走ろう会	03:18:04	▼
18	原田 藤春	雪印横浜走友会	03:19:14	▼
19	染谷 篤郎	多摩走友会	03:19:16	▼
20	小平 安保	茅野楽走会	03:20:14	△
21	酒井 竹男	小川走友会	03:21:49	△
22	瀧尾 豊	大同特殊鋼	03:21:53	
23	笠岡 俊之	大濠ランナーズ	03:22:05	
24	藤田 一寿	あざみ野走友会	03:22:42	▼

	氏名	所属クラブ
1050	鈴田 智康	
1051	田村 実	大岡団地走ろ会
1052	加納 光一	
1053	吉田 新作	小金井公園走友
1054	大川 武志	千代田走友会
1055	中島 稔範	235走志会
1056	西村 進	
1057	秋田 哲治	ディゴクラブ
1058	原口 照夫	静岡県島田商高
1059	佐々木 徹	
1060	小田部 勝雄	
1061	川瀬 誠一	新潟日報RC
1062	野口 武	
1063	山口 人士	
1064	米屋 邦雄	
1065	川田 哲男	杉並走友会
1066	K. VOLK	
1067	根 征喜	東工所JC
1068	福家 孝之	笠取走友会
1069	石根 要二	成蹊小学校
1070	緒形 之正	蓼風走
1071	伊藤 彰	三宿走ろう会
1072	大池 徳夫	NTT城北
1073	松本 敏明	大同RC
1074	中井 信也	JICA RC
1075	小野島 荘太	オノジマコマス
1076	高木 博	ATC
1077	新井 正義	王子信金運走会
1078	豊泉 保雄	中部体育会
1079	山下 弘一	

Soon after our return to Maine, I paid a visit to MCCP and delivered the most recent round of checks. Most of them had arrived during our absence. (I also presented the organization with a purloined banner.) The additional checks received while we were in Japan had brought my total contribution to just under $8,000, which was enormously encouraging and gratifying to a guy who'd just run his hindquarters off in the Land of the Rising Sun.

My mailing list was growing fast and so was the amount of money flowing in. But I had to be circumspect about the trophy I'd carried home. As I presented the MCCP managers with their Japanese banner, I carefully avoided mentioning any details about how it had been obtained. They accepted the gift with their usual graciousness . . . and it was soon enshrined in the MCCP waiting room for all to admire.

A week later I received the following note from MCCP:

> *Dear Ken,*
>
> *The banner is beautiful! What a wonderful memento of your Run and ALL the money you raised for us!*
>
> *The banner is a GREAT addition to the walls at the center.*
>
> *You and Diane are terrific friends!*
>
> *Thanks a bunch,*
> *Your pals at MCCP*

Running the Japan marathon had required a huge effort . . . but as I read and reread that letter, I knew that all the stress and all the grueling hours on the road had paid off beyond my wildest hopes. My dream of running a marathon on each of the seven continents while raising funds for sick children was beginning to come true . . . and now it was on to Melbourne for the next chapter of what had become a thrilling saga, indeed!

THE MELBOURNE MARATHON

AUSTRALIA - MAY 31, 1992

Three marathons down, four to go!

By the time I returned to Portland from Japan, my determination to raise "major money" for the MCCP was soaring off the charts. From morning to night, I talked to everyone I met about my quest . . . while hoping they'd get the hint and donate generously to the struggling pediatric cancer patients of the great state of Maine. Full of passion for the cause I'd adopted, I had never felt so energized.

Fortunately for me (and for the children I yearned to help), most people proved to be very understanding – and my list of donors grew larger each day.

Portland is a small city by national standards, and word traveled fast. Soon the local newspapers got wind of my efforts, along with the local radio and television stations. And this growing media attention helped a lot. Example: From time to time, brief stories about my campaign would appear in the sports section of the paper, and these spurred donations from readers who'd been touched by the effort to raise funds for sick kids.

One day I received a call from a gentleman named Bill Green. Bill was the local sportscaster on our NBC television affiliate, and he wanted to interview me and do a piece on my efforts. We met on a sunny afternoon at a running path around the Back Bay of Portland, and the production crew taped the two of us as we jogged along and talked about my marathons and my fundraising.

When I asked when the spot would appear on television, Bill told me I could expect it that evening "as long as a plane doesn't hit the oil tanks." The tanks he was referring to were large petroleum storage vessels situated right beside the Portland airport. Well, a plane didn't "hit the tanks" that evening . . . but President Bush *did* choose that night to make a major address to the nation at six p.m. As a result, the piece on me which had been scheduled to run for three minutes was cut down to less than a single minute.

So much for the media stardom I'd been expecting! Still, there's no such thing as "bad publicity" – and I was grateful for Bill's efforts. Encouraged and energized, I continued writing letters and exhorting potential contributors, and the donations continued to roll in.

Trust me: There's no greater satisfaction than delivering money to a worthwhile charity – and especially one that focuses on the needs of kids with cancer.

For Diane and me, the Australia marathon will always be a "family affair."

Why? It's simple: Our daughter, Allison, a junior at the University of Pennsylvania in Philadelphia, had decided to follow her mother's example – by spending her junior year abroad. Diane had loved her year in France, of course . . . but the free-spirited Allison had ideas of her own.

Allison's destination? You guessed it: the wide-open blue skies of Australia!

At first glance, it seemed like a strange choice. But when Allison explained the reasons behind her "Aussie" move, we quickly understood. As it turned out, all of her friends were going the "traditional" route – meaning that they had opted for London or Paris. That was fine for them, but as usual, the independent- minded Allison had ideas of her own.

Hungry for a new experience, she came upon a one-semester academic program that was based in Melbourne. And knowing that, I didn't have to think very hard in order to decide when and where I wanted to complete my Australian marathon.

Melbourne, here we come!

As I would soon discover, it was an excellent choice – and not only because it would connect me so powerfully with Allison. Melbourne is a beautiful city, but smaller and more laid-back than Sydney; in many ways, comparing Melbourne and Sydney is like comparing Boston and New York. The two cities also share the same kind of rivalry that exists between Beantown and the Big Apple.

Allison had done her research well – and even though none of her college professors had ever had a student choose Australia for foreign study, she was able to work out a powerfully appealing curriculum of studies there. Much of her time would be spent exploring the physical landscape . . . in an Independent Study Program (or ISP) which called for her to write a paper that would serve as her Senior Thesis as a sociology major at Penn. The Thesis was required for graduation, and hers could be based on Australian culture, or on the people of the country, or on an event of historical interest.

She chose to write about an earthquake that had occurred in the town of Newcastle, a small suburb of Sydney. What made this event so compelling was that the earthquake hadn't been expected, since Newcastle isn't located on a "fault line."

Along with writing the paper, Allison would engage in a series of extensive travels throughout the country. (Jokingly, she and her fellow students often referred to the program as the "I Study on Planes" program.)

I'm not sure just how much "traditional education" Allison received in Australia, but the experience was well worth the tuition. Moving swiftly and efficiently, she'd soon arrived in Melbourne and had been assigned a family for the semester. Upon arriving at their home, she discovered that it was a Hasidic Jewish family steeped in that ultra-religious tradition. Her hosts also had two small children, with a third on the way. Staying with this family would require her to live in the far suburbs of Melbourne, in an area where many members of the Hasidic faith had chosen to make their homes.

And there was more. Since the strict orthodox creed of her hosts prohibited riding in automobiles on the Sabbath, Allison would have to be home by sundown on Friday. Saturdays would be spent in solemn prayer. And even on the days when she wouldn't be bound by religious restrictions, bus transportation to her area shut down about ten o'clock each evening. This wasn't exactly what she'd had in mind while making her plans; if she'd wanted this kind of "foreign study" experience, she would have gone to Israel!

What to do? After a few tearful trans-Pacific telephone calls between Melbourne and Vail, Colorado (we were there for our annual Sheet Plant Owners and Operators "golf, ski and eat" meeting), Allison spoke with the program director and was able to change her host family. These families are paid a small stipend for taking in students, and this one was quite upset to learn that Allison was leaving. Unfortunately, there were some angry words, and Allison wound up feeling that the miffed family wanted a student primarily for the income, and also to perform as a baby sitter.

Allison couldn't escape from that home fast enough – and she soon made her way to a new residence, located just minutes from downtown Melbourne. Her "Australian Parents" were Dick and Sandy Sutcliffe. Dick was an anesthesiologist and Sandy a nurse. They didn't take students in for the money; instead, they were genuinely interested in meeting new people and broadening their horizons. They had two children, Andrew (now an accountant) and

Julie, both of whom were students. In addition, Sandy's mother – "Granny" – lived in their beautiful house.

They welcomed Allison into their home as another daughter and, in the same way that Diane's "French Family" had embraced her and included her in all family activities, they made our daughter an important part of their family life. My only concern at the time was that Allison and Andrew (or any other Aussie, for that matter!) might bond . . . and then my daughter would end up living in Australia with my grandchildren. I think that's a fear experienced by most parents of students who live abroad . . . and I also think it's entirely understandable.

In this case, however, my anxiety proved to be groundless. Andrew later received his M.B.A. from the University of Florida, and the Sutcliffe family journeyed all the way to Maine in order to attend Allison's wedding to Drew Isaacman. The two families have remained in close contact, and in 2010, Allison, Drew, and their three children (Emily, Max and Zachary) traveled to Melbourne to "relive" Allison's experience and meet her adopted family.

The Sutcliffes were gracious hosts, as expected, and they offered Allison and her family the use of their beach home while they were in the Melbourne vicinity. My daughter and her crew also stayed with Andrew and his family while in Melbourne, and both sets of children were able to get acquainted. Understandably enough, Allison and her family were delighted to have been so fortunate as to see some of Australia through the eyes of Australians. Allison was soon able to reciprocate, when Andrew and his family visited her in San Diego in the fall of 2010.

So much for the background. While I thoroughly enjoyed hearing about Allison's "Australian Adventure," I also understood that I needed to get my act together for the fast-approaching Melbourne Marathon. Fortunately, I had some time to prepare. Unlike what had happened in Paris, I knew far in advance when the event would occur – and I was able to begin my training relatively early.

I hoped to build my strength up slowly, by adding the same 10 minutes a week until I was able to run 15 miles without much strain. Then, on February 28th, three months prior to the race, I would again begin the arduous process of conditioning my body for a regimen that would culminate in running 22 miles, two weeks before race day.

My first "official" training day was on a Saturday and I met my running partners – Al Mack and Bill Davenny – at the University of Maine gymnasium on Falmouth Street in Portland. We ran five or six miles at a leisurely pace and then they peeled off to head back to the gym so Al could open his business for the day. It was a beautiful morning and I felt wonderful, so I decided to continue for another four or five miles. As I trotted down Falmouth Street, I was thinking about how terrific I felt.

Was it fate? Had I angered the running gods by boasting about my physical well-being? All I know is that at that very moment, I felt a noticeable pull in my left hamstring. I continued on – but it soon became apparent that my running was over for that day. I iced the area down and hoped for the best . . . but when there was no improvement over the following week, I gave in to my usual impatience and quickly presented myself at the office of my orthopedic surgeon, Doug Brown.

I asked for an immediate evaluation, since my medical coverage required a referral for physical therapy. Having been through this same experience with my left calf – while preparing for the Lake Kawaguchi Marathon – I knew instinctively that Doug was going to order a regimen of physical therapy. And I was right. All too soon, I found myself back at Saco Bay Physical Therapy for "P.T." with my "personal physical therapist," Kurt Jepson.

It was frustrating, to say the least. Of course I also winced when I saw the bills . . . and I couldn't help wondering if Kurt was beginning to look at me as his "annuity." If it were up to him, I'd run five or ten marathons a year! But there was no way around it, so I did my best to put up with the heat treatments, the stretching and the ultrasound therapy . . . all of which was coupled with regular workouts at the University of New England pool and gym. Each morning I headed from Portland to Biddeford to run in place in the pool for an hour and then, on prescribed days, I trekked back to Saco Bay Physical Therapy for more treatment.

Maybe if I hadn't been in the "Clydesdale Division" of runners (those over 200 pounds), I could have withstood the rigors of training. But I wasn't about to give up my evening martini with the cheese and crackers on the side. No way! Hey, I figured that the running "washed out" the martini . . . and the cocktail hour was certainly worth it . . . even if it *did* mean that I'd have to train harder, run longer and be more tired at the end of each run. (By the way: I continue to enjoy my evening martini even at this writing. Some things will never change!)

Of course, I readily admit that running in the water at 6 a.m. is probably one of the most boring activities ever invented by humans. Still, it kept me in reasonable shape until I could resume my outside running. After about two weeks, I felt well enough to wave goodbye to UNE and test the leg outside.

I ran slowly and gingerly at first, but I couldn't wait to return to serious training. After putting in another restless and impatient week of preparation, I finally decided that I was healthy enough to rejoin my running partners. And the rest of my training was of the very best kind: injury-free!

Marathon Day. May 31, 1992. (Warning to readers: This is going to be a very short paragraph!) As I write this memoir, I must confess that I have no recollection whatsoever of anything memorable occurring during the marathon.

However, I do remember the start of the race at the Olympic Village in Melbourne. The route passed the National Tennis Centre, home of the Australian Open Tennis Tournament, and the

Melbourne Cricket Grounds; then it wound through the suburbs of Melbourne before finally arriving at the Eiffel Tower replica, which is a major landmark in the Victorian Arts Centre at Melbourne Center.

Ken and Allison at the finish line.

For the most part, it was a very forgettable event. What I *do* recall, though, is that it was difficult for Allison and Diane to follow me along the course of the run. I can also say with certainty that I finished in 4:13:20 – less than one minute behind my time thirteen years before. I didn't realize it then, of course, but I was destined to break the five-hour mark only one more time . . . and by a margin of only about a minute.

Although I drew little inspiration from the passing landscape, I did have a powerful motivator on the Melbourne run. Only the previous July, our first grandchild had been born . . . and so I'd pinned a cute photo of little Dylan to my singlet. I knew his smile would give me the boost I needed whenever the going got tough! Each time I felt like I had nothing left in my legs, I'd tilt his picture up to my face and gain major inspiration. Looking at his vivid features and recalling my fundraising efforts of the past months – along with my reasons for making them – gave me *plenty* of determination to complete the grueling marathon.

This "Dylan Strategy" worked very well . . . and it soon evolved into a pleasing tradition in which I would carry pictures of Dylan and his sister, Mariah, with me on all my runs to double my inspiration. Like the fabled "post-marathon tradition" that Diane and I had so thoroughly enjoyed, this new ritual would play an important part in my future marathons.

Success can be measured in many different ways, and in my case, success was achieved by making sure I was effective in fundraising – along with simply finishing the marathons and also basking in the continuing love and support I got from my entire family.

The Australian event was deeply satisfying, but later I was so fatigued from the run that I could barely keep my eyes open. At Melbourne, in fact, my exhaustion was so pronounced that Diane and I even had to forgo our "post-race tradition." After returning to our hotel and showering, we simply headed out to meet Allison for dinner. It was a delightful meal, but as I dug into my steak and nipped at the red wine we'd ordered (another post-race ritual), I could feel the fatigue throbbing in every one of my muscles.

This may sound hard to believe . . . but as we were walking back to the hotel after our sumptuous meal, I actually fell asleep while walking! I'd never thought it possible, but when I started lagging behind Diane and Allison, they looked back at me and realized I was fast asleep but still erect and walking. I did make it back to the hotel while awake – but the same thing occurred while we were going up in the elevator. Fortunately, I didn't fall down; Diane gently nudged me awake and took my arm as we walked to our room.

Good night, sweet prince! Dead-tired to the bone, I slept like a man who'd been drugged.

The next morning, the three of us bade goodbye to the Sutcliffes and boarded a train to Horsham for a visit to a working sheep ranch. Known as the Glenisla Homestead and located adjacent to the Grampion Mountains National Park, the grazing land was owned and operated by Eric and Evelyn Barber, whose Australian roots reach all the way back to the founding of the area by the original settlers.

The Barber ranch is classified as a National Historic Trust and there's even a plaque commemorating "Evie's" ancestors along the road. The original founders, the Carter family, built the homestead in 1843. It isn't a large ranch – not by Australian standards – but it does occupy a lucrative niche as a producer of some of the world's finest wool for the manufacture of high-priced clothing. The layout consists of a main house surrounded by connected bunkhouses for guests and workers.

Our visit was quite pleasant. All our meals were included – we ate with the family – and we enjoyed a cocktail before dinner. (About that aspect, they didn't have to ask me twice!) The discussion was also lively and interesting. Example: As we gabbed away happily one evening, I happened to ask our host if he ever had to put up with "disagreeable guests." He thought for a minute . . . and then informed me that he "automatically added ten percent" to his price when reserving accommodations for visitors from New York. (My apologies to my New York-based children – hey, I'm only reporting what he told me . . . so please don't "shoot the messenger!")

When I asked our soft-spoken rancher why he hiked the fee

for New Yorkers, he simply shrugged his shoulders and asked me why he couldn't. I had no answer to that. His next comment was: "I don't care. They can stay home if they don't like it." This seemed like a pretty independent attitude, but I guess he felt entitled. His roots were pretty deep in Australia, after all. To understand how he felt, imagine belonging to a family whose ancestors had included residents of the original Thirteen Colonies of the United States. In that situation, a Yankee Blueblood might feel he was allowed a certain degree of smugness and arrogance, don't you think?

At any rate, this crusty gentleman was obviously a major-league curmudgeon. And he *did* have a thing about New Yorkers, whom he described as "never satisfied." He pointed out that no matter how hard he and Evie tried to please them, they inevitably complained that they were being short-changed as guests. On one famous occasion, for example, as Eric was guiding a Big Apple guest through the countryside, the Aussie host spotted a koala nestled in a tree.

When he stopped to give the greenhorns (his guests) a better look, this particular tourist decided that a view from ground level wasn't enough. He wanted an "up close and personal" look at the koala – and obtaining it would require him to climb a nearby tree.

Eric shrugged; who was he to question his guest's big-city wisdom? So up the tree the loudmouth visitor went. What Eric failed to explain, however, was that one of the koala's key defenses is its remarkable ability to spray attackers with urine. And this isn't just *any* old urine; when it comes to the koala, we're talking about an effluent that smells like month-old skunk!

Can you picture the scene? As the poor, unsuspecting New Yorker climbed closer to the koala, the uneasy animal kept glaring at him and shifting his position. And then it happened. With the climber located directly beneath him, the koala cut loose with a torrent of reeking piss! And the torrent landed with deadly accuracy on the head and torso of Mr. New York!

Raging and bellowing, the offended "Mr. Disagreeable" scampered down . . . and was forced to remove all his clothes before being allowed to re-enter the tourist van. Eric found the incident hysterical – and who could blame him?

During the hours of daylight, Diane, Allison and I took long walks on country roads and over fields that contained thousands of sheep, along with the occasional platoon of cavorting kangaroos and emus. It's often been said that "there are more sheep than people in Australia" . . . and based on what we saw during our strolls, that estimate is entirely accurate.

As we passed their flocks, the sheep took notice and stopped grazing in order to watch us pass. And the effect was quite comical; it was like watching the spectators at a tennis match as their heads swiveled back and forth in response to the flight of the ball. We also got a good laugh when the ranch-owner took us on a truck ride around his spread . . . and wound up chasing a panicked emu across the terrain at a blistering 20 miles an hour! (He wanted to show off the speed of this amazing bird.)

We had a blast. After two days of decompressing from the marathon, we said goodbye to our hosts and headed to the airport for the flight to Alice Springs, home of the great monolith – Ayers Rock – that dominates the center of Australia. We enjoyed an uneventful flight (the best kind), then retrieved our rental car and took off toward the Sheraton Resort Ayers Rock. My job was to transport the luggage while Diane handled the logistics of checking in. Allison helped me unload, and then we headed off to the registration desk to find Diane.

And then it happened. As I was walking along with our two bags, I heard a "Psst! Psst! Dad!" I looked over and saw Allison beckoning with an index finger and then pointing down at the floor. Was there a problem? Puzzled, I followed my daughter's stricken gaze . . . and discovered that I had traipsed right into the middle of a huge painting being worked on by one of the Australian Aborigine women. (Their paintings are composed of a series of multi-colored dots arranged very precisely on the canvas to create the effect the artist desires.)

As I stared back at Allison, horrified at what I'd done, I spotted the artist sitting cross-legged on the floor with a look of sheer hatred on her face. If this lady had had a gun, she'd have used it in a New York nano-second. What a gaffe! Moving as carefully and gingerly as possible, I tiptoed off her artwork and beat a fast retreat to the front desk, without ever looking back. Thinking about my blunder later, I fervently hoped that I'd done no damage to the masterpiece . . . and I contemplated the idea of purchasing the artwork myself, in order to make amends.

But then I priced some much smaller works in the hotel gift shop, and I realized that as much as I didn't want to look like the "Ugly American," there was no way I could afford to buy this artisan's huge rendering! And besides, I rationalized: The painting hadn't exactly been fenced off, had it? Had there even been any warning signs? Was it really my fault that I'd stepped on the damn thing?

In the end, I managed to convince myself that I was blameless in the incident. Still, I did make it a point to avoid the ticked-off *artiste* during the rest of our stay in Alice Springs. I'm sure my fears were baseless . . . but I couldn't shake the mental image of her arriving with her relatives – all of them outfitted with vicious-looking spears – in order to exact vengeance against the destroyer of her precious art!

Ayers Rock is a sacred site for the Aborigines of Australia. Rising to a majestic height of 863 meters (2,831 feet) above sea level, this is the second-highest monolith in the world (after Mount Augustus, which is two-and-a-half times larger and also located in Australia). Like an enormous iceberg, Ayers Rock penetrates the earth to a depth of 3.5 miles – so it's not surprising to learn that the Aborigines regard this great landmark as a symbol of creation and also treat it with the utmost reverence.

According to the geologists, the monolith was formed over a period of more than 500 million years. A well-known landmark in the Uluru National Park, Ayers Rock is often said to be positioned at the exact geographical center of the country . . . and for many years, climbing the vast sandstone hulk was strictly prohibited out of respect for the Aborigines.

All of that changed in 1983, however, when then-Prime Minister Bob Hawke transferred the title of Ayers Rock to its original owners – the Aborigines – with the condition that visitors to Australia would henceforth be permitted to climb the geological icon under careful supervision. As expected, the appeal of this famous landmark was widespread. One of its most attractive features can be found at sunset, when the giant mass of stone reflects spectacular shades of orange, red and purple. The experience isn't completely enjoyable, however, since visitors are required to wear mosquito nets while watching the sun disappear over the horizon. Fighting off the swarming "skeeters" is a bit of a bummer, but most visitors to Australia agree that the rock is a "must see" if your travels take you anywhere near Alice Springs.

On the morning after our arrival, we awoke early in order to beat the crowd and the heat. Our goal was a challenging one: We hoped to climb all the way to the summit of The Rock.

The first part of the trek was the toughest, as we gritted our teeth and battled our way across 200 to 300 yards of remarkably steep terrain. It was no easy assignment, but the presence of a "climbing rope" made the task somewhat less formidable.

Allison had already climbed to the top on another occasion, and Diane soon decided that the enormous effort wouldn't be worth the payoff . . . so the two of them called it quits at the halfway point and headed back down the slope. I mustered on, however, determined to reach the summit. Once past the initial steep section, the climb upward became more leisurely and I "summated" rather easily. From the top you could see for miles around – although in all honesty, there wasn't much to see except many miles of barren-looking, desert-like flatlands.

After about 20 minutes of strolling around the summit and having my photo taken by another climber, I headed back down to reunite with Diane and Allison. As I was descending, I couldn't help applauding myself a little bit for the rigorous physical conditioning that had allowed me to meet this stern uphill challenge. Yes, I was feeling pretty good about myself at that moment – as a highly trained marathoner who'd demonstrated that he could take on the most demanding physical tests and live to tell the tale!

Wouldn't you know it? Even as I was mentally patting myself on the back, I came upon a narrow ditch. Unconcerned, I vaulted the obstacle . . . and heard a distinct "pop" in my right calf. I didn't know if I'd torn a calf muscle or simply pulled one – but what I *did* know was that I could no longer walk in a normal "heel to toe" manner. All at once, I discovered that my right foot had to be pointed out to the right, if I expected to cover any ground. I also was forced to take very short steps in order to proceed.

Unbelievable! There I was, only a hundred yards below the summit – and now I would have to limp my way down the rock-face in a series of tiny baby steps, each of which triggered a blast of searing pain. To this day, I don't know how I made it back to Diane and Allison. Once there, however, and while groaning in misery, I made my way to a tour bus in order to see if they might have any ice available for their passengers. One did, and I immediately began applying ice to the area in the hope of avoiding swelling and further damage to the calf.

After taking these immediate first-aid steps, I headed off to visit a local "Doc in a Box" for a full-fledged medical evaluation. Thankfully, the medico didn't suspect a muscle tear and simply recommended that I continue the icing routine. Apparently, I'd escaped what would have been a very damaging and painful tear. Still, it took about a week before I could resume jogging. Thankfully, what I'd experienced was simply a bad muscle pull – and I was soon able to resume my daily running. (Although I didn't realize it at the time, this was to be the first of many visits I would make to doctors in foreign countries. Diane maintains that the visits took place because I like to "spread the wealth.")

Our next stop was the Coburg Peninsula, perched 150 nautical miles off the coast of Australia, where we planned to enjoy a few days of R&R at Seven Spirit Bay Resort. A spectacular setting with equally spectacular accommodations, Seven Spirit Bay offers a leisurely atmosphere . . . while also providing its guests with plenty of optional activities. The Peninsula is the home of some of the best reef and tropical sports fishing in the world, and its promotional brochure brags about the "totally unique experience, incorporating luxury accommodations and superb food and wines, all set in the wilderness of the Gurig National Park" that can be enjoyed by the spoiled visitors to these posh precincts.

To reach Seven Spirit Bay, you have to board a small, one-engine plane, then fly over the Timor Sea and land on a runway made of dirt and gravel.

To digress momentarily: For years, whenever our family had traveled to Florida over the Christmas holiday, Diane had insisted on flying only on the "big jets." No "turbo props" for her! (The fact that for many years all commercial jet planes had *been* turbos – and that they'd proven to be very reliable aircraft – simply had no bearing on the case!) Because of Diane's strange attitude about the turbo props, we often found ourselves flying from Palm Beach to Boston . . . and then having to wait three hours for the next "big" jet from there to Portland.

There was usually, however, a turbo prop which left Boston for Portland about 30 minutes after we arrived in the Massachusetts city. Fat chance! Inevitably, I found myself crawling with impatience . . . since our post-Florida journey usually coincided with either the National Football League playoffs or the college football bowl season. I really hated waiting in Boston any longer than necessary – so on many occasions, I'd take the small plane home alone, watch the football game while enjoying a refreshing martini and awaiting Diane's call announcing that she'd arrived safely in Portland. (Secretly, of course, I often hoped she'd experience a major delay – just so I could prove my point!)

Anyway . . . the comical fact here is that on our Australian jaunt to Seven Spirit Bay, we were required to board a small, one-engine plane piloted by a kid who looked to me to be about 13 years old! Was this baby-faced youngster really going to fly us over crocodile-infested waters? Yes, he was. And amazingly enough, Diane didn't seem to mind; defying all human logic, she seemed to regard the little kid at the controls (it looked to me as if he'd never used a shaving razor) as the full equivalent of two Delta co-pilots and their combined decades of flight experience.

Somehow, the airborne tyro got us to our destination, while the utterly relaxed and utterly unconcerned Diane sat reading a magazine and enjoying the flight!

Seven Spirit Bay Resort was all that its propaganda had built it up to be. Each guest was housed in a personal "habitat" overlooking the ocean and facing east for a view of the sunset. No air conditioning was needed, and wooden louvers provided the necessary privacy – even though no unit looked directly out on another. All meals were provided, and the easygoing experience proved to be a wonderful respite from the very active trip we'd been having up to that point.

Each morning a list of activities – such as bushwalking, fishing or sailing on the resort's 50-foot yacht, the *Touché* – was posted, and the delighted guests could opt for anything that appealed to them. Or they could do nothing. One day a bicycle trip through the jungle was on the menu, and Diane and I signed up immediately. (Allison chose to take a hike.) The bikes weren't high-tech, and the challenge presented by the terrain certainly was demanding – so it didn't take Diane long to decide that brains were better than brawn, and then to head straight back to the lodge. After her departure, I was left with the guide and two female tourists, a mother and her daughter, who hailed from Denmark.

The ride was both beautiful and exhilarating and we worked up a pretty good sweat, before finally arriving at a clearing and a deserted beach. The guide asked if any of us were interested in a swim – and the two ladies jumped eagerly at the idea of cooling off. Fine, said the guide . . . but first, he needed to check the area for crocodiles. (All of us quickly agreed that, yes, a quick crocodile-check was probably a sensible idea!)

As we walked along the beach, the guide pointed to the outlines of crocodiles which had slept there in the recent past. Then he showed us the footprints they'd left behind, as they made their way back to the water. (You can be sure that we were thoroughly impressed.) Once the area was declared safe, however, the two Danes didn't hesitate; in a flash, they were out of their clothing and into the water. No problem. After slightly revising that old epigram ("When in Denmark, you must . . ."), the guide and I quickly joined them. Soon all of us were frolicking happily in the beautiful warm water.

I made sure to stay on the shore side of the guide, however, figuring that if we didn't see any crocodiles on our way out, they'd have to encounter the guide before they encountered me. (When it comes to devising anti-crocodile strategies, I'm usually pretty quick on my feet.)

Actually, we had a lot of fun. After too brief a liquid sojourn, we exited the water, dressed and headed back to "civilization." (Dinner that evening was rather interesting, since the two frolicsome Danes were seated at the next table; at times I found it difficult to focus on the food.)

But then I sobered up – in a hurry – as Diane and I realized that Allison hadn't yet returned from her hike . . . and that she'd set out alone and unguided on her foray into the unknown. Not good! We immediately alerted the hotel, and they sent out a search party to locate her. And it turned out to be the right move at the right time . . . because Allison had indeed lost her way for a while. After a few moments of real panic, Diane and I were immensely relieved by the news that she'd been found safe and was headed back to the resort. She didn't seem too concerned about her adventure, but her parents had gotten a major scare, at least briefly. Trust me: this was the kind of "excitement" that parents can do without!

It was soon time to depart Seven Spirit Bay and head back to civilization, so back on the one-engine Piper Cub we went – with "Junior" once again serving as our pilot. I was no less nervous on this leg of our trip than I'd been on the first . . . but I figured that if nothing else, at least the kid had to know the route. My fears proved baseless, however, and we arrived safely in Darwin, where we could then enjoy the luxury of boarding a regular-sized plane for Cairns and a visit to the Great Barrier Reef.

During one of Allison's "I study on planes" trips, our daughter had visited Cairns and the reef, and she had loudly sung the praises of both. Make no mistake: For anyone visiting Australia, this is a definite "required destination." Our delightful and thrilling stop-off there would eventually become one of our most treasured memories of the sprawling country . . . even though I nearly had a heart attack when I saw how far I would have to go in order to have what Allison described as "some real fun."

The thrilling (and terrifying) challenge began one morning in February, just as I was leaving to head to the gym for a run. It was 5:30 a.m. – and I could hardly believe that the telephone was ringing. I mean, anybody with a brain was still asleep . . . and a phone call at that early hour was enough to cause immediate panic, especially for those with elderly parents.

Surprisingly, the caller was Allison – and I can recall her exact words, even though 18 years have passed. "Dad! You can't believe what just happened to me!"

My heart sank, of course. All I could imagine was that my beautiful daughter had been a rape victim, or worse. Well, looking back, I'm tempted to believe that something "worse" may indeed have occurred that day . . . because Allison proceeded to tell me that she'd just completed a "bungee jump" off a 185-foot-high platform in Cairns!

Listening to her excited description of the leap, I started considering just where she should be institutionalized, once she returned home. And what about that money I'd sent to the University of Pennsylvania? Clearly, the entire sum had been wasted, since I'd soon be visiting my daughter in "the home."

As I listened to her delirious description of the leap, however, I gradually realized that she was actually quite safe, and also quite happy. Then I did the dumbest thing imaginable: I blurted out that when we came to Australia, I, too, would jump off that same idiotic platform. If she could do it, so could I!

Of course, as a sane human being with a keen instinct for self-preservation, I'd forgotten all about my vow as we traveled through Australia with Allison.

And now here we were, entering Cairns. Until this moment, the promise I'd made Allison back in February had been locked away in the darkest area of my brain. But then she ruined my peace of mind completely, as we approached the area that contained the bungee-jump facility, by pointing out that I'd made a solemn vow to her: "I will jump!"

Never one to go back on my word, I accepted the inevitable: I was soon to be annihilated in a maniacal bungee jump.

What can I tell you? Like a Paris aristocrat on the way to the guillotine, I groaned with dread as we lined up for the event. First I was weighed; the poundage was then stamped on my arm. (This step would allow the bungee-operators to adjust the device to the correct "level of tension," whatever that meant.)

Desperate for moral support, I tried to interest Diane in jumping with me, but she's no dope. Not a chance. She was very happy to take my picture, however, while watching from the ground.

I was on my own. Imagine my response when I was asked if I would "like to touch the water."

"Not on purpose," I quipped by way of a response.

The way I saw things, it was one thing to bounce around on the end of a giant rubber band (and then to be lowered into a nearby boat). That much, I could live with. But having your head hit the water after a fall of 185 feet? Forget about it!

Why was I doing this, anyway? Frantic with fear, I quickly reviewed the "bungee research" I'd performed the night before. Recognized as a sport in 1979, the roots of bungee-jumping go back to 1955, when *National Geographic* depicted it in a documentary on the Indians of the South Pacific island of Pentecost. Apparently, those addled Indians had long enjoyed a ritual in which the males jumped from banyan trees tied to vines.

It didn't sound very encouraging. Nor was I comforted by an article on sports medicine and bungee-jumping that had been penned by Drs. Mario Cesar Moreira de Araujo and Marcelo Riccio Facio. These two bold thinkers had divided your basic bungee jump into three stages: free fall, body deceleration and upward movement. During the free fall, "stress hormones" (such as beta-endorphin, growth hormone and adrenaline) are released. This phenomenon supposedly explains the feelings of exhilaration and well-being that occur during and sometimes for several days after a jump.

The body deceleration state, on the other hand, occurs due to the elastic properties of the cord. The intensity of the deceleration depends upon the kind of elastic line used, along with the altitude of the jump. (The more intense the deceleration, the higher the risk of injury.)

During this stage, the good doctors noted, an increasing "headward fluid shift" takes place and the hydrostatic pressure in the blood vessels of the eye becomes dangerously high. Because of the head-down position, a sudden rise in "intra-thoracic pressure" also occurs, and this process ranks as one of the major causes of "damage events."

The third stage, upward movement, is characterized by an upward movement in a head-down position. Intra-thoracic and head blood vessel pressures may rapidly increase in this stage, and hemorrhages may occur as a result. But the most common fatal accident occurs when the individual becomes entangled with the cord. In these unfortunate situations, the body can end up being suspended by the neck – with compression of the trachea, carotid arteries, jugular vein and cervical vertebrae leading to "severe asphyxia, consciousness decline and death."

Also, the miscalculation of the elasticity of the bungee cord may allow the impact of the head with the bungee pad to occur, and this misstep is frequently fatal. Non-fatal injuries such as compression fractures, near-hanging and quadriplegia are also possible.

And this is what I had agreed to attempt? In hindsight, I'm wondering why someone didn't check me into a mental facility before I could make the leap.

Showtime! Up the stairs I climbed, until I reached the platform area from which I would do a header straight down. Note for would-be participants: Unless you've done multiple jumps, you're required to dive head-first. This may sound like twisted logic (wouldn't it be safer to jump feet-first?) . . . but if you leap into space with your feet pointing downhill, you'll be flipped into a head-first position at the moment of impact. Surprisingly, it's much easier to simply dive from the platform. It's also less frightening, remarkably enough.

Oh, well, I told myself as my turn approached, *you only die once, right?* Actually, I was feeling rather cocky. Was this simply because I'd accepted the idea that my life was over, and that there was nothing I could do about it? As I watched others taking the leap from the platform, however, the "moment of truth" didn't look all that tough. Surely I could handle this brief plunge into rapid acceleration and deceleration? But my confidence evaporated the moment I mounted the platform and saw what lay ahead.

I've always been good at climbing, mind you. Going *up*, even in heart-stopping locales such as the Grand Canyon, is no problem for me; it's the *descent* that I find difficult. To be blunt, making that downhill climb is what scares the crap out of me! And now here I was, 185 feet in the air, and nothing below me but a small pool of water and a couple of tiny specks . . . which turned out to be people on the ground who were watching the idiots above.

There was no escape; it was time to bid the world adieu. I watched with mounting horror as the attendant secured my ankles together and then attached the proper (I hoped!) cord, so that the water and I would not become close friends during the next few seconds.

Feeling like a trussed Thanksgiving turkey, I jiggled and twitched my way out onto the platform. I was in my bare feet, and I was *very* nervous about the possibility that my ankle truss might slip off . . . so I kept my feet together and pointed up toward my shins. My strategy here was a simple one: I hoped that if my ankle truss started to slide, *it wouldn't slide all the way*.

Just imagine walking the plank in the olden pirate days – but not into the ocean. Instead of the deep blue sea (and the usual circle of hungry sharks), my target would be a tiny pool of water no more than 25 feet in diameter. Contemplating all of this, I simply shrugged: *okay, let's do it*. Since we'd paid for a video (Allison had also requested one), I was asked if I had anything to say before my leap into the unknown.

I thought for a moment. Then, brightly: "Ahh . . . where's the nearest bathroom, please?"

The attendant laughed heartily . . . and then told me he was going to "count down from five," and that when he got to zero and said, "Jump," I was to head out into the wild blue yonder.

Well, no way was I going to wait for "zero." If he got that far, I knew I'd be heading back to the platform – intent on making my way back down the stairs toward the sane people below. So when he hit the "two" I was *out* of there.

How can I describe what followed? Actually, the whole thing is over very quickly . . . and the sensation of a sudden "stop and jerk" doesn't happen. Instead, you get a very gradual slowing down of the cord and when it reaches its limit, you're catapulted back up about 60 percent of the way. After that, it's up and down and up and down until the cord has finally had enough and quivers to a stop.

Once you're hanging motionless in the air, a boat stationed at the edge of the pool meanders over and you're lowered head-first into it for the ride back to solid footing. It is actually a very enjoyable experience, in spite of the pre-event jitters. And the best part of all is the moment when you realize that you've *survived.*

No . . . scratch all that. As I write this line, my conscience is telling me that I should be honest – and that bungee-jumping is the most frightening and idiotic thing I've ever done! Look, I've pulled some pretty dumb stunts over the years, but that Australian leap takes the cake. And whenever I think about the moment just before I went over the side, two often-quoted words flash instantly into my shuddering mind:

"Never again!"

On we traveled to the Sheraton Mirage in Port Douglas for our visit to the Great Barrier Reef. This amazing and living world beneath the waves, located in the Coral Sea, is the largest of its kind in the world. It includes more than 3,000 individual reef systems and 900 islands that cover more than 1,600 square miles.

To visit the reef, you must first take a one-hour boat ride. After arriving on the scene, you're provided with snorkel gear that will allow you to view the various species of fish at close range. When Diane and I had previously traveled to Maui, we'd snorkeled and fed bread to the fish. And since this experience obviously qualified me as an "expert," I headed to the dining room and loaded up plenty of bread in my bathing suit pockets and even beneath the suit.

So far, so good. But as I walked down the gangplank to dive in, one of the attendants noticed the bread in my hand. When I told him it was to feed the fish, he replied that the "fish are very aggressive." Well, I was pretty cocky – a real expert in "fish feeding" – so I thanked him for his concern and dove right in.

Whoa! I was immediately engulfed by what seemed to be thousands of fish . . . and every one of them was pecking frantically at me for the bread, while also trying to get under my suit and into my pockets. Panicked, I couldn't throw the bread far enough away – that's how desperate I was to get those fish off my tail. Diane thought it was hysterical . . . but as the fish were swarming me and doing their best to invade my suit, I was asking myself a vitally important question: What if they took a nip in the wrong place and part of my anatomy either disappeared or shrank?

Diane was howling with laughter at this point, and she still thinks it's funny. But I wasn't amused, and I told her so. Fortunately, the ravenous sea-feeders moved away – once they saw that I'd dumped all of my bread products – and after that, they left me alone.

Diane, Allison and I then had a wonderful time viewing multicolored fish in their natural habitat. But you know me: I can always find something to worry about . . . and I had noticed that the ship's personnel hadn't done a head-count as people dove into the water. So I kept a constant vigil – and I hawked that boat relentlessly, fearful that it might leave us behind.

Some years later, you may recall, that ghastly scenario *did* happen – and a honeymooning couple was left to drown. The poor souls were left behind, and their absence wasn't noticed until the dive-ship returned to port. These days, of course, it's standard practice to conduct head counts before and after the ships move. That strategy makes good sense, obviously . . . but it came too late to save the unfortunate honeymooners from a terrible fate.

Once you've visited the reef, there really isn't much else to see in Port Douglas, so we departed for Brisbane and a visit to O'Reilly's Guest House in the Lamington National Park. At the same time, we felt a moment of sadness, as we said farewell to Allison, who needed to get back to Melbourne to complete her foreign-study program.

O'Reilly's was founded in 1911 by five brothers who trekked up the McPherson Range outside Brisbane and then laid claim to 100 acres of land at the top of a cliff at Moran's Bluff. For this unusual swath of real estate, they paid the grand sum of thirty-five shillings – which was to be repaid over a period of thirty years at 5 percent interest. The only condition was that the land had to be used for dairy farming.

Over the years that followed, a guest house was constructed and local residents soon began making the two-day trip up the mountain to view the myriad species of birds native to the area. Life in the guest house was quite pleasant and enjoyable, and each day started with the same ritual: At breakfast, a member of the O'Reilly family would approach each of the family-style tables and announce the day's planned activities. You could opt to do it all . . . or you could simply kick back and relax. Either way, how could you go wrong?

On our first day, however, we chose to go on a guided bird-watch through the forest. Neither Diane nor I can tell the difference between a robin and a bluebird (actually, we do know *that* much, but not much more) . . . and on this foray, we would be hiking with experienced watchers – all of whom were equipped with binoculars, bird books and personal notebooks in which to record careful notes about any interesting species they came across.

These veteran birders are quite passionate about their sport. They compare notes meticulously, and they all live by that famous bird-watching maxim: "He who hath seeneth the mostest birds winneth the prize!" (Okay, I made the maxim up – but I'm sure you catch my drift.) This particular hike was led by one of the sons of the current O'Reilly proprietors, and the procession wound its way on and off the paths wherever the call of a bird was heard. It was a remarkable performance . . . especially when you realize that our fearless leader was doing this barefooted!

As soon as he heard the cry of a bird, or spotted one in the flesh, the valiant guide would raise one hand and quietly tell his group what he'd heard and where that particular species came from. It was an impressive display, and the longtime birders oohed and aahed each time the guide announced another major find. Meanwhile, the two greenhorns from the U.S. (aka Ken and Diane) were gazing vacantly into the bright sunshine with no idea on earth of what we were looking for or where to find it.

Speaking in a low voice that was nearly a whisper, the guide would say something like, "Listen! That's the yellow-tailed flinglehoffer" – and everyone would gasp loudly (*a flinglehoffer!*) and then reach for the binoculars. After several minutes of studying the landscape (no birds were ever visible), they'd nod wisely and begin scribbling frantically in their little notebooks. Apparently, this was very serious stuff!

Diane and I didn't want to be rude or make fun of the bird watchers, but it was difficult to keep ourselves from hooting with laughter at their excitement. (Sorry, owls!) I'm sure they could all tell that when it came to distinguishing a snowy egret from a ruby-throated hummingbird, poor Diane and I were totally clueless!

Two days at O'Reilly's were enough for us; after all, there are only so many different bird species out there to be observed.

Still chuckling with merriment, we headed back down the mountain for our last stop, Sydney, which turned out to be an extraordinarily beautiful city. Sydney is the "New York of Australia," no question about it. As the financial capital of the country, it's a very lively place . . . with people constantly on the move and lots of activity. The famed Opera House overlooks Sydney Harbor and was designed by the great Danish architect, Jorn Utzon. It was quickly obvious why it had won architecture's most prestigious award, the Pritzker Prize, in 2003.

Originally budgeted at a cost of $7 million, it was already 47 weeks behind schedule after only a year and a half of construction. Eventually, this magnificent structure would cost more than $102 million – a truly staggering sum in the early 1960s. Its formal opening by Queen Elizabeth of England occurred in October 1973. Most famously known for its shelled roof, the facility provides regular tours of the premises – which Diane and I quickly took advantage of. (Unfortunately, it wasn't opera season, so we had to content ourselves with viewing the building while it was unoccupied.)

Like New York, Sydney is a "walking city" – in that it's very easy to simply walk around the metropolis in order to soak up its ambiance. On our last morning, I left our hotel for a short jog around the harbor area. For some time, I'd been noticing pennants hanging from the light poles and I thought a Sydney pennant would look just as good in our house on Sebago Lake, Maine, as the Kawaguchi pennant looked!

I stopped to ask the workers what the flags stood for, and they told me the banners commemorated the victory of the Allies in the Battle of the Coral Sea. As it turned out, this was the 50-year anniversary of that decisive battle in the Pacific. Had the Japanese been victorious, an invasion of Australia was scheduled as the next item on the Japanese agenda. Interestingly, the Australians had long understood that they didn't have the resources to stop a Japanese invasion . . . so they had created an "imaginary line" that bisected the country from east to west, starting near Brisbane.

This was to have been their "no trespassing" line. It would have preserved the key cities of Melbourne, Perth and Sydney for the free world, while ceding control of Darwin and the country's northern population to the Japanese. The Battle of the Coral Sea turned the tide toward the Allies, however, since the Japanese were repulsed and thus deterred from implementing their invasion plans. When I asked the city workers if I could have a flag, they told me they'd lose their jobs if they accommodated me. But they also went on to tell me whom I might call if I wanted one as a souvenir.

One of them said, "If you were Japanese, there would be no chance of your ever obtaining one of these." Needless to say, there's no love lost between the Australians and the Japanese, even to this day.

I returned to the hotel as Diane was finishing our packing and made the call to City Hall to the individual in charge. I really wanted a flag . . . and I'm embarrassed to say that I told a bit of a "white lie," in that I mentioned how my father had participated in the Battle of the Coral Sea, and how it would "mean a lot to him" to have a flag. They were more than happy to accommodate my request, and Diane and I detoured to City Hall to pick up our coveted keepsake.

I have to exonerate Diane from any complicity in my scheme, however. I'm totally to blame for the fib! But the strategy worked quite well because the flag was boxed up and waiting for us when we arrived. I asked if I could pay for it, and they were most gracious in refusing any payment – while also wishing my father well and thanking him for his participation. I felt like a bit of a fraud, but I did want that flag! It seemed unusually heavy, compared to our Kawaguchi flag, though, and we soon discovered why. When we got back home and unfolded it, we realized that it was more than 20 feet long!

Unfortunately, there was no place to display such a huge banner, so to this day it still sits in its carrying case, waiting for a home. But we were very grateful for the gift, and we felt certain that the Australians would be our friends forever.

Our great Pacific Ocean adventure had finally ended . . . and by the time we reached the airport outside Sydney, I was already planning for my next marathon – a thrilling run that was destined to unfold somewhere on the great continent of South America.

QANTAS
3MP

Brasilia Marathon

SOUTH AMERICA - APRIL 18, 1993

If ever the time comes for someone to give the world an enema, then Brasilia will be the logical "insertion area" for the nozzle. Do I seem harsh in my assessment of the Brazilian capital? Let me tell you about this city of 3.6 million – the city where I ran the South American leg of my marathon challenge – and then you can decide for yourself whether I'm being fair or not.

First of all, it should be noted that Brasilia is a "planned city" – an urban metropolis that was originally designed back in the 1950s to ease the population load on teeming Rio de Janeiro. The buildings in the new megalopolis were constructed of cement – and many of them were showing very visible structural cracks when I arrived there in the spring of 1993.

Since this was a new city erected from scratch on open land, the planners and architects were working with a blank slate and could design the layout as they saw fit. The result was a city that consisted of carefully organized sectors – with each of the neighborhood squares catering to a specific service. For example, one square might contain eyeglass providers. Another would be inhabited entirely by restaurants. In the beginning, traffic was supposed to flow so easily that no traffic lights would ever be needed. But that didn't happen. Instead, the population grew at a much faster rate than expected.

Workers were imported to help build the "perfect city," and once they arrived, they stayed – primarily because most of them lacked the resources that would have been required to pay their way back home. Another problem was that many of the residents of Brasilia didn't seem to *like* the place; all too often, government employees and embassy personnel would flee the city on the weekends and during vacations in order to enjoy much pleasanter surroundings in Sao Paulo or Rio.

Site-development work on the city began in 1956, and the actual construction kicked off the following year. The new metropolis was officially dedicated on April 22, 1960. Think of it: In only four short years . . . *voila!* A brand-new capital city had sprung up out of thin air, with a populace that exceeded 3.5 million. Unfortunately, however, the drab surroundings and the searing heat and humidity often made life in the new capital seem like a punishment . . . for business people, for bored government workers and disaffected natives alike.

Sadly enough, this was the site I'd chosen for my fifth marathon . . . in my ongoing quest to become the first person to successfully complete the 26-mile event on all seven of the world's continents.

As I prepared physically for the run in Brazil, my efforts were continuing on behalf of MCCP. By 1993, the fast-growing non-profit had helped to provide care to more than 200 families and was capable of servicing about 50 new cases each year. My donor list was also expanding nicely, due to some terrific publicity we received in the local newspapers. We also scored a nice hit in *USA Today*. What a thrill it was to see my name in a national newspaper! Here's the clipping, so you can see for yourself how the coverage went.

Marathoner takes distance seriously

When Ken Volk went to the Brazilian consulate to apply for a visa recently, he was asked his reason. "To run a marathon," said the 55-year-old businessman from Portland, Maine.

"The guy looked at me like I was from the moon."

Volk's goal is to run a marathon on all seven continents – four down and three to go – and raise money for the Maine Children's Cancer Program. He's hoping the marathon in Brasilia April 18 will raise about $8,000.

"I've got three children and a grandchild," says Volk, who owns a corrugated box company. "We've never been touched by the disease. I feel very fortunate. I want to give back."

Volk, 55, who has completed marathons in the USA, France, Japan and Australia, is a plodder. "I tell people I run 3 hours, 71 minutes," he says. "Everybody talks about PRs [personal records]. I talk about LTs –live-throughs. My goal is to finish in good health and raise money for the kids."

After the race in Brazil, Volk will lack marathons in Africa and Antarctica. For the run in the ice and snow, he's considering running in a building.

Talk about getting weird looks.

Contributions can be made through the Maine Children's Cancer Program at 207-775-5481.

After this article appeared I received a copy in the mail from my brother, Roger, who had altered the title of the article to "Marathoner takes condoms seriously." But the fund-raising was taken seriously, and almost $10,000 was donated, in addition to a gift from Volk Packaging of $12,500. That money would be dedicated to sponsoring a new treatment room in the new quarters of MCCP, which had now outgrown its original layout. I like to think I helped make a small contribution to the organization's rapid growth and success. As you might imagine, I felt good inside with every check received and delivered!

To help with my planning, I enlisted the support of our U.S. Senator, George Mitchell. He, in turn, wrote to the U.S. Ambassador to Brazil, the Hon. Richard H. Melton, asking if he would extend me any and all courtesies. Senator Mitchell wrote Ambassador Melton on February 1st and received a prompt reply on February 12th. (That lightning response is a true indicator of the immense power wielded by the U.S. Senate!)

In his letter to the senator, the American ambassador provided me with a wrong date for the running of the marathon (it was only off by three days!). He also made mistakes in listing the various U.S. Consulates located throughout Brazil. Still, he *did* make a hugely important contribution to my run . . . by assigning U.S. Embassy staffer Wesley Hubbell the task of serving as our guide throughout our Brazil stay.

Wes was also running in the race, so he understood the trials we faced and the worries that troubled each and every participant. He was kind enough to meet Diane and me at the airport and then to invite us to have dinner with him and other staff members at a local restaurant. That sounded like a great idea . . . until we walked into the eatery and got hit with the powerful aroma of the native foods that were being cooked there. Was it really the cooking? Or was it the malaria pills we'd been taking right before our departure from the U.S.? Whatever the cause, the unfortunate fact is that Diane became extremely nauseous soon after we entered the restaurant, and we were forced to leave the gathering and return to our hotel for a light snack.

Not a good beginning to our trip! But things began to look better the following afternoon, when we joined several embassy personnel for a very diverting event that was known as a "Hash." This was a kind of specialized race in which the participants must follow a series of clues in order to discover their route and end up in the winner's circle. (No one except the organizer knows the running route before the takeoff – a wrinkle that adds lots of suspense to a road race.)

The concept of the "Hash" was reportedly invented in one of the Far East embassies, and it has proved to be very popular at U.S. installations all around the globe. There's even a book of registered "Hashers" available for traveling Americans, who often refer to it in order to meet some of their fellow U.S. citizens in foreign realms. (As a matter of fact, I myself am now listed as a Hasher from the great state of Maine!)

As I soon learned in Brasilia, newly inducted Hash members are required to drink a large container of beer non-stop, with any left-over brew poured over the head of the inductee. Yes, I'm proud to tell you that I survived my beer bath – and that I was quickly accepted as a dedicated member of the "Hash House Harriers." Proud of my new status – and still soaking wet – I waited eagerly for the Brasilia Marathon (my personal name for it was "Marathon Number Five") to finally get underway.

Marathon Day! Diane and I awoke early, but for no real reason except nerves – since the run wasn't scheduled to begin until 3:30 in the afternoon. When I asked Wes Hubbell why the event started so late, he explained that the Brazilians simply hated to get out of bed early!

As always, I was desperately eager to get the running torture underway. (The sooner we got started, I figured, the sooner the agonizing endurance race would be over!) After a light breakfast of scrambled eggs, Diane and I wandered around aimlessly, until at last the time came for us to depart for the race.

I was hyperventilating a bit by then, but at least I knew I was well-prepared for the struggle that lay ahead. Example: Joan Benoit Samuelson had called before we'd departed the U.S. and had asked if she could give me some protein drink in powder form. The plan was to mix the stuff with water; Diane would then carry it along the marathon route and make it available to me during my various pit stops.

We'd also been warned about drinking the water, so we'd included a case of Poland Spring Water in our luggage, and we'd been using it to brush our teeth and for drinking. No sense in taking any chances with "Montezuma's Revenge!"

At last it was time to face the music. Off we trudged to the starting line, while the sun beat a tattoo of searing heat on our heads. By the time we'd reached the start, I was afloat on a sea of perspiration and wondering what on earth I was doing running a marathon in 88-degree heat! On the black tar of the road, the temperature had to be approaching 100 degrees and my feet were already burning up.

But at last the starting gun sounded – to everyone's immense relief – and along with 3,000 of my closest South American friends, I headed off into the unknown. Normally, the first five miles or so of a marathon are relatively easy; after all, the fatigue, the cramps, the aches and the pains haven't set in yet.

However, this race bared its fangs very early. As I ran along the treeless avenues – they offered no shade whatsoever from the brutal heat – the road veered to the right and under an underpass. Things looked pretty grim at that point, let me tell you. There I was, less than a mile into a grueling 26-mile event, and I already felt ready to quit. But then, with a burst of sudden insight, I realized what I had to do . . . and I made an important executive decision.

I could either continue running on this blistering asphalt surface (by now the runners had begun climbing up a slight incline) . . . or I could decide to walk rather than run, in order to finish this race alive. It was not a very difficult decision, mind you. Within a few seconds, I found myself in a very unusual situation – walking along at a moderate, easygoing pace . . . with 25 miles of the Brasilia Marathon still in front of me.

Walk, don't run! Yes, it was a bit deflating and discouraging, to be walking already at this early stage. And yet I knew in my heart that my decision was the correct one. I also felt some consolation in the fact that I certainly wasn't the only one walking. After all, my objective had always been to *finish* these marathons on the seven continents of the world. My goal had never been to set any speed records. Freed of the necessity to "prove myself" as a marathoner, I could take solace in the fact that at least I'd be crossing the finish line.

As I reached the top of a little hill, volunteers were busily handing out water. I asked for more . . . and then *more* . . . and was promptly warned by one of the workers to be careful about my water consumption – too much H2O would make me ill! I'd never heard of anything so idiotic in my life, but I thanked my spontaneous advisor and continued drinking. (A few years later, after some marathoners dropped dead during races, it was determined that too much water intake can deplete a runner's supply of electrolytes . . . even to the point of death. So my Brazilian friend hadn't been so "idiotic," after all.)

Anyway, I trudged slowly along, feeling worse by the minute and seeking out shade on every block . . . even though in doing so, I sometimes added distance to my run. As I struggled along the route, I knew Diane was trying to figure out where she could meet me. Unfortunately, there was no public transportation, and it hadn't occurred to either of us to hire a driver. But the persistent Diane was finally able to communicate with one of the locals, who directed her to the ten-mile mark. There we met for the first time – thanks to the fact that she'd come upon one of the Embassy staff with whom we'd had dinner the previous night.

He had been following his own running friends and was kind enough to drive Diane to a point on the route at which I hadn't yet arrived. Meanwhile I consumed some of Joan Samuelson's protein concoction in the remote hope that I would begin to feel human again. By then, I was a mindless robot. One step. And then another. And another . . . while the sweat ran down my face from the searing, unmerciful heat. These damn Brazilians! Three-thirty in the afternoon is an ungodly hour in which to begin a two-mile fun run, let alone a full-length marathon.

It was still broad daylight in Brasilia and I was facing another 16 miles, as my body began to ache all over. My feet were suffering from the beginnings of blisters caused by perspiration and the rubbing of my socks against my toes. I could tell that Diane was becoming very concerned, but the thought of aborting the run never occurred to me. One thing only I knew for certain: I didn't want a return trip to Brazil – or to any other South American country. This was going to be my South American marathon and that was that!

Mile thirteen for me has always been a turning point. Up to No. 13 – the halfway point in a 26-mile marathon – I would count upwards in my head. But from No. 13 on, I would count *down* – which seemed a hell of a lot easier, for some reason. Don't ask me why, but counting down instead of up gave a huge boost to my psyche. *I'm now on my way home,* I would tell myself. *I've got a long trek still ahead of me, but I'm on my way!*

Fortunately (or *unfortunately,* depending on how you look at it), I was running so slowly that I wound up benefiting more from sundown than the elite runners. By Mile 15, the sun had retreated behind some clouds and the first shade of the day had come to my rescue. I had no idea where Diane was, and I learned later that she was also unaware of my whereabouts – while sweltering alone on a pre-arranged corner. Unfortunately, she had no way of knowing whether I'd passed her rendezvous-point or not.

Meanwhile, the embassy staffer who'd accompanied her at the start of the race had left her to follow his friends . . . meaning that she was now on her own and hopelessly lost. I, on the other hand, felt utterly isolated as well. By this time the spectators had disapeared, for the most part. They'd headed off to dinner, and I only wished that I'd been able to join them! I knew I was on the right route,

MAINE
TRACK CLUB
104

however, since I could see the trash that had been left by runners ahead of me – but that was my only clue. Even the aid and water station volunteers had departed the scene. Well, so be it. I trudged on and on, with my teeth gritted and my eyes locked on the road.

At mile 20, I hit "the wall." This term describes an imaginary (but very real) mark in a marathon. Here your energy sags to its lowest point and every ache and pain makes you wonder if those final six miles are really doable. There isn't a bone or muscle in your body that doesn't scream for relief. But there was to be no relief in sight for me – all I could do was continue to grind it out and hope for the best.

Then I got a miracle. As I approached another underpass, I suddenly noticed Diane standing just above. Up until now, she'd been just as lost as I was on the dark and deserted marathon route. To say that she'd felt frightened – and convinced that she'd never find her way back to civilization – would be a major understatement. By taking advantage of her fluent French, however, she'd been able to communicate with a lone Brazilian street cleaner who'd directed her to a strategic spot on the route. The road up there was well lit . . . but she was still alone and she was still scared.

She spotted me instantly – my staggering shuffle was hard to miss, after all – and ran to greet me. What a wonderful sight she was, as I watched her waving to me. We embraced warmly, and our brief moment together gave me the impetus to head back out into the darkness and resume my struggle toward the finish line. By sheer luck, she then met another of the Embassy employees, who was kind enough to drive her to the finish to await my arrival.

It was brutal, to say the least. By now I was beginning to suspect that the race organizers were moving the finish line back as I ran, and as I desperately counted off the remaining miles.

At last the end was in sight. As I had during past runs, I put on a blinding (yeah, right!) burst of speed and crossed the line in exactly 4:58:49 – a truly stellar time that was good enough to earn me 696th place out of an estimated 3,000 starters. But that number turned out to be deceptive; in fact, only 785 runners actually completed the entire course. What can I say? Apparently, Brazilians are not only reluctant to get out of bed early in the morning, they're also not terribly fond of running in extreme heat. Indeed, simply finishing that run made me very proud . . . especially when I considered the fact that 2,304 runners (according to local newspaper reports) had either finished behind me or had just plain quit.

As Diane joined me, we hugged fiercely and I couldn't hold back the tears. Completing a marathon has to be one of the most personally satisfying accomplishments that one may ever enjoy. Suddenly, all the hours of training and all the pain took on a new meaning, as I celebrated victory in Brasilia.

Wes picked us up at our hotel early the following morning, in order to ferry us to the airport for our trip to Rio de Janeiro and then home. In Rio we had a long layover, however – so Diane and I took a room in an airport-area hotel in order to pass the time. We enjoyed ourselves thoroughly, and the "Post-Marathon Tradition" was resumed with a vengeance.

Upon our return to Maine I received the following letter from Ambassador Melton:

> *Dear Mr. Volk:*
>
> *I am very pleased to congratulate you on your participation in Brasilia's Third Annual Marathon on April 18, 1993. Considering that you traveled over 5,500 miles to participate certainly makes you one of the more committed runners.*
>
> *I admire your efforts to raise money for charity by running in a marathon on each continent and extend*

my best wishes for your continued success in this endeavor.

Sincerely,
Richard H. Melton

On to Africa! Five down, and two to go. And another $22,500 for The Maine Children's Cancer Program!

The Pyramids Marathon

CAIRO, EGYPT - AFRICA
JANUARY 28, 1994

Five down, two to go. Diane and I had never visited Morocco, so at first that country seemed like a logical choice for my African marathon. It was also easy to get to – and there were many inexpensive tour packages to Marrakech, where I'd been told that a well-attended marathon took place each year. It took some time and energy, but eventually I located a Canadian tour company that conducted trips to Marrakech, and the itinerary included the marathon there. But the event was shrouded in uncertainty, according to the very up-front Canadian travel agent with whom I spoke. He told me that the year before the race had been scheduled, cancelled, re-scheduled, cancelled, and then finally run.

I listened carefully to his description of marathon chaos in Marrakech – and quickly decided that the event represented far too much of a gamble on my part, given the amount of training that would be required and the fact that I'd already started soliciting new donations for MCCP.

Thanks, but no thanks. I thanked the agent for his honesty and said goodbye. Suddenly I was back to Square One.

Back I went to my local advisor on exotic marathons, Joan Samuelson. She had some information about a marathon in Cairo . . . but she also had a suggestion for me. Why not postpone my African marathon and run the Antarctica leg of my odyssey instead? That way, she could join me on the African run – and the delay on Africa would also give me more time to raise additional funds for MCCP.

Although I was flattered that an Olympic champion runner would even consider accompanying me on a marathon, I responded to her by saying: "Joan, the starting gun would sound and I'd never see you again. And within a very short time, you'd be relaxing back in your hotel with Scott, already having showered and changed – while I was still struggling through Mile 13!"

We had a good laugh together, and I respectfully declined her offer and went back to searching for the perfect African marathon.

My first call went to Marathon Tours in Charlestown, a tour agency that specialized in marathon events all over the world. While they couldn't help me with an African marathon that fit my schedule, my contact there did mention that they were in the midst of organizing a marathon in the Antarctic for the following year. My excitement at hearing this news was unbounded. I had a deposit check written and in the envelope before concluding our conversation . . . and immediately began celebrating the fact that I was all set for the final installment in my Seven Continents Quest.

Then I went back to working on Africa. After considerable research on my part, I finally reached a woman in Baltimore, Marie Frances, who specialized in organizing African and other trips for runners who wanted to experience "The Most Exotic Run in the World." Yes! She also managed the "Mt. Kilimanjaro Marathon and Climb," so I felt very comfortable in throwing in my lot with her. Apparently, this widely traveled entrepreneur had considerable experience in dealing with Third World countries. As I eyeballed her marathon itineraries and the other particulars in her globe-trotting program, I liked what I saw. For one thing, the date of her Cairo marathon junket fit my *own* schedule perfectly. With the Cairo event set for late January, I could commence training in late October – and the running conditions wouldn't be as harsh as those I would have faced in a January-through-March training period.

An added benefit, of course, was that Diane had always wanted to visit Israel – and a Cairo Marathon could be combined easily with a trip to the Holy Land. All at once, it looked as if we were in business.

I had maintained a fairly demanding regimen of training during the past couple of years, so I was already in decent shape. Per my usual plan of attack, I began training in earnest for Cairo exactly three months before the event was scheduled to take place.

It soon became obvious, however, that my assumptions about "moderate" weather in the late fall and early winter of 1993 weren't even *close* to being accurate. As a matter of fact, the beginning of winter featured some of the coldest days on record. Example: One memorable evening in mid-December, Bill Davenny and I left the University of Maine gymnasium for what was to be a 20-mile run to Falmouth, Maine and back.

There were a few light snowflakes falling as we departed, with the temperature hovering at around 10 degrees. By the time we'd completed eight miles, however, the temperature had dropped to just below zero, and the snow had turned into a cold, miserable sleet. Now, snow normally rides harmlessly on my nylon gear – but sleet is a different animal altogether. Drenched to the skin and running flat-footed in order to avoid the treacherous ice that had accumulated on the road, I was truly miserable.

Bill, my devoted running partner, was equally uncomfortable – but he was willing to soldier on because he understood the importance of the long runs for my training program. He didn't want to be the one to cause me to abort! Well, it was pitch-black outside, and there was no moon to provide light. The only illumination came from the light poles that sporadically flanked the road.

Remember, this was Maine, not New York City, and we were in a rural area where lights weren't exactly a high priority.

It was a recipe for disaster . . . and it wasn't long before I skidded on a patch of black ice and crashed. My hands, which had broken my fall, were now freezing – literally – and I had difficulty in opening and closing my fists.

It was at this point that I made another key "executive decision" – and the two of us took the first turn-off that led back to the gym. Bill wasn't unhappy about my move, either. The run would be shortened from 20 miles to 12 . . . but we both felt that with the conditions as they were, those 12 miles were easily the equivalent of a 20-miler.

And then: ka-boom! About three miles from the gym, I went down for the second time, with just about the same results. And this fall left me aching all over. Frost-bitten hands were the least of my worries at this point. Right then, all I wanted was to survive! Fortunately for the two of us, we came upon a variety store just about to close as we grew near the gym. I couldn't go on another foot, so into the store we limped. Once inside that zone of blessed warmth, we asked permission to use the phone.

The proprietor was very kind and thoughtful, and she seemed to be touched by the condition of the two ragamuffins who'd just crossed her threshold. Summoned by my call, Diane drove right over and we dropped Bill off at his car. Wracked with pain, I was too sore to move and in no shape to drive, so I simply left my car at the gym. All the way home, I dreamed of sliding into a hot bath. But once in our garage, I discovered that I could barely move. With Diane's help, I was able to mount the stairs into the house and then head for that bath I had been dreaming about.

Under normal circumstances, the word "bath" isn't in my lexicon. I'm a "shower guy" – but this had to be the best "tub time" ever enjoyed by any human anywhere! As I luxuriated in the warm water, however, I had no idea what was in store for me during the next four months.

After retrieving the car the next morning, I resolved to take a couple of training days off to recuperate.

By now my fundraising for MCCP was becoming more sophisticated, and I felt I was doing a much better job of building my request list. This fact was borne out when I ultimately raised almost $10,000 for the children I was now referring to as "My Kids." I felt like Jerry Lewis fighting for Muscular Dystrophy, only on a somewhat smaller scale!

The key to my success was that although I hadn't achieved a major increase in the number of letters I sent out, the average gift I received was increasing . . . even if by a relatively small increment. I'd also begun to attract notice in the press – everything from the local Portland and Biddeford, Maine newspapers to the Palm Beach Post and a national runner's newsletter, *Stride for Stride*. Donations were now arriving from all corners of the country, and perhaps the most touching one of all came from the mother of a young cancer victim whose treatment hadn't been successful, and who had subsequently died.

The note that mother sent along with her donation tore me to shreds. I admit that I'm a pretty emotional guy (I cry when the organ plays, "Here Comes the Bride," even if the bride is ugly!), and this loving message from the departed child's mother left me swamped beneath a tidal wave of grief and affection for her. If I'd needed any inspiration or encouragement to continue, that single letter would have provided it, and then some.

In October of 1993, my parents celebrated their 57th wedding anniversary. Our family (and now even our extended family, with all the in-laws included) has always been proud of the closeness we share. We're very connected, and one of the major reasons for that was my mother's lifelong insistence that we remain close to each other. One of her favorite sayings – still indelibly etched in her three sons' minds – was: "It is better to lose with your brother on your side than to win against him."

I'm not sure where that epigram originated, but she preached it to us over and over again. So it was in that spirit of closeness that our folks decided to celebrate their anniversary – by taking the entire family on a cruise from Miami to Mexico during the Christmas school vacation period. And since none of us had ever been on a cruise, we all looked forward to being together and celebrating a wonderful occasion en masse.

One of the most anticipated stops was Key West on the return leg of the cruise. Since Diane and I had already visited "Cayo Hueso" as a couple (and since we'd found it to be little more than a collection of tourist t-shirt stores), my plan was to disembark and run around the circumference of the island, which I estimated would involve a distance of about 13 miles. In the meantime, while steaming along at sea, I was determined to maintain my running schedule with short, one-hour jaunts on which I trotted contentedly around the ship.

This plan worked very well for a few days . . . but then one morning after returning to my cabin and removing my running shoes, I felt a sharp pain in my right heel. It felt as if I'd stepped on a small rock in my bare feet. The pain was localized, and I could put my finger on the exact spot from which it seemed to be emanating. But since nobody trains for or runs a marathon without having to endure some aches and pains, I didn't pay much attention to this latest ailment.

The discomfort refused to go away, however. The day after it first appeared, when our boat docked in Key West, I took off on my run around the Spanish-named "Isle of Bone." The foot still hurt, but I was now in my final four weeks of training – and I needed these miles if I were to be successful in Cairo. As I zipped along the island roads, I could feel the heel begin to throb. I was in continual pain, but I managed to complete the circuit I'd laid out for myself.

What I *didn't* realize, of course, was that this would be my final run before departing for Africa and the marathon. At first I assumed that I was dealing with just another "minor" injury – just another example of the physical wear and tear that inevitably occurs during training. But the pain persisted. And then it got worse. Soon I was struggling to get around at all . . . so that with only four weeks left before Cairo, I'd begun to worry about my ability to walk, let alone participate in a 26-mile run.

The pain was dogging me steadily now. Even after we returned to our condo in Boynton Beach, Florida for the balance of our December vacation with our children, it continued to make my life miserable. Instead of seeing improvement in my foot, I felt that I was losing ground in the race to get well. Grudgingly, I began to face up to the possibility that I might not be able to make the Cairo race at all.

On January fifth, upon our return to Maine (and with only 23 days left until Race Day), I finally gave in to the pain and went to visit my favorite physical therapist, Kurt Jepson at Saco Bay Physical Therapy. His diagnosis was as follows:

"On 1/5/94, Mr. Ken Volk presented at this facility with complaints of (R) heel pain. He stated that he had recently run 10 and then 20 miles on a 'cruise ship' and had some moderate (R) heel pain with radiation into the distal calf with this activity. However, this did not alter his training. Subsequent runs on dry land seemed to exacerbate his problem and made weight-bearing very difficult. All of his symptoms now are specific to the plantar aspect of the (R) heel and are increased with weight-bearing. He has been utilizing ice as well as over-the-counter NSAID as needed at home. He has altered his running mileage at this point and is cross training. He would like to resolve his problems as soon as possible as he has a marathon coming up within three weeks."

Kurt and I became very close "friends," as I visited him for treatment on every day of the week that led up to our departure.

My routine was to head directly to the University of New England for an hour of running in their pool, followed by electrical stimulation and ice massage for another hour. I was also using a cane in an effort to take some of the pressure off my foot. But that pressure, although painful, didn't compare to the pressure building between my ears. Incredibly stressed, I was doing my best to come to grips with a deeply disturbing insight: This next marathon wasn't going to be a pleasant experience!

On January 15th, ready or not, Diane and I arrived in Israel to tour and "relax" (fat chance!) prior to our visit to Cairo.

We'd arranged for a guide to escort us throughout our entire stay. That gentleman, a highly patriotic American named David Perlmutter, had immigrated to Israel – where he bravely defended his new country by serving in its Tank Force. As is true of most of the guides in his adopted nation, David was a fount of knowledge. Under his savvy tutelage, we traveled Israel from its northern Golan Heights to the Dead Sea in the south.

Diane felt very relaxed (she wasn't preparing for a marathon!) and seemed to be enjoying the various tourist sites much more than I was. And no wonder: Walking with a cane on cobblestone streets isn't exactly my idea of "relaxation." Typically, Diane and David would walk ahead at a normal pace, while he explained the significance of a particular site. Meanwhile, I trudged gamely along behind them, taking in whatever knowledge I could. But it wasn't easy; there's so much history in Israel that trying to grasp and understand it all is like trying to catch a firefly with your bare hands.

Diane was soaking up information like a sponge and loving every minute of the tour. But my situation was very different; most of the time I was simply trying to move without pain. I was also struggling with the fear of injuring myself further. What would happen if I slipped and fell on these iron-hard stones . . . or if I walked too far and damaged my ailing foot even more as a result? At this point, running to "maintain my conditioning" was an impossible dream. Dazed with pain and anxiety, I did my best to keep up with the torrent of information that poured from the lips of our super-knowledgeable guide. But my concentration was muddled and fuzzy . . . and each time David asked me about something he'd explained the previous day, I responded by saying: "David, I listen to everything you tell us, but then I go on immediately to the next story you're telling. The stories go by so quickly . . . that I make no effort to try to remember them."

I don't think he was too happy with my answer – but hey, I was in "survival mode" at this point. It was exactly like my "survival shuffle," in which I put one foot in front of the other until I reach my destination. In this case, however, my brain cells were restricted to fretting about Cairo. To be quite honest, I simply didn't have the mental space to deal with more than one historical saga at a time!

In spite of my struggles and lack of focus at times, there were certainly some memorable moments during our visit to Israel. Example: One day David asked me if there was anything in particular that I'd like to see. I told him I wanted to visit the super-secret Negev Nuclear Research Center in Dimona, home of the alleged Israeli nuclear arsenal. I was pulling his leg, of course, but I was only half kidding. Why? Because most of our friends who'd visited Israel in recent years had come home with marvelous stories about how their guides had taken them to visit "insider" locales which "no one who visits Israel ever gets a chance to see."

Deep down, I wanted to wow them with my own story, and I also figured this would be a good test for David, the super-guide! But I wasn't terribly surprised when my request was refused . . . although our trusty shepherd did point out that he had once visited the site with his Israeli Tank Force. Can you imagine – I made only one simple request, and it was *denied*? Oh, well. Disappointed as we were, Diane and I finally accepted the fact that we'd have to be content with the same "touristy" experiences that are so familiar to most voyagers who wander the Holy Land.

I did my best to enjoy the sojourn, however. And although my attention span was necessarily limited, there were a few encounters that I did find thrillingly memorable.

Unforgettable was our visit to Yad Vashem. A "must visit" for foreign dignitaries and tourists alike, it is Israel's official memorial to the Jewish victims of the Holocaust. Established in 1953, Yad Vashem is a doleful reminder of the unspeakable crimes that were committed against millions of Jews – and it's also Israel's second most visited tourist site after the Western Wall. The 45-acre layout includes the Holocaust History Museum, the Children's Memorial and a special exhibit known as the Hall of Remembrance.

Diane and I were most moved by an area containing small plaques inscribed with the names of non-Jews who saved Jews during the genocide. These brave souls often took huge personal risks – and they are rightly honored as "Righteous Among the Nations." We could only imagine the perils they endured and the terror they overcame while endangering their entire families to save people whom they hardly knew. What heroes!

Masada, the desert fortress overlooking the Dead Sea, was a wonder to behold. A place of gaunt and majestic beauty, the fortress was built between 37 and 31 BCE by Herod the Great. Looming 450 meters above the Dead Sea, it was thought to be impregnable to foreign invaders. However, in 66 CE, a group of Jewish rebels, subjects of the Romans, seized control. Responding with the full fury of the Empire, the Roman governor Flavius Silva marched against Masada in 73 CE – with units that included thousands of Jewish prisoners-of-war. The attackers established camps at the base of the mountain, laid siege to it and then built a circumvallation wall. After that they constructed a rampart made of thousands of tons of stones – and in the spring of the year 74 CE, they moved a battering ram up the rampart and breached the wall of the fortress.

The fatal blow had been struck. Realizing the futility of their defense and knowing it is against the Jewish religion to commit suicide, the desperate Jews drew lots to choose 10 men who would kill the remainder. These 10 then chose among themselves the one man who would kill the other nine survivors. The last man standing then killed himself. More than 900 Jewish fighters died in the onslaught.

For someone like me who was in "Marathon condition," climbing Masada would have provided a wonderful memory. That feat was not destined to occur, however; because of my foot injury and the looming marathon, we reached the top of Masada via a cable car. I was a bit disappointed, of course, but the grandeur of Masada soon lifted my spirits. To stand atop the majestic summit and imagine what those courageous fighters had endured so many centuries ago was awe-inspiring – and it left me more determined than ever to contribute to the good of this world by doing what I could for the children of Maine.

From Masada we drove to the Dead Sea, where it is a tradition for tourists to bathe in the salty water and lather themselves with gallons of soothing black mud.

A highlight of any trip to Israel is the visit to Jerusalem. This great city is the birthplace of the three major religions of the world – and you can't walk for more than a block in any direction without encountering a landmark of historical significance. For the Jewish people, this is the Biblical Aion, the City of David, the site of Solomon's Temple and the eternal capital of the Israelite nation. For Christians, this is where the young Jesus impressed the sages at the Jewish Temple, where he spent the last days of his ministry, and where the Last Supper, the Crucifixion and the Resurrection all took place. And for Muslims, the ancient city is where the prophet Muhammad ascended to heaven. Is it any wonder – when you think about Jerusalem's historic pedigree – that this ancient metropolis is so often described as the "holiest of cities?"

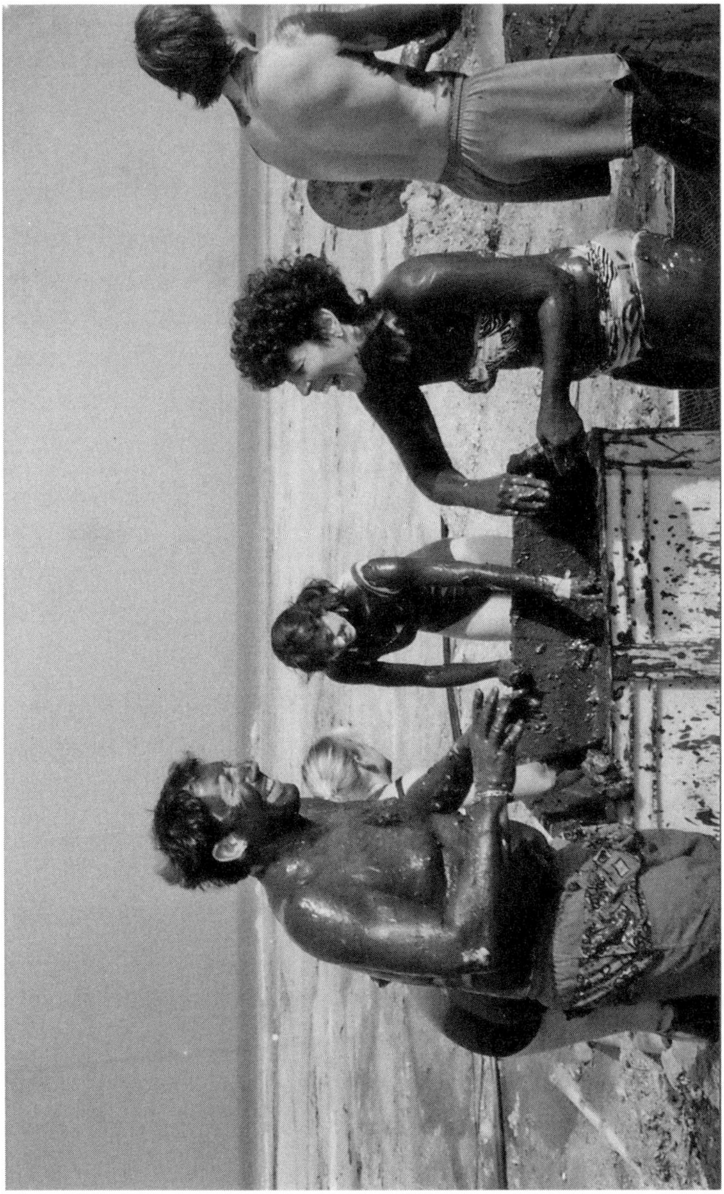

At the Dead Sea

With its wide array of sacred sites, its cobbled streets and its frenetic citizenry, Jerusalem is rightly regarded as the highlight of any trip to the Holy Land. And no visit to Israel would be complete without paying one's respects at the Western Wall. Built by King Herod in 20 BC, this famous monument is all that remains of the Second Temple. Until the Six Day War of 1967, the site had been under the control of Jordan.

We also visited the Temple Mount, which is considered by Judaism to be the place where God chose the Divine Presence to rest. According to ancient teaching, it was from this spot that God gathered the dust He would use in creating the first man, Adam. But Jerusalem is also the third holiest site in Islam. You can imagine the fascination and excitement Diane and I experienced as we meandered around this beautiful city, while taking in the sights and enjoying the sweet aromas of falafel and other ethnic foods being sold by the local street vendors.

The Golan Heights, formerly known as the Syrian Heights, may very well be the biggest bone of territorial contention in the world. Overlooking Israel from the north and controlled by Syria through successive regimes from time immemorial, the Heights have long provided a strategic launching point for a potential invasion of Israel by Arab forces. In addition, the area contributes significantly to the water resources of the region. Its strategic importance simply cannot be overstated. During the Six Day War of 1967, it was captured by Israel – a momentous event that has helped to change the balance of power in the Arab-Israeli conflict, since it gave the Israelis a significant boost in their quest for national security.

After the war, the United Nations adopted Resolution 242, which calls for "safe and recognized boundaries free from threats or acts of force." This historic resolution is the basis upon which Israel justifies its continuing control of the area. But the same resolution calls for "the withdrawal of Israel's armed forces from territories occupied in the Six Day War." These two conflicting declarations are clearly paradoxical; they also serve as a typical example of how the gutless U.N. so often tries to please all sides in a dispute. As usual, the result is that the U.N. posture fails to solve the problem. On the one hand, the world body declares that Israel should have safe borders; on the other, it demands that the Golan Heights must be returned to Syria – a recommendation that would make safe Israeli borders impossible!

Given the U.N.'s weak-minded vacillation, is it any wonder that the Golan Heights region has been locked in bitter dispute for the past 43 years, with no successful resolution in sight?

In 1973 the Syrians – along with their Arab allies – attacked Israel without warning during its holiest of holidays, Yom Kippur. One story, unverified but interesting to relate, is that the Syrian General commanding the forces ordered to re-take the Golan was expected to complete his conquest in 24 hours and then call for further orders. He was able to complete his mission in a matter of a few hours, since the Israelis had been caught totally unprepared.

Once in control, however, he failed to follow up on the victory . . . and instead of calling for his new marching orders, he waited the full 24 hours as instructed. The delay allowed the Israeli forces to mount a counter-attack and retake the Heights. It was a turning point in the war. I love that story! Israel later returned one-third of the captured land to the Syrians during the late 1970's but has continued to build settlements in the area it still controls there. The Golan Heights are now considered home to approximately 40,000 Jewish residents and more than 75,000 Syrians.

Since Resolution 242 is so ambiguous, it's entirely understandable that no agreement between the warring countries has been reached. Technically, in fact, Israel and the Arab nations of the region (with the exception of Jordan and Egypt) are still in a state of war, since no peace treaty has ever been signed. Today the United Nations, along with all of the Arab nations, considers the area "annexed" or "occupied." The Israeli government views the Golan as essential to its security and its water resources, however. As a result, the conflict over the Golan remains insoluble, and few analysts of the region expect a solution in the near future.

It was in this context, then, that Diane and I walked the area. Deeply touched by the historic nature of the place, we surveyed the inactive gun emplacements and gained our first views of both Syria and Lebanon from above. It's difficult to convey the emotion we felt as we stood on ground from which the Syrians had rained shells onto neighboring Israeli cities below. That experience must have been hellish, and it's hard to imagine the terror that the parents and grandparents of the Israeli youth living directly below the Golan must have felt as shells dropped from the sky on their settlements. It was painful to imagine their desperate anxiety, as they fled to the bomb shelters where they were forced to hunker down for hours at a time, while doing their best to comfort their traumatized children.

The days were passing quickly now, but my ailing foot wasn't getting any better. The pain continued unchecked, and I felt more dejected with each passing hour. Meanwhile, I couldn't help wondering if the incessant walking required for our role as tourists might be adding to my injury.

All too soon, it was January 24th and time for us to depart Israel for our Air Sinai flight to Cairo. My pilot's cap of choice has "Delta" or "United" written above the visor – so I wasn't entirely comfortable to see that our only choice of transportation to Egypt was named "Air Sinai!" There was no other alternative, however. I didn't like it, but I steeled myself for the flight. In order to remain calm, I kept reminding myself that Diane and I had managed to survive the "boy pilot" of Australia. At least the pilots would be *grownups* on this flight. Perhaps, if we were very lucky, they'd even be able to get us safely down to the runway in Cairo – so that I could then die of pain and exhaustion in my approaching marathon!

My fears proved to be unfounded, and the Air Sinai flight

turned out to be of the very best kind: uneventful. Diane and I had arranged for a driver to meet us at the airport and take us to our hotel, the Helnan Shepherd, the oldest hotel in Cairo. This charming edifice had been recently renovated, and it was a truly delightful place to stay. Our room included a balcony that overlooked a vast boulevard and the River Nile.

Being in Egypt was amazing. All of my young life, I'd been reading about and hearing about my ancestors and their battles with the Pharaohs . . . about Moses being hidden away in a reed-woven basket on the Nile, and about the building of the majestic pyramids. I had thrilled to the stories – but I had never imagined that I would one day be permitted to visit these ancient and historic locales in person.

On the drive in from the airport, I noticed that there were monuments dotting the landscape at virtually every intersection, and that Cairo itself was also full of these somber memorials. I asked our English-speaking driver about their significance, and he told us that they'd been erected in order to honor Egypt's many war veterans. He seemed to be particularly impressed with a large obelisk that memorialized the Yom Kippur War of 1973. I found that a bit ironic – since it hadn't been one of Egypt's most successful ventures – but politeness kept me from asking any further questions about the memorial.

Cairo is a city of 16 million teeming, sweating and bustling people . . . with at least two million additional commuters arriving by train, car, bus and camel each day. The buses were so crowded that the bus company stationed individuals at each stop, where their job was to help stuff passengers into each jammed vehicle. Amazingly, the Egyptians rode both inside and *outside* the buses, with the out-riders hanging on for dear life. Nor did there seem to be any speed limits. As we watched the traffic on the boulevard below our balcony, we marveled at the close calls that were happening each moment. Somehow, the accidents were always averted at the last instant, however, and we didn't witness as much as a minor "fender bender."

With 16 million people crammed into a single city (not counting the commuters who drive cars), parking in Cairo is at a premium – and especially parking on the street. There are no meters, but over the years an elaborate system has been worked out. It seems that each city block has a "boss," and he runs the parking on that block. In order to park, a driver signals the boss that he wants a parking spot. A gratuity is then required, before the new arrival is permitted to back into his space. Inevitably, however, the driver must stop halfway through the parking process – after discovering that the space simply isn't big enough for his car.

Time for another tip! After pocketing this second gratuity, the "boss" will manually push the cars bracketing the space backwards or forwards until the new car can be accommodated. (All of the autos are left in "neutral" by their owners, as part of a clever strategy that allows them to be pushed at will.) Next step: Once the new car is in place, the vehicles in front of it and behind it are then pushed in close – ensuring that no exit will be possible without moving them again. The same ritual (and yet another tip) occurs whenever a car leaves a space.

It sounds pretty crazy, but the Cairo parking system actually seems to work – provided that the tips keep on flowing!

Our Marathon Director, Marie Frances, met us at the hotel and informed us that she had arranged for us to have a personal guide during our stay in Cairo. It was included in our total package, thanks to the very fair-minded agreement the two of us had worked out. What happened was that she had wanted to provide the air portion of our travel (ensuring her commission for same)... while I wanted to use our Frequent Flyer miles so we could fly First Class. The truth is that I'd become spoiled and would only fly Business Class or First Class when going overseas. Why? Because these flights are too long – and because the coach section is always too crowded with foreign nationals returning home. Hey, I'm not really xenophobic – I just don't like to be crowded! (Plus, we usually had plenty of miles to spare in our Frequent Flyer program.)

Could we reach a compromise? Yes, we could. Since Marie Frances hoped to make some money on the plane tickets, I simply told her to add what would have been her profit on the airline tickets to her fee – and that I would trust her to make a fair-minded calculation. I think she appreciated my gesture, and she couldn't have been more accommodating.

So far, so good. Our guide for the week was scheduled to meet us the following day, Tuesday, and the marathon was on Friday so we opted to take a walk along the Nile to stretch our legs and get a feel for the city. Central Cairo, where we were located, was a very safe area – but as we walked along the beautiful promenade we were continually accosted by local vendors, each of whom would greet us with the exact same words:

"Hello. My name Muhammad. I your brother. I have factory. Would you please come with me and I show you my [whatever he was selling]." These high-powered street merchants were pretty insistent, and once they'd latched onto you, it was difficult to escape without being rude. We soon learned that we could say "no" in as many nice ways as possible . . . but the pitch-man would continue to walk stride for stride beside us. We did our best to pay no attention to the ongoing spiel, until at last the pesky merchant would give up and start looking for another hapless mark.

The following morning, after a beautifully served breakfast in the hotel dining room, we were met by our guide, Akila, a pretty 20-something young girl who spoke perfect English. Our first stop was Giza, home of the Great Pyramid of Giza – also known as "The Pyramid of Cheops," the fourth-dynasty Egyptian Pharaoh. The oldest of the Seven Wonders of the Ancient World and the only one to remain largely intact, this fabulous monument had been the tallest man-made structure in the world for more than 3,800 years.

All during my life as a young Hebrew school student (although not a very good one!), I'd read about the pyramids and how the evil Pharaohs had used Jewish slave laborers to construct them. And now I found myself, as an adult, standing right beside the greatest pyramid of them all!

It was awe-inspiring, especially as my eyes wandered down the hill and suddenly discovered, in full view, the mighty Sphinx. This was a pretty impressive neighborhood, to say the least, and when I looked up some facts about the Cheops pyramid, I was even more astonished. According to the historians, the structure had been built over a 20-year period by 100,000 men – and it's estimated to weigh nearly 6 million tons. Since the Great Pyramid consists of 2.3 million blocks, completing it within 20 years must have required moving more than 12 blocks with an average weight of 2.5 tons each into place every hour, day and night, during the entire 20 years of construction!

I was able to enter the pyramid by climbing down a steep, ladder-type stairway into an inner chamber. But the tight enclosure made me feel rather claustrophobic . . . so it wasn't long before I was clambering back into the bright sunlight of Giza, happy to be back on terra firma and out of the tomb.

Since the Three Pyramids of Giza are a prime tourist attraction in greater Cairo, a swarm of local camel drivers shows up each day to offer rides from the Great Pyramid down the hill to the Sphinx. Prices for the rides are based on the negotiating skills of the tourist, and they can vary widely. Knowing this, the loyal Akila kindly volunteered to be our "agent" in the negotiation process. After three protracted and animated bargaining sessions, she directed us to our host for the ride down the hill.

I thought it would be fun if Diane and I rode together (big mistake!) so we hopped on our supine camel and then hung on as the driver prodded the creature in order to make it rise.

Uh-oh. The camel hadn't looked so tall, while stretched out flat in the dirt . . . but when he stuck out his front legs, tilted us forward, and then extended his hind legs to rise to his full height, it felt like we were suddenly 22 stories high! My only means of support (and balance) was the death-grip I managed to secure on Diane's waist. She, meanwhile, had the advantage of clinging to the reins and stirrups for support. Trust me: I did not look terribly dignified at that moment. For one thing, my feet were dangling in space . . . and as the animal loped downhill, I was rolling from one side of his broad back to the other – with nothing to break my fall if I should tilt too far in one direction and then slide right off the beast!

It was a horrific – and comical – moment. Had I gone over the side, there would have been no way for me to right myself in order to land feet first. Was this the end? Strangely enough, the only thought that crossed my mind – as I pictured myself landing on my noggin and then being declared "dead on arrival" at the nearest Egyptian hospital – was that I would have to utter that dreaded phrase: "Goodbye, marathon!"

Stricken with terror (no marathon meant no more funds for my kids in Maine), I had begun to perspire profusely – while also yelling my damn head off. Diane found this hysterically funny (almost as funny, in fact, as the "fish-nibbling attack" at the Great Barrier Reef, which had nearly ended in my total emasculation). Convulsed with merriment, my treacherous mate enjoyed the comedy for all it was worth . . . and did almost nothing to help me.

Frantic, I bellowed at Mohammed (or whatever his name was): "Do you hear me? I want off *now*!" It seemed to take forever, but I finally managed to make myself understood. With unspeakable relief, I watched the camel jockey order his charge to stand down and release me. Somehow, I had managed to survive this encounter with the tallest camel in the history of Egypt.

Diane continued on to the Sphinx – good riddance! – while I rejoined Akila for the short automobile ride that would allow me to catch up with my still-chuckling mate. As we rolled toward the

Atop our "22 Story Camel" (Before he started to move!)

great monument, I was singing the praises of Henry Ford for all I was worth – and if I never see a camel again, it will be too soon!

Whenever there's a new construction project in Egypt, you can be almost certain that the digging will unearth one archeological treasure after the next. Such was the case with the Sphinx, which was completely excavated between 1925 and 1936. (The chest of the great monument had been excavated way back in 1817.) Built in approximately 2500 BC by the pharaoh Khafra, the Sphinx remains one of Egypt's primary tourist attractions. The head is believed to resemble that of Khafra himself – although many archeologists consider it to have prominent Negroid features. Regardless, it provides a wonderful photo op . . . with the Sphinx looming in the foreground and the pyramid of Khafra in the background.

Since the pyramids and Sphinx were the two attractions I'd most wanted to visit, I was in no hurry to leave. But there were many other attractions waiting for us out there on the Egyptian landscape, and Akila soon had us on our way.

During our ride together to meet Diane – immediately after the Great Camel Ride Disaster – Akila and I had become close buddies, and she had even taken to calling me "Dad." When I asked her why, she told me that I reminded her of her father. (I quickly assumed she was paying me a compliment.) She then proceeded to tell me that her father was a retired Egyptian Army General who'd been wounded during the Yom Kippur War of 1973. I felt uneasy for a moment . . . but then decided that if she was comfortable enough with me to call me "Dad," it would probably be okay to ask her a potentially troublesome question about recent Egyptian history.

As you may recall, I had been struck by the numerous wartime monuments that were scattered around Cairo . . . and by the fact that so many seemed to refer to the disastrous (for the Egyptians) Yom Kippur War. Gathering my nerve, I now asked my high-spirited guide directly: "Akila, I'm puzzled by something. If the Yom Kippur War – when Israel was attacked on its holiest of days and then proceeded to decimate the combined armed forces of the Arab nations, while totally surrounding the Egyptian Second Army in the Sinai Desert – was such a disaster for Egypt, why are there all those monuments commemorating that particular war? After all, it was hardly one of the most shining moments in Egyptian history!"

I felt a tad uneasy asking Akila this question – her father had been a prominent Egyptian general in the war, remember – but she didn't seem fazed by my query. Responding, she gave me a big smile and without blinking an eyelash said: "Because it was that war which brought Egypt to the realization that Israel was here to stay and that peace must be made. It was that war that brought Anwar Sadat to Israel, and it led to the eventual signing of a peace treaty between the two countries.

"It was also the war which brought my father to retirement and to advise my brother that a life in the army was not his choice for him." What a wonderful and gracious answer – as I listened to her, I wanted to hug that girl!

The next few days leading up to Marathon Day were devoted to additional sightseeing. Meanwhile, my foot continued to ache without letup . . . which left me worrying almost non-stop about my prospects for success in a 26.2-mile run. My cane was providing some relief . . . but it's impossible to walk very far when all you've got is a cane and one foot. Unfortunately, *both* feet need to touch the ground on each step – and you don't have to be a member of the Mensa Society to understand that when one of your feet refuses to bear any weight, there's something *wrong* with it.

Luckily for me (and unlike what had happened during our visit to Israel), the Cairo tour was conducted mostly by car. There wasn't much walking required, thankfully, and I soon realized that since there was nothing I could do about the pain, I might as well not waste my brain cells by worrying about it. I also realized, early on, that the Cairo Marathon would have to be run in "survival shuffle" from start to finish. It was a grim prospect – but I also knew for certain that I was gonna cross that finish line, come hell or high water . . . or both!

The Egyptian Museum, home of many of King Tut's treasures, was situated directly across the street from our hotel – so Diane and I dropped by for a visit one afternoon. The layout was impressive, but we were amazed by the lack of climate control in a building housing such important artifacts. Windows had been broken and left open, and there was no visible humidity control at all. When we asked why, the answer came back immediately: "No money."

Amazing. Can you imagine visiting the Smithsonian or Guggenheim Museums in America and finding broken windows and fetid heat and humidity swirling through the building? As we wandered around the facility, we were also struck by the paucity of the exhibits – although we soon learned that many of King Tut's treasures (along with his sarcophagus) are actually located in Luxor. Since we knew we'd be visiting Luxor on the day after the race, we weren't terribly disappointed by the relatively meager offerings at the Egyptian Museum.

Akila knew we were Jewish, so she made certain to escort us to the Ben Ezra Synagogue, the oldest such temple in Egypt – and also the site, according to legend, at which the baby Moses had been found. (I'd always thought he'd been discovered after floating down the Nile in a reed-woven basket, but who am I to argue with local lore?)

It was all very interesting. And in what appeared to be an ecumenical gesture, Akila then led us to the spot where the baby Jesus (accompanied by Mary and Joseph) had been hidden from the marauding King Herod. The Old Testament tells us that the Three Wise Men had told the king that a star had risen in the east, signifying that a new *king* had been born. Concerned about maintaining his term in office, the Egyptian monarch (definitely not a nice man) had then decided that this troublesome baby had to be eliminated, and pronto. Since he didn't know which baby was the one who might threaten his throne, he'd simply announced that all baby boys under the age of two were to be immediately slain.

Not good. But Mary and Joseph managed to elude the monster by fleeing with the baby Jesus to Egypt, where they'd hidden themselves away. It was a thrilling story – and now here we were, standing on that exact spot. Actually, the setting seemed just a bit mundane, since the entry to the famous hiding place looked more like a boarded-up New York Subway entrance than an exalted landmark. Still, we knew we were observing a moment of important history . . . and we experienced the same surge of emotion we'd felt when we shook the hand of Pope John Paul II during our "private audience," back in 1984.

We concluded our tour with visits to the Mohammad Ali Mosque, which houses his tomb and dates back to 1830. This fabled landmark was relatively new by Egyptian standards. After paying our respects, we visited the Citadel of Saladin, the oldest Catholic Church in Egypt, and then bade a fond farewell to our lovely guide for the week, the cheerful and tireless Akila.

As the day of the marathon approached, I was struggling with a growing feeling of anxiety. Fretful and uncertain of what lay ahead, I knew that it would soon be time to test the ailing foot. More than anything else in the world right then, I just wanted to get through the marathon and achieve the original purpose of our visit – by finding the strength and the endurance that would be required to make it across the finish line.

Friday morning, January 28th, was upon us now. The weather wasn't bad, really; today would be a typical January day, with a high temperature of 55 degrees and relative humidity of 43 percent. It was perfect for running . . . although I understood that in my case, no running would be involved. For me, the marathon would be a matter of "putting the left foot down and then gingerly putting the right foot down" . . . and then wincing as the pain went zooming up my trunk and scorched my eyeballs! It would be an agonizing sequence, and I would have to perform it over and over again, for 26.2 miles.

On Marathon Eve the runners gathered and Marie Frances handed out our "bib numbers" for the race. Perhaps she took pity on me (after watching me hobble around – but without complaining – for a solid week before the run). Whatever her motivation, Marie surprised me by assigning me Number One as my bib number.

Was she touched by the way I had refused to moan and groan about my foot ailment? Maybe. But the credit for my valorous refusal to whine about my injury actually belonged to my old grandmother – a stalwart lady who believed that complaining used up too much energy without ever producing any results. As she so often liked to say, in accents that recalled the Old Country of her long-ago birth and upbringing: "Vat vas, *vas*!" (Loose translation: "What was, *was*!") And this pithy statement would inevitably be followed by a second: "Vat iss, *iss*!" ("What is, *is*!")

Thanks to Grandma, I had long ago decided that I wouldn't complain about my problems or setbacks. And now, apparently, this noble posture had earned me the respect of Marie Frances, who had crowned me Number One. Actually, my low number wasn't really all that prestigious . . . since, as it turned out, there were only to be about a dozen runners participating in the event!

(When I referred to our pre-race powwow as a "small gathering" a minute ago, I wasn't kidding.) Why the tiny turnout? When we asked her about this, Marie Frances told us that she'd originally had more than 100 entrants – but because the idiot Muslim fundamentalists in the south of Egypt were at that time killing and looting innocents and tourists, only 12 hearty souls had decided to stick their necks out by engaging in a lengthy public run.

Oh, well. The bottom line was clear, and it left me feeling kind of proud, if also a little silly.

The Bottom Line: I was *Numero Uno,* and I was rarin' to go!

After a light breakfast of tea and toast, we boarded the two vans that had been hired to take the entire entourage to our starting point near the three pyramids in Giza. As the takeoff grew near, I wondered what would happen next. Let's face it: my foot was a mess. During the past few days, it had become more and more difficult to recover the full mobility and use of the ailing extremity – especially during the first hour or so after awakening from the previous night's sleep. And this day was no exception. Increasingly agitated, I waggled the balky thing back and forth and up and down. Gradually, I was able to work the stiffness out of it, as we drove the fifteen minutes to our destination.

At last we arrived. Then the twelve of us hovered around, waiting anxiously, while Marie Frances looked for a starting gun. Once she had it in hand, we lined up at a makeshift ribbon. This was the first marathon in which I hadn't been required to seed myself – and it was quite a thrill to begin a race in the very front row! Of course, this was also the first marathon in which I knew each competitor by first and last name . . . since we'd all been staying at the same hotel and taking the same tours of Cairo.

BOOM! The gun sounded and the competitors took off like gazelles down the hill. Bounding along on an initial surge of energy, we tooled past the Sphinx and into the Cairo traffic. With only twelve runners participating, not much traffic control was required. . . .

But hang on; let me back up for a second. And let me point out, quite honestly: There weren't really "12 gazelles" running down the hill, but only 11. Nor did I "bound." I think the more appropriate verb would be "limp." Having given Diane my cane just before takeoff, I was now doing my best to even *walk* . . . as my running colleagues rapidly vanished into the hazy distance.

Walking on flat surfaces was painful, and I had developed a very distinctive limp in an effort to reduce some of the pressure on my right foot. But running down a hill, with my heel hitting the ground before the ball of my foot, was absolutely excruciating. I did my best to concentrate on what was up ahead, one step at a time, and at this point, I think my previous marathon runs were a great educational resource. As they say, "Experience is the best teacher," and I had five unforgettable "experiences" to draw upon.

Diane and I had finally learned our lesson. For this event, we had hired a driver, Abdul, to transport her along the route. In addition, it was the policy of the marathon that an ambulance with two in attendance would follow the last runner in the race. This procedure had been designed to ensure prompt medical attention for any runner in distress. (That would be me, of course.)

On we went. And there I was – Number One! – creeping along with the ambulance and a big black official-looking Mercedes in close pursuit. By the time I reached Mile One, not one of my fellow runners was in sight. Their disappearance was entirely understandable . . . since my 12-13 minutes-per-mile pace was hardly the norm for this event. My first inclination was to wave the ambulance in close and then advise the driver to take it on ahead, in order to help other runners who might need it. Being followed by two vehicles was somewhat disconcerting, and I also felt that I was holding the ambulance back.

All too soon, however, I realized that the ambulance was a good thing, and not a bad thing. The ambulance was my friend! I also began to appreciate the presence of the Mercedes . . . since they'd stocked it with plenty of water, and since there were few water stops along the route. As the marathon unfolded at a glacial rate (for me, anyway), I became increasingly comfortable about stopping frequently in order to request additional liquid refreshment.

Out of Giza I plodded, and I was soon trudging on dirt roads in the farm country of greater Cairo. The route took me out to Saqqara, the burial ground of the ancient Egyptian Capital, Memphis, and the home of the famous Djoser Step Pyramid. Loping along these dirt roads gave me a sense of peace, as I witnessed the locals milking cows and tending their fields – obviously without a clue as to what this idiot was doing, or why he was being pursued by an ambulance and a Mercedes. But they were all very friendly and waved to me as I passed. When I could summon the strength to lift my arm, I would wave back and smile with a thankful nod.

Onward! Soon I had been on the road for about two hours, but I had yet to see the halfway point, the Step Pyramid. By this time my bladder had expanded from all of the water I'd been consuming, but there was no restroom in sight. What to do? As I analyzed the problem, it seemed very doubtful that these farmers would walk all the way home each time they needed a bathroom break . . . so I started looking for trees that weren't overlooked by homes or farmers.

Both the Mercedes and ambulance stopped to wait each time I conducted my business. By this time, however, Diane was also feeling the urge. A quandary! Thus far, you see, we hadn't noticed all that many Exxon stations or Burger Kings. So she asked Abdul about the chances of finding a bathroom. "No problem," he replied and promptly stopped the car and then scurried into a nearby home.

With a big smile on his face he returned and motioned Diane to follow him. She did, and he escorted her into a house filled with women and young children. One of the ladies, whom she assumed to be the matron of the house, took her by the hand and out the rear door to a hole in the ground covered by a grate. This quaint facility was located directly next to the chicken coop, and not far from a tethered donkey and several doves' nests. The hole was covered by a roof (I could only assume that Egyptians don't like peeing in the rain), supported by four poles. But there were no sides and no door.

The lady smiled at Diane, grabbed a nearby hose and washed down the grate. As is so often said on the high seas, "Any old port in a storm will do!" The matron politely left Diane to her "privacy." A short time later, Diane returned inside and offered to pay the women for their kindness but they wouldn't hear of it. Smiling happily, they waved her off and bid her well and she and Abdul were soon hurrying to catch up to me – not a difficult task, given my foot speed in this event.

It was a remarkable situation, to put it mildly. From beginning to end, I didn't see a single automobile other than those supporting the runners. Nor was there a single traffic light over the course of the entire 26.2 miles.

I staggered on. At last I could see the distant pyramids denoting the 13-mile mark of the race. Right then I truly wished the Pharaohs hadn't felt the need to build their tombs at the tops of hills – but Djoser and his two pals, Unas and Userkaf, had been interred at the very top of what looked like Mt. Everest.

Up I climbed. By now I was concentrating so much on relieving the pain in my foot that I barely noticed the magnificent Step Pyramid to my left. What I *did* notice, however, was that from the top of the hill I could see the three Great Pyramids – the *finish line* – in the far distance. Only thirteen miles to go, but those pyramids looked like they were in France!

The one positive note was that now, instead of counting "up" on the mileage, I could count "down," as each step brought me closer to the end of the ordeal. On I went. Noontime on Friday in Egypt begins their Sabbath . . . so as I returned along the same dirt roads I'd already traveled, I could hear the *Adhan,* the Muslim Call to Prayer, rising from the small, local mosques in the vicinity. The *Adhan* has a great deal of tradition associated with it. As legend has it, the ancient prophets were discussing ways to call the faithful to prayer. One suggested using a bell, similar to that employed by the Christians. Another suggested a ram's horn, following Jewish practice. Then it was suggested that one person, called a muezzin, should mount the minaret of the mosque and in a loud voice summon the worshippers.

These days, however, it's not necessary for the muezzin to climb to the top of the mosque, since loudspeakers routinely blare out the summons for all to hear. The Call to Prayer is heard five times each day: at dawn, at midday, in the middle of the afternoon, just after sunset and at nightfall (about two hours after sunset). To the uninitiated like me, it sounds like a continual drone – but that wailing voice was something to occupy my mind as I continued on my journey.

All work in the fields had ceased by now, and the only human beings in sight were those heading off to prayer. Most were dressed in white robes as they ambled slowly along toward the mosque. One gentleman (you'll find him gracing the cover of this book) was walking his water buffalo and two goats. I can honestly say that I don't recall whether I was passing the buffalo or he was passing me (total exhaustion tends to weaken the mind) – but what I do recall, quite vividly, is that these water buffalo sure can leave a mess on the roads!

Soon my bladder was giving me hints that it needed relief, and once again I found myself positioned near a secluded tree in order to provide it with some personal watering. But as I left my spot and ran back to the road, my feet suddenly went out from under me. All at once I was struggling to keep my balance.

I'm sure you can imagine my dismay . . . when I looked down and saw that I'd skidded on a pile of water buffalo dung. What next? And what was I to do . . . now that my custom-made Hersey running shoes were crap-covered and emitting a fiercely pungent odor of the barnyard variety?

Along the Route

Groaning with aggravation, I banged my feet as hard as I could on the ground, hoping to knock off the excess dung. But in spite of my huge efforts, much remained. Make no mistake: My struggles were sharp and unrelenting – and my poor mate was *also* grappling with adversity, although I didn't know it at the time. Understand, please, that Diane and I had been married for 31 years . . . and after so much time together, our body clocks seem to work in sync. Which meant that even as I was limping through the buffalo poop, Diane was feeling the call of nature herself.

She, too, needed relief. So she asked Abdul for a suggestion. He was happy to oblige, and soon pulled over and repeated his routine of entering a house and then returning to summon Diane. No problem. But as she entered the living area of the home, she noticed one gentleman who hadn't yet departed for prayer. He was surrounded by women and children – all of whom were relaxing on beautiful Oriental rugs.

It was a bit of a delicate situation. Since there was a man in the house, Abdul explained, one of the women would be required to personally escort her to the outhouse. This facility turned out to be fancier than the last one, however. It had sides, for example. And it also had some holes near the top of the four walls; they were located where you would normally expect to find windows. Once again, Diane's escort hosed down the grate and then departed, in order to ensure her privacy. (And once again, Diane offered some money that was graciously refused.)

At approximately Mile 16, I was joined by two young girls on donkeys. They thought it quite funny that I was out in their part of the world and running along in short pants. They were awfully cute and fun to talk to, and I could tell they enjoyed practicing their English on me. Diane and Abdul pulled ahead of me in an effort to get a photo of the girls . . . but before the picture-taking could begin, Diane was admonished by our guide, who explained that she must obtain permission from her subjects before the photo shoot could begin.

The girls were most willing, however, and they posed happily. Apparently, people in this part of the world like to be photographed. More than once, in fact, Diane had asked Abdul to stop the car so she could secure an unposed photograph of the natives as they worked the fields . . . and on every occasion, as the locals spotted her adjusting her camera, the subjects would wave happily and smile at the lens. We could only conclude that there was no such thing as a "natural photo" in this part of the world!

By this time all of my fellow competitors had obviously completed the run, and I was now alone on the route and followed only by my two chase cars. Since the other runners had long passed by, everyone who saw me chugging along had to figure that with "Number One" on my shirt and nobody else in sight, I was leading in the race. From time to time, the crowds of people walking or sitting along the road would burst into spontaneous applause. I grinned happily back at them, of course, thanking one and all for saluting my hard-earned lead!

Diane, meanwhile, could see the toll the run was taking on my body. She sensed the pain that was oozing from my pores, and she was deeply worried about my health. Was I doing permanent damage to my body? Would I be unable to run again? Play golf? Ski? Travel? Would the joy we'd always felt in our shared physical activities be destroyed because of my stubbornness and refusal to quit? And what would living with me be like, if I could no longer be an active participant in outdoor sports?

I'd always preached to my children that the easiest thing in the world to do is *quit* – while letting them know that this despised word simply isn't in my vocabulary!

Crazy or not, I had no intention of giving up. With agonizing slowness, the miles melted away step by painful step. Somehow I hung in there – until at last I was back in civilization with the Three Great Pyramids in sight. What a wonderful feeling! Daring to hope now, I rounded the bend and worked my way around the traffic to enter the area housing the Sphinx and Pyramids. It was time to begin my climb to the finish line. Somehow, even though the pain going down the hill had been much greater than going up (your heel hits the ground harder), the climb to the top seemed to take much longer. It was about a mile to the summit, and I felt every inch.

To my great amazement, I soon discovered that a few of the racers had already finished running and had retired to the hotel to rest and shower . . . before returning to the course to root me home. What a nice gesture on their part, and totally unexpected. And this is one of the best things about long-distance running – the way the runners all become members of a fraternity, and the way everyone roots for each other. I'm sure that kind of brotherly ritual doesn't take place during the Olympics – or among the elite runners in the Boston or New York Marathons – but on our level, with no prize money at stake, we all root for each other to do well.

What a moment! With the cheers and applause of my well-wishers ringing in my ears, and feeling more dead than alive, I finally dragged myself across the finish line. Diane was waiting for me, as always; she had passed me on the hill, and now we were embracing in a blizzard of hugs, kisses, tears and overwhelming relief.

It was also a highly comical moment, however. Somehow, Marie Frances had even arranged for two cheering people to hold a tape that I could break as I finished. I was dead last – Number 12 out of 12 runners. But I'm sure I was the happiest – and the proudest – of them all. The fact that it had taken me 5 hours, 42 minutes and 10 seconds to cover the distance was of no importance now.

I had finished the marathon, and I was still standing upright (at least for the moment).

Abdul drove Diane and me back to our hotel and with the aid of my cane, I followed her back to our room. As we walked down the corridor, we could smell the water buffalo remains that were still percolating on my sneakers. I might add that these running shoes, fabled Herseys, had been custom-made by a craftsman named Bart Hersey in Farmington, Maine. As you might imagine, they weren't inexpensive – and understandably so, since they'd been individually crafted to accommodate my feet, my particular orthotics . . . and also the plastic gel heel pads I always wore while running. As costly as they were, however, there was no way that these particular shoes were ever going to make it back to the United States. Hey, I wasn't even going to wear them in my room! In the end, I left them outside my door . . . and I often wonder if there's an Egyptian out there somewhere, even today, jogging contentedly along in my once-upon-a-time running shoes!

I'd experienced some raw feelings after previous marathons, but nothing compared to what I felt after Cairo. For starters, I could barely walk – even with the cane. But I knew that I needed to keep moving, in order to rid my body of the lactic acid that builds up during a long run. Running itself, of course, was now impossible; at this point, I was praying that I would be able to *walk*. And trying to navigate a flight of stairs was completely out of the question.

After a shower and nap (by the way, did I mention that the "Post-Marathon Tradition" was now the farthest thing from my mind?), Diane and I descended to the lobby of the hotel so we could call home and report to our children that Daddy had actually finished the race. My other call was to my brother, Douglas, my partner in business. He congratulated me and I thanked him – and then I asked him to call my orthopedist, Doug Brown, for a consultation on the day after our arrival in Portland.

At seven o'clock that evening, Marie Frances had arranged for a post-marathon banquet, during which she presented parchment-like certificates to all. In addition, she'd gone to the considerable trouble of locating a trophy, which she presented to me as the "Most Courageous Runner." It was very sweet of her to think of me – given all that she had on her mind in producing and coordinating a marathon.

After that, we feasted. I don't know how the Egyptians go about making hummus, lamb, olives, baba ganoush and pita bread, but the food was delicious. The olives were especially tasty. Enjoying myself thoroughly, I alternated between the lamb, the olives and the pita bread covered with hummus. Delightful! But then it happened: As I ate and talked with my new friends, I wasn't paying enough attention to the items on my plate. After scooping up and then spreading some hummus onto a pita slice, I bit into the delicacy and heard a loud "crunch.

It was the sound of my teeth colliding with a large olive pit that I'd inadvertently taken in, along with the hummus. As I reached into my mouth and removed one-half of a large tooth, I could only wonder what misfortune was going to befall me next! Luckily, the root of the tooth wasn't exposed, so I wasn't in pain. But now I would have to ask my brother to make a second appointment – this time with my dentist, Lenny Brennan, in Portland. (Only $3,000 and a root canal-with-permanent-cap later, my mouth was good to go. Let's just say it was an expensive banquet and leave it at that.)

As badly as I felt the following morning, I knew I had to get moving. Diane and I had booked an early flight to Luxor, the home of the Valley of the Kings and the Valley of the Queens. We had a return flight set for late in the evening, but I was in no condition to do any touring . . . so we cancelled our plans and forfeited our plane fare. This was probably a wise decision, though – since the area of Egypt we were scheduled to visit had been experiencing the same kinds of kidnappings and random killings that had caused most of Marie Frances' marathon runners to cancel.

Missing out on Luxor didn't exactly break my heart. By this time, I'd seen enough tombs and artifacts to last a lifetime. All I wanted right then was to get off my foot and not move. Still, I knew that sitting idle wasn't the right move, medically . . . so Diane and I used the day to go to an open air market where the most beautiful olives and dates we'd ever seen were being sold.

(Diane had begun using dates as her "substitute chocolate" and was restricting herself one date a day as a special treat.) We spent the balance of that final day waiting for it to *end* – so we could board our plane for Tel Aviv and the return journey home.

Early the next morning, a taxi arrived to convey us to the airport for the beginning of our last leg home. There wasn't much traffic on a Sunday morning, so our driver drove about as fast as humanly possible to the airport. It seemed like he was daring other drivers to challenge him, as he tore through intersections and ignored the few working traffic lights. All too soon, we had arrived at the airport.

And then, unbelievably, we experienced another startling mishap. What happened was that the driver pulled our taxi up to one of the terminals – in order to let a third passenger disembark – and when he opened the door, we heard a loud *Clunk*!

Another taxi had just smashed into the opened door.

We just stared and shook our heads. All week we'd been witnessing "close encounters of the traffic kind"—but without ever seeing an actual accident. And now we were *in* one! I couldn't help

The Day After

but laugh at the sheer idiocy of it all. While sitting at a full stop, we'd been nailed in a nasty fender-bender.

Fortunately, no one was hurt, and even our taxi driver didn't seem too concerned. He and the other driver talked for a few moments – but no papers were signed or passed back and forth. Then he simply jammed the door back into place until it held, although it wasn't completely closed. He then told us (as if such guidance were necessary), that we should exit from the other side. A few minutes later, he was depositing us at our terminal without further mishap.

Back in Tel Aviv, we checked into our hotel and waited for a 3 a.m. wakeup call in order to start our journey back to Ben Gurion Airport and home. Our plane didn't actually leave until 8 a.m., but we'd been told that we needed to arrive four hours ahead of our scheduled flight, due to security requirements. For the record, I should point out that "departure times" in Israel are very different from those in the United States. In this country, an 8 a.m. departure time means that you'll probably take off pretty close to that time. In Israel, however, it means you'll leave "whenever we decide to take off." Could be earlier. Could be later.

That approach makes good sense, in a place like Israel – because it's actually a strategy for knocking potential terrorists off their game plan. So we adhered to the familiar adage, "When in Israel, do as the Israelis."

We lifted off eventually, and I watched the landscape around Tel Aviv recede with a joyful heart.

We were headed home at last. And I was very glad to be leaving . . . because I certainly didn't want to miss my dates with my orthopedist and my dentist!

The Agony of Da Feet

Back on U.S. soil after my Cairo adventure, my first order of business was to see if I could solve my chronic foot problem. I also needed some routine maintenance in the dental area, which meant that I would have to set up appointments ASAP with a dentist, an oral surgeon and a periodontist who could attend to some unpleasant issues along my gum-line. Oh, and one other thing: At some point, obviously, I had to return to my office in Biddeford and start selling some boxes!

At this point in my Seven Continents quest, my head was still spinning with the elation of having completed my next-to-last marathon. But I was also feeling no small amount of dread over the future of my perpetually malfunctioning foot. To be honest, I was deathly afraid that I'd damaged the unfortunate extremity beyond repair – and that the doctor, responding to that unhappy fact, would advise me to stop running marathons once and for all.

What to do? Each time I thought about the problem, I realized all over again that I couldn't quit. Regardless of the ultimate impact on my ailing foot, I knew I wouldn't be able to abort this mission – not with final success so tantalizingly near!

My first appointment with my orthopedist, Doug Brown, was

scheduled for the day after my arrival home. Doug was intimately familiar with all my aches and pains, and no wonder: I'd been a patient of his since he'd established his practice in Portland. But I did feel at ease in his care – since he'd served admirably as the team physician for the U.S. Olympic Committee at the National Sports Festival in 1982 and also at the World University Games in 1985. In addition, Doug had distinguished himself as a team physician for various Men's Olympic and Men's National Soccer Teams . . . and as the head team physician for the Women's National Soccer Team during two World Cups.

Given that stellar background, the good Dr. Brown seemed eminently qualified to care for my foot injury and help me fend off the nasty waves of pain that still radiated from it. One of the first things he suggested was x-rays . . . but when they turned out to be inconclusive (there had been no fracture, according to the photos), he concluded that the only effective remedy would be physical therapy – a strategy that would require more trips to Kurt Jepson at Saco Bay Physical Therapy.

By this time, of course, I knew the routine all too well: ride the stationary bike for 20 minutes and then brace yourself for electric stimulation and hot packs.

I followed the P.T. program carefully, but when it failed to provide any measurable relief, I decided to seek a second opinion and scheduled a visit to Dr. Richard Needleman at the Ortho Foot and Ankle Center in South Portland, Maine. His assessment went as follows:

> Perhaps bruising to the medial aspect of the
> calcaneotuberosity.
> Small nerve impingement of the small nerve
> to the ADQ muscle.
> Plantar fasciitis at origin.

He scheduled a follow-up for three weeks later and then sent me back to physical therapy. To my knowledge, this was the first time plantar fasciitis had been mentioned as a possible diagnosis, but the treatment for that condition still failed to bring me any significant relief. Maddeningly, my foot continued to feel especially sore when I awoke each morning, after it had spent the previous six to eight hours resting in the same position. (This phenomenon is a classic symptom of plantar fasciitis, by the way.)

What a bummer! Writhing with impatience, I managed to wait for three weeks – while doing my best to be a "good patient" and never missing a single P.T. appointment. Then I returned to Dr. Needleman for further examination. To say I was becoming a bit "discouraged" at my lack of progress would be a humongous understatement! I was unable to run, after all. As a matter of fact, I couldn't even walk without major pain. And that was truly aggravating. During this unhappy period, I wasn't the most light-hearted or engaging figure in our household, to be sure. (But more on my surly, bear-like behavior later in this chapter.)

If you know anything about orthopedic specialists, you probably know that they don't like to inject the foot. But we were becoming increasingly desperate . . . and Dr. Needleman finally decided on a last-ditch strategy that called for him to inject a combination of Depo Medrol and Lidocaine directly into the localized area of pain. I was all for this treatment plan, of course; at the very least, after countless failures, we would be attempting something *different*!

Let's face it: I'm not exactly regarded as the most patient individual on our crowded planet! As a matter of fact, my poor mother was forever complaining, as I raced about the house nonstop: "Kenny, your problem is that you have no patience." And my reply was always the same: "Ma, patience is *not* a virtue!" (We never came to an agreement on that particular dispute, however.)

Anyway, the sad fact is that the injection didn't do the trick, either. After another three weeks had passed and the Lidocaine and Depo Medrol (whatever that is) had done their thing – with no visible signs of improvement – I felt strongly that it was time to head in a different direction and seek help elsewhere.

I was referred next to a Dr. Mark Mizel of the Boston Foot and Ankle Center at the New England Baptist Hospital, and I had high hopes that he would provide the "magic bullet" of a complete cure . . . since many of Boston's top professional athletes relied on him to treat their foot injuries. Dr. Mizel's diagnosis was as follows:

"This fifty-five-year-old white male comes in with pain in his right heel region. The patient is an avid marathon runner, having run marathons on six continents, and he was practicing jogging on a boat while preparing for a marathon in Egypt, and he noted a great deal of pain in his right heel region. The patient cut down his running to approximately four to six miles per day.

"The patient has been treated by Dr. Needleman, including a cortisone injection in the medial heel region which helped him for several days. The patient notes the pain is worse over the course of the day with standing and walking, as well as throbbing when his foot hangs down. Nothing makes it better. The patient denies any history of significant trauma to the right foot or ankle or previous problems with it. The patient denies diabetes mellitus, rheumatoid arthritis, gout or pseudogout."

Dr. Mizel then went on to note that "X-rays of the right foot including axial views show no acute fractures leading to possible stress fracture of the right foot or a right heel inflammatory process. The patient will be placed in a removable cast to be worn twenty-three and a half hours a day. We will obtain a bone scan of the patient's right foot and ankle and probably a CT scan. The patient will be seen and re-evaluated in approximately six weeks time."

The bone scan and CT scans were done immediately following my initial visit with Dr. Mizel, and they indicated no evidence of a stress fracture – although a small bone spur was discovered near my Achilles' heel. Once it was clear that I hadn't sustained any fractures, I was immediately ushered to the cast room, where I was fitted for what is known as a "Bledsoe Boot." This is a black boot that extends from the foot to just below the knee. The device is secured by three Velcro straps and includes a rocker extension in the middle of the sole which relieves all pressure on the heel.

Thanks to the clever design of this very helpful therapeutic tool, my right foot would land on the rocker with every step – in a sequence that prevented my heel from ever making contact with the ground. But the Bledsoe Boot did have one major drawback: It required a great deal of adjustment on the part of the patient. For me, that radical adjustment began immediately after I left the hospital and climbed behind the wheel of my car. Within a few seconds, it was clear that with my right foot totally immobilized inside the boot, I'd have to drive with my left foot.

Suddenly, I was struggling to manipulate both the accelerator and the brake pedal with the "wrong" foot! In a flash I saw that the learning curve was going to be steep . . . and that I would have to master it quickly, since I was 100 miles from Portland and my car was my only means of getting home. (It's amazing how quickly you can adjust to adversity when you have to: Within a few miles, I was very comfortable using my left foot to get down the expressway!)

Dr. Mizel was very explicit in his instructions to me, and the third from the last sentence in his prescription turned out to be the most challenging part of the therapy: "The patient will be placed in a removable cast to be worn twenty-three and a half hours a day." Why twenty-three and a half hours? Simple: This thoughtful medico in his great wisdom had allowed me 30 minutes in which to shower each day. Otherwise: *Wear the Bledsoe Boot, Mr. Volk!*

He meant it, too. Amazed, I now understood that I was not only being told to *sleep* with the damn thing on . . . but even to make *love* with it on. You can imagine how nervously Diane and I approached each other during our romantic interludes and how much I feared causing her serious injury in my wildly rocking boot.

And yet this deep anxiety did not dissuade me from pursuing my amorous intentions, and to this day I celebrate the depth and richness of a relationship that could survive such stress. It's true that Diane protested once or twice, as she fearfully eyed the boot (while even crying out, on at least one occasion, "It's all about *you,* isn't it?") . . . but I managed to overlook that moment of understandable human weakness for the sake of the greater good that was our blissful marriage!)

Learning to live in a Bledsoe Boot was a major physical challenge, for sure, and it required the talents of a Houdini-like escape artist. Example: When taking a shower, I soon developed a routine of standing on one foot, washing, and then upon exiting the tub, hopping furiously across the room in order to flop down on the toilet and dry off. And the first step in that process was to dry the incarcerated foot and leg, and then immediately replace the boot.

As always, I was a stickler for following the rules. In the entire six weeks prior to my follow-up visit with Dr. Mizel, I never (not even once) deterred from this remarkable regimen. My attitude was that I wanted to get *better,* period. And I also understood a key fact about my situation . . . which was that if I didn't follow my instructions to the letter and then the Bledsoe Boot didn't work, I'd never know if the failure had occurred because the therapy was no good, or because I hadn't really given it a *chance* to be good.

I would like to say that the six weeks "passed like a flash" before my eyes, but that would be an outright lie. Actually, that month and a half of "wearing the boot" seemed like an eternity. I was, however, feeling a little better each day – and I was also becoming more accustomed to conducting my daily activities. From time to time, hoping to measure my progress, I would gingerly place my troubled foot on the tiles in the shower and exert slight pressure. Sometimes there was no pain, and sometimes there was only a little. Either way, it now seemed clear that progress was being made. Buoyed by my growing optimism, I returned to Dr. Mizel in the first week of May

– and I returned full of hope that I'd soon be able to resume the full range of my activities. To be honest, in fact, I was expecting to be able to leave Dr. Mizel's office, return home, and then immediately resume my regular running and training regimen.

Our consultation went something like this, and I can almost quote it verbatim.

> Dr. Mizel: "How are you feeling?"
>
> Ken: "Pretty good."
>
> Dr. Mizel: "Pretty good? Does it hurt?"
>
> Ken: "Just a little when I put my heel down. But not always."
>
> Dr. Mizel: "Come back in six weeks. Keep wearing the boot."
>
> Ken: "Are you kidding me?"
>
> Dr. Mizel: "Do you want to get rid of this thing?"
>
> End of discussion. End of consult.
>
> Back to Maine in the boot.

I wanted to cry – but I knew in my heart that I wasn't 100 percent cured, so I immediately returned to the "23 and a half hours *on*, 30 minutes *off*" routine. But then I made an alarming discovery: When I dropped by the orthopedic clinic's scheduling office to set up my next six-week physical exam, I realized that in six weeks Diane and I were scheduled to take off on a trip to Prague, Vienna, Budapest and Paris. The trip had been planned for some time, and we would be accompanied by four of our dear friends from the SPOOC trade group: Lois and Steve Eisen from Winnetka, Illinois and Lois and Don Mayol from Modesto, California.

With a sinking feeling of disgust, I realized that I was going to have to wear the boot while touring the four cities on our itinerary.

I didn't like that fact, but there it was. And since I was determined to follow my doctor's instructions to the letter, I understood that I had no choice.

Off we went. All six of us met in Prague, and we were delighted to be soaking up the ambience of the immortal Franz Kafka's native city. But then, somewhere in the middle of our very first night in town, I awoke with what I can only describe as a "banging and throbbing" in my left arm. I looked at the elbow in the mirror and saw that it was considerably swollen. But of course, I figured the problem would be "gone by morning." No such luck. Now, I don't have a regular physician on call in many of the Eastern European countries . . . so I wasn't sure what step to take next. But then I remembered the great help I'd gotten from the American embassy during my Brazil marathon (thanks to a kind word from Maine Senator George Mitchell), and a light bulb went on in my head.

Instead of joining our friends for the morning tour of beautiful downtown Prague, I jumped on the phone and called the American Embassy . . . where a helpful staffer quickly referred me to a hospital across town that often treated Embassy employees.

Diane and I hopped into a taxi and drove across Prague to a sprawling, bleakly gray series of buildings which reportedly housed the most prestigious hospital in all of Czechoslovakia. After I explained our predicament as concisely and clearly as possible to the attendant (while also displaying the swollen elbow), we were escorted to the Dermatology Department. To my dismay, however, the on-duty dermatologist took a single look at the swollen joint and then exclaimed in broken English: "My, this is not for my department. You need to see a surgeon."

She personally conducted us to the Surgery Department, where I was seen almost immediately. One look from the surgeon told me that I was in trouble – and I wasn't at all pleased to see him removing surgical instruments from paper wrapping.

More than a little alarmed, I turned to Diane: "They're not

going to do any surgery on me in this place!" But before all of the words were out of my mouth, the doctor had lanced the infection and it was draining down my arm. After cleaning up the mess he'd triggered, the clinician swabbed the area with a thick, black solution and bandaged the entire arm from my elbow to my wrist. He then informed me that he was going to put me in a permanent cast so that the arm would remain elevated.

Wait a minute! A plaster cast was the *last* thing I wanted, so I begged for a sling . . . while promising him fervently that I would be a good boy and not take my arm out of it. He wasn't easy to convince, however. And his concern was entirely understandable – once he explained that I had a serious staph infection. In the end he agreed to the sling, provided that I make sure my arm didn't move about inside it.

I agreed, and he began to write out a prescription for an antibiotic. But when Diane mentioned that we had some erythromycin with us, the surgeon was impressed. After pointing out that "we don't have that medicine here in Prague," he recommended it enthusiastically. Soon we were back at the hotel, and I was my shaking my head in wonder at my continuing bad luck. There I was, a man wearing both a sling and a boot – and a man who was about to begin taking the first of the antibiotics he'd be gulping down for the next ten days! (And not only that: I'd also been stung for a cab ride across the city which ended up costing more than the hospital visit!)

Annoyed almost to the point of no return, I did my best to hang on to my rapidly dwindling equanimity. But what could I do? Once again, I followed my instructions as best I could . . . and by the time we reached Vienna, I was feeling confident that I'd at least rid myself of the infection. Just to be certain, however (since I knew our next stop would be in another Third World Country – aka "Hungary" –) we again availed ourselves of the American Embassy. This time, a helpful staffer at Uncle Sam's foreign mission in Vienna referred us to a nearby clinic for a consultation.

Fortunately, this facility was within walking distance of our hotel, so we meandered slowly on over to our appointment. And on every step I felt more confident that the doctor would tell me to "throw away the sling and have a nice trip."

Wrong again, Mr. V! Instead, he ordered me to keep the arm in its sling and to go ahead and take the second ten-day dosage of erythromycin that we'd brought along, just to be on the safe side. He also explained that the black antibiotic solution I'd been wearing – thick goo that smelled like pungently smoked meat, I might add – was totally useless. (His grandmother had used it on him, years before, and it hadn't worked then, either.) You can imagine how I felt, when I realized that for days I'd been giving off the gamey, unsettling aroma of a sausage-maker on holiday from his kielbasa factory . . . without gaining the slightest medical benefit in return!

Half crazed with frustration by now, I decided to try and calm my nerves by treating myself to a manicure. Relaxing in the chair, I took a deep breath and settled back. But then the manicurist – a sweet little Viennese girl – suddenly asked me if I'd "been in a car accident."

All at once, the reality of my situation came crashing in on me. I was a guy in a foot-boot and an arm-sling, and I smelled like week-old *braunschweiger*! And to add insult to injury, Diane seemed to be rather *amused* by the entire scenario. Instead of cradling my poor head in her arms and soothing me with gentle caresses, she had taken to telling everyone we met that there was "never a dull moment, when you're traveling with Ken Volk!"

Upon our return to Portland, I immediately scheduled an appointment with my family doctor, Peter Gordon, with whom we'd been in touch by telephone while we were away and undergoing treatment. After assuring me that the infection had disappeared, he asked me in an offhand manner: "By the way, while you were on the erythromycin, I assume you *stopped* taking your Seldane [my allergy medicine]. Am I correct?"

I stared at him for a moment. Then I told him that I'd continued taking the Seldane along with the antibiotic.

He blanched. Watching him, *I* blanched. It seems that erythromycin and Seldane, when taken in concert, had caused sudden death in some individuals. (Seldane would soon be removed from the market by the FDA, for just this reason.)

Fortunately, I felt fairly certain that I wasn't dead at that moment. The doctor agreed . . . and then assured me that I was no longer in any danger. Apparently, I'd just dodged a whistling bullet. Maybe my luck wasn't so bad after all!

Now that we were back home in Portland, it was time for my next consult with Dr. Mizel. I had been a very good boy, I was feeling absolutely no pain, and it had been seven weeks since I'd last seen Dr. Mizel . . . so I was eagerly looking forward to the visit. This consultation took about the same amount of time as the last:

> Dr. Mizel: "How are you feeling?"
>
> Ken: "Fine. I have no pain even when I put pressure on the heel while out of the boot in the shower."
>
> Dr. Mizel's written follow-up report read as follows: "The patient comes in doing well regarding his foot. He has no pain and no tenderness. He is happy with his result. He will slowly increase his activities and be seen in the future on an as needed basis."

Free at last! Thank God I'm free at last! Dr. Martin Luther King said this before me, but it describes my emotions perfectly. Cost of the plantar fasciitis:

Dr. Brown:	$ 475.00
Dr. Needleman:	$ 350.00
Saco Bay P.T.	$ 1241.00
Dr. Mizel:	$ 3915.00
TOTAL:	$ 5981.00

And I didn't even get to enjoy it! *And who ever said that running doesn't cost anything?*

During this period my son Derek joined my brother Douglas and me at Volk Packaging Corporation, and we became a third-generation company. It gives me great pride to know that my son and my brother now own and manage the company founded by my dad and me in 1967. Today I'm fully retired and enjoying every minute of my retirement – while basking in the knowledge that something I helped start 43 years ago is still operating and becoming a better company with each passing day.

I might also add that my former partner Douglas was of immeasurable support in my quest, never begrudging me the time I took off to run and travel (not to mention the time I spent in the office not doing "Volk business" but soliciting money for MCCP). Douglas had run the Casco Bay Marathon with me and had even completed another marathon in Kennebunk, Maine, so he was well aware of the trials one faces during the training period.

We were also blessed with the first two of what would ultimately be ten grandchildren. Being a grandparent is an entirely different experience from being a parent – and as I watched these two new additions to our family and made my trips to the MCCP offices, I felt so blessed to be able to give something back.

My foot miseries and elbow miseries were over, at least for now, and life seemed warm and promising again. But all too soon, it was time to restart my training and prepare for the ultimate adventure: running a 26-mile marathon on the frozen tundra and the wind-blasted glaciers of vast Antarctica.

"The Last Marathon"

ANTARCTICA - FEBRUARY 5, 1995

Men wanted for hazardous journey. Small wages, extreme danger, months of darkness. Chances of safe return doubtful; fame and recognition if successful.

– Sir Ernest Shackleton, 1913

Having recovered fully from my debilitating plantar fasciitis – the cause of the foot misery I'd endured in Egypt – I now turned my attention to my next challenge: running on the frozen tundra of the Antarctic Continent. Managing the logistics for this event would be a formidable task, and I felt very fortunate that I'd been able to connect with Thom Gilligan and his company, Marathon Tours. Thom's was the official travel agency for marathons all over the world and his outfit had a great deal of experience in leading marathoners to exotic locations. With his skilled hand on the tiller, I felt confident that the final piece of my marathon puzzle would fall into its place without complication.

I must admit that after having successfully completed six marathons, I was feeling a bit cocky about my ability to finish my worldwide quest. In an effort to avoid injury during the run-up to Antarctica, I hired a local trainer, Steve Fleuret, who devised a personal conditioning regimen for me. Included in each day's run was speed work. And it didn't take me long to come to the conclusion that the words "speed" and "Ken Volk" don't mix very well. My idea of "speed" is a "continuous lope," and I was deathly afraid of pulling a muscle or tearing something that might prevent me from running.

Fearful as I was, I soon decided that the first item to be eliminated on the training agenda was in fact anything connected with "speed." The second item for the discard pile would be my perpetual compulsion to adhere to a five-day-a-week schedule, along with my fanatical insistence that I never miss a training run. The third discard item would be my highly restrictive diet, and the fourth would be my chronic refusal to engage in pre-run stretching.

My dislike for limbering up before a long-distance workout was totally irrational, of course. As much as I know that proper stretching is a basic "must" for runners and athletes alike, I've never been a big fan of this tedious activity. And that's pretty sad – when you realize that many of my injuries could have been avoided, had I only been able to commit to a proper stretching program. Unfortunately, however, my Type A personality wouldn't permit me to take a few minutes for "preliminary" activity.

For me, it was always the same drill. Upon arriving at the gym, I would be desperate to hit the road immediately. And no matter how often my mind told me to "stretch, stretch!" my heart just wouldn't listen. Shame on me! How could I have ignored such vitally important pre-training steps as eating a healthily balanced diet or stretching before setting out on a long run? Such short-sightedness was a recipe for disaster . . . but I continued to kid myself, while insisting that I'd be able to finish the 26.2 miles, one way or another, which was all I really cared about. I knew I didn't want to make a second trip to the Antarctic, and so my goal quickly became limited to simply finishing the race – so that I could head off into the sunset with my Seven Continents out of the way and my fund-raising for

MCCP successfully accomplished.

The training regimen was similar to the one I'd used in my previous six races. Why change something if it ain't broke? Per usual, I gradually increased my weekly long run by 10 minutes per week . . . and the training was mostly uneventful, with the exception of one poor run I experienced in Florida. It happened about two weeks before our departure date, after I'd scheduled a 20-mile run along Route A1A, from Boynton Beach to my previously parked automobile. This is my favorite Florida run, since it flanks a series of beautiful homes and offers a nearly uninterrupted view of the ocean.

But let me back up for a second and explain how the snafu developed. On the night before any run longer than ten miles, my practice has always been to drive the route and stash water at various stops along the way. And that's exactly what I did in Florida. Still, a highly threatening problem nonetheless emerged: Even though I drank my water every five miles or so, I became seriously dehydrated by the 15-mile mark. My condition was so bad, in fact, that I had difficulty even walking. Suddenly I was in trouble, and I knew it.

Since discretion is the better part of valor, I quickly made an executive decision. Just as I was passing the Ocean Ridge Police Department headquarters, I concluded that this wasn't my day, and that I'd had more than enough, thank you. Luckily, a squad car was pulling out of the parking lot – and I quickly flagged it down and explained my predicament. The officer behind the wheel listened, then explained that the police are not a "taxi service." At first he simply refused my request for a ride. But after I pleaded my case and explained my urgent problem, he relented and put me into the rear of the squad car . . . right behind the bullet-proof shield and between the doors with no handles.

It's a very odd experience – simulating the ride that the criminals of this world must take when being transported to the lockup – and I was grateful when he dropped me off at my car and pulled away to resume his official duties. As I reached for the door, I was already dreaming of standing beneath a hot shower in my own little bathroom.

There was one problem, however: The little packet that I always attach to one of my running shoes (it holds my car key, I.D. and a few dollars) had somehow broken free and fallen off. Suddenly, I had no means of getting home except by taxi. Diane was on the golf course, so I limped down to a nearby convenience store and phoned my mother (she lived in the same development) and asked her to go to our condo and bring me my extra set of keys. She did so, and I still thank her for it! Saved by Ever-Faithful Mom, I hurried home, took a steamy shower – and then slept for an entire day. After awakening, I sent a letter of thanks (and a nice donation) to the Ocean Ridge Police Department.

Since this was to be my final solicitation on behalf of MCCP, I put a "full-court press" on my fundraising. By now I had no compunctions whatsoever about asking for money, and so I explained to each of my potential donors that this was "it" – and that they wouldn't be hearing from me again, except for a thank-you note. I was nearing the magic $50,000 mark by now, and I didn't want to fall short. And it was also true that MCCP had outgrown its current facility in Portland. They'd moved to larger quarters, and as you might imagine, the move was costly. To cover their expenses, they'd embarked on a major fund drive. And one of their fund-raising strategies had been especially effective; it consisted of offering to "name" the various rooms in their new facility in honor of supporters who donated $25,000 or more.

When they told me that L.L. Bean had already contributed $12,500, I suddenly had a bright idea. Within a few days, I approached my two business partners – my brother Douglas and my son Derek (he was by now a manager and a stockholder) – and suggested to them that Volk Packaging could partner with Bean, and the two firms could *together* provide the $25,000 for the "honorary room." I wasn't surprised to find that they were very enthusiastic about my proposal – and we sent the check in immediately.

Thanks to their kindness and generous support, my fundraising total was now just shy of $60,000! And since I'd claimed no expenses at all for my fundraising, every dime went directly to MCCP. As you might expect, I'm still immensely grateful for the opportunity to have helped the kids, and I regard my efforts as one of the highlights of my life.

Soon it was time to embark on the first leg of our journey: Miami, Florida to Buenos Aires, Argentina. I was fired up and ready to rock . . . even though I knew I'd be carrying a few extra pounds on my person. At 205 pounds – some of it outright blubber – I certainly qualified for the "Clydesdale Division!"

The flight to Argentina was included in our tour package, but Diane and I had opted to upgrade to Business Class on Argentine Airlines for an additional $1,700. This was the first of our marathon trips in which the airfare wouldn't be paid for with Frequent Flyer Miles. But we rationalized that when amortized, all five of our previous overseas marathons had cost us less than $300 each for the airfare. Having saved a small fortune by then, we felt we were entitled to splurge on a bit of comfort!

All those on the tour were staying at the same hotel, The Inter-Continental, in Buenos Aires . . . and a training run was quickly arranged so that we could loosen everyone up after our long flight. As we milled around shaking our legs and stretching, I noticed a fellow runner standing nearby who wore the same brand of running shoes as I did. My jogging shoes had been hand-made by Bart Hersey of Wilton, Maine, and they fit my feet perfectly – with room for orthotics and rubber heel cups.

Bart had left New Balance Shoes to start his own company, and I'd been wearing his running shoes during my past three marathons. For this race, he'd removed the existing soles and had glued on new ones containing large rubber cleats that would provide traction in the snow. I'd had two pairs altered but hadn't used them for fear of wearing down the treads unnecessarily . . . but when it came time in this first warm-up run to put them on, I realized that I'd made a huge mistake. They were so heavy due to the excess rubber that my legs felt as if they were dragging lead weights through every step. Too late! The idea had been a good one; the only hitch was the final result. And now I was stuck with the weighted shoes.

Anyway, my fellow runner with the Hersey shoes was from Mississippi, and in the course of our discussion about my heavyweight shoes, he informed me that he was the subject of a study by Dr. Kenneth Cooper of Dallas, Texas, the renowned expert on cardiovascular conditioning. Interestingly enough, Dr. Cooper was trying to determine if inveterate runners suffered from carbon monoxide poisoning, due to breathing in excessive amounts of the noxious gas from automobile emissions. My new friend was traveling with his family and had run all over the world. When he explained that he "worked in a bank," I quickly came to the conclusion that "his daddy must *be* the bank!" And I later discovered that I'd been correct in my assumption; his bank in Jackson, Mississippi was the leading bank in the state, and he was its President.

I mention this fact simply in order to emphasize that all of my fellow runners on this trip seemed to have something special lurking in their resumes. It was to be an interesting and diverse group with whom Diane and I would spend our next two weeks. Many of the runners had been in the Armed Forces and had run marathons all over the world in the course of their deployments. One especially accomplished strider, Wally Herman from Canada, had run more than 400 marathons already. He worked for the Canadian Postal Service, and whenever he had time off, he would book an unlimited ticket on Greyhound and travel to marathons wherever they were held. He'd run two of the long-distance events on a weekend, and he didn't require the usual training period . . . since his runs consisted almost entirely of 26.2 mile jaunts. Wally was in his sixties and carried a cane, but I had the distinct feeling that the cane was actually a prop, as well as an attention grabber. (Once again, as with my banker friend, I was correct in my assumption.)

The training run over, we all returned to the hotel, showered, and met for a group dinner that included instructions from Thom and gave all of us an opportunity to mingle. The next day we departed early for our flight to Ushuaia, Argentina – the southernmost city in the world. Here we would hunker down for one night, before finally heading out to sea.

The following morning, as the group boarded the buses for our ship, the tension was palpable. Although we'd been a boisterous bunch up until then, we were now remarkably quiet. Nor was there any of the usual bravado emanating from the runners. Indeed, all of us now seemed thoroughly preoccupied with what lay ahead. Feeling uneasy and uncertain, we arrived at our ship, the *Vavilov,* with a double sense of trepidation. Understandably enough, we were wondering if we'd able to complete a 26-mile marathon on the driest, coldest place on Earth – the "White Continent." But we were also asking ourselves: Could we survive the notorious Drake Passage, which contains some of the world's most treacherous waters?

Thom Gilligan, the owner of Marathon Tours, had conceived the idea of conducting a marathon in the Antarctic entirely by chance. In 1993 his company had been featured in a national travel magazine, and Thom had casually mentioned that he'd led tours all over the world, with the exception of Antarctica. Soon after the article ran, he received a call from an executive at Marine Expeditions of Toronto, Canada asking if he'd be interested in leasing a ship for a marathon tour to the Antarctic.

Would he ever! The seed had been planted, and after he described the upcoming adventure in his company newsletter, 159 applicants had signed up in just six weeks. Amazingly, the roster was now large enough to fill not one but *two* ships. It was an eclectic group consisting of lawyers, doctors, government workers, ex-servicemen, etc. – all of whom possessed Type A compulsive personalities. One gentleman, a professor at George Washington University Medical School, was quoted as saying, "We're all three standard deviations off some norm and probably representative of some obsessive group." (Sounds pretty impressive, right – even if, like me, you have no idea what it means!)

Understandably enough, Marine Expeditions owned leases on two Russian "ice breakers" which made regular visits to the Antarctic. I placed quotation marks around "ice breaker" – because although they may have been ice breakers in a technical sense, their original and primary purpose had been as Russian spy ships . . . or as the Russkies like to call them, "listening ships" whose primary targets were U.S. submarines. Ice breaking ability was still required, however, since sailing in and around the Antarctic Sea was treacherous and the sailors never knew what lay ahead.

About one-third the size of a typical ocean liner (or 375 feet long by 60 feet wide), these sturdy vessels were also nimble enough to handle the unsteady waters of the Drake Passage. Many of the rooms were locked and inaccessible, however, and we soon discovered that the ship was manned entirely by Russian sailors. Since the end of the Cold War, the Soviet Union's hunger for hard currency had intensified dramatically, and rather than mothball their ships, the Russians were now leasing them out to companies such as Marine Expeditions.

During the ship's earlier incarnation as a spy vessel, the sailors who manned her had obviously lived a Spartan life. In other words: Any resemblances between a luxury liner and the Vavilov were purely coincidental! Diane and I had booked the second-best suite, the "Drake Suite" (we'd missed the premium "Captain's Suite" by one day and there were no others) . . . and soon after boarding our new quarters, we were treated to a rude awakening.

The entry to our suite led to a bedroom about 8 feet wide and 20 feet long. Immediately to the right of the door was a single cot located directly under a permanent and immovable shelf about four feet over the bed. This stark resting place was to be my sleeping pod throughout the trip, and it presented a significant hazard – because any quick "sit-up" in the middle of the night (for a bathroom run, let's say) would undoubtedly result in a major concussion. Just to the left of this area, a second door led to what was to be Diane's "bedroom," which was merely another single bed.

So much for a sexy crossing to the tundra of the Antarctic! The door to Diane's quarters opened directly into her room, while the door to the bathroom (just off her chamber) opened outward – and directly into the entry door. The bottom line was that every time I needed to use the bathroom, I would end up banging the two doors together as I maneuvered my way into the single-occupant stall. This meant, of course, that I would inevitably awaken Diane, since the clanging of the doors was unavoidable.

What to do? After wracking my brain for a while, I came up with a tactic that the military would describe as "field expediency." The solution, in a few words: I simply used our emptied water bottles as a urinal – and then emptied them out in the morning through our porthole, directly into the sea. Or at least I *thought* it was into the sea. But since we never bothered to extend our heads beyond that porthole window, we didn't realize that there was actually a walkway directly below our window.

I'm sure I came very close at times to pouring the contents directly on a crewman or passenger. That was a scary thought . . . but at least I never woke Diane.

The Antarctic is populated by research bases from seven different countries, and all of them claim to own territorial areas in their zones of influence. In addition, forty additional countries have recorded "claims" in the past, but these nations no longer maintain these kinds of research bases. Each of these seven major countries is still hanging onto its base, however, and they're all very careful to maintain a physical presence on the continent. Of course their attitude makes very good sense: They want to be ready to occupy their territories fully, in the event that widespread development ever begins to occur.

Their attitude about development was easy to understand, since the region contains large deposits of gold, copper and oil. Knowing that fact, no country wants to be left out in the event that the riches are ever exploited. But the activity of the participants is regulated by protocols, and the bases must be used solely for peaceful research purposes. At the same time, any prospecting for minerals or development is strictly prohibited. Governed by the Antarctic Treaty and signed by 46 nations, the ruling treaty sets aside Antarctica as a "scientific preserve." It also establishes freedom of scientific investigation and bans military activity on the continent. And indeed, it was these key countries – the ones who control the continent at present – from which Thom had been required to secure permission for the marathon tour.

The largest of the bases, the United States base at McMurdo Bay on the southern tip of Ross Island, had shown little enthusiasm for hosting Thom's marathon tour. Apparently, the powers representing the United States' interests weren't interested in encouraging tourism. His next option, he figured, was the Argentine Station at Esperanza on Hope Bay. But when the Argentines also denied permission, he was forced to resort to "Plan C." After much haggling and negotiation, the doggedly determined Thom was able to secure permission from Uruguay, China, Russia and Chile for the use of their territories on King George Island, the largest of the South Shetland Islands, which extend just off the peninsula.

Their only stipulation was that we pass directly by each base on our route. Interestingly enough, there's a rule on the Continent that there can be no more than 100 people congregating in any one place at any one time – but somehow Thom was able to circumvent it.

Did you know that the Antarctic is the coldest place on earth, and that it was the site of the coldest temperature ever recorded (-128.6 F)? And did you *also* know that this vast and windswept realm is technically a desert? It's true. The average precipitation is only 6.5 inches a year – but the snow on the surface never melts and it's eventually compressed into an enormous glacial ice sheet.

Originally, and until about 200 million years ago, Antarctica was connected to Africa, South America, India, Australia and New Zealand and was part of a huge continent known as "Gondwana." According to what geologists refer to as the "plate tectonics theory," the Antarctic eventually split off and gradually floated to its present location. If its ice sheets ever melted, the world's oceans would rise over 200 feet. Another interesting fact: The climate of Antarctica is so dry – and its Dry Valleys are so similar to those of the planet Mars – that NASA conducted numerous tests and experiments there in order to prepare for its Viking Mission to the Red Planet.

Talk about a longstanding drought: These dry valleys haven't seen rain in at least two million years! Nor have they seen many visitors; in 1995 it was estimated that fewer than 70,000 people had ever set foot on the Antarctic.

About 30 million years ago, the Drake Passage was opened and that was precisely where we were headed on our 44-hour voyage. "The Drake," as it's affectionately known, is the roughest water in the world – a 300-mile stretch of turbulent, swirling foam that surges relentlessly between Tierra del Fuego and the Antarctic. In this roaring maelstrom, three major bodies of water converge: the Atlantic, the Pacific and the Drake Passage. Thom, in one of his informational letters to us, happily noted: "Just plan for the wildest trip of your life. Everyone should be prepared to prevent sea sickness. I never heard of anyone who liked the Drake Passage. You can't run a marathon after being dark green for 48 hours. Bring patches, bracelets, pills or a teddy bear if you know it works. And keep your stomach full, even if you are not hungry. The Captain of the ship recommended brandy. It worked for me."

Diane and I took his advice to heart, of course, and purchased seasick patches for behind our ears. We also took the additional step of obtaining pressure bracelets, which we wore on our wrists. Each bracelet contained a little "ball" that was placed carefully between the veins leading from the wrist to the hand. Unfortunately for Diane, the device cut off the circulation to her hands . . . which quickly turned blue and then went numb. Too bad for her; in the end she was forced to rely entirely on the patch.

After settling into our fancy accommodations, we bade goodbye to the South American continent, and soon the ship was meandering down the Strait of Magellan. Off to our right, and not far away on the starboard side, we could see Chile. To our left (or port) side, we could observe Argentina. These two countries aren't terribly fond of each other, but we were soon out of their neighborhood and headed toward the open seas. We were about to pass Cape Horn and then enter the dreaded Drake Passage during the evening hours.

To ease the tension, we did our best to enjoy our "happy hour" at 4 p.m. This agreeable ritual was immediately followed by a "carbo-loaded" pasta dinner, after which all of us looked forward to an early-to-bed night. Around 1 a.m., however, I was awakened by what I can only describe as a loud banging and cracking noise. What was going on? Had a violent storm come up, or what?

No . . . the boat was actually pitching and yawing on the high seas of The Drake. Every time it climbed a wave and headed down again, the next oncoming swell would smash the hull of the ship with a resounding explosion that echoed throughout the ship. We were in 28- to 30-foot seas with a 45-mph wind. Later, these stormy conditions were estimated at "8" on a scale of 10 by the crew! Well, I just had to see what was happening . . . so I climbed the stairs to the sixth deck, where the bridge of the ship was located.

I'm not exaggerating when I tell you that getting up those stairs was a major challenge. As I staggered along, I didn't know if I was headed up or down – or if I would be flung against the sidewalls of the stairwell like a helpless rag doll. I was hanging onto the railing for dear life! Finally I reached the bridge, where one small night light illuminated the entire room. Facing me was the great wheel used for steering, but there was no one manning it! Twenty-eight to thirty-foot seas! Forty-five mile-an-hour wind! And no one at the helm! Was I still asleep and in the middle of a "lost at sea" nightmare? I looked wildly around the bridge . . . but the only two people up there were two Russian sailors in a corner, and they must have been telling each other a series of jokes – because they were both laughing their heads off.

To say that I felt some alarm would be putting it too mildly. Who the hell was in *charge* here? It was extremely dark, since there was no moon, but I could see waves barreling over our heads as we rode each one down into the trough, even though we were six stories high. To have placed a ship on automatic steering in this type of sea without fear of broaching was beyond my comprehension – was the captain out of his mind, or merely loaded on powerful Russian vodka?

After worrying my head off about the situation for half an hour, I finally realized that there was nothing I could do. The whole thing was out of my hands. Realizing that my fate belonged to the gods (but not the God of Vodka, I hoped!), I did what any normal human being would do: I hurried back to my room and went straight back to sleep.

The following morning at breakfast we noticed that attendance was sparse and that there appeared to be lots of greenish-looking people wandering about like lost souls. Many had spent the previous evening "carbo un-loading," as the brutal forces of seasickness claimed one victim after the next. Fortunately for Diane and me, we were unaffected, probably due to the precautions we'd taken. Those who had been sick were very nervous, however; they feared that the ailment's accompanying dehydration would rob them of the strength and vitality needed for our upcoming endurance run. But their fears proved groundless; thanks to some very good luck, the seas calmed after we had crossed The Drake. In the end, everyone recovered nicely – and all of us were then able to take part in and enjoy the daily program of lectures on the history, wildlife and geology of the areas where we'd soon be making landfall.

Time passed quickly and soon we were summoned to the deck for our first view of the Antarctic. Suddenly, the entire enterprise had become very real – and all of us were feeling more than a little squeamish. And why not? As we divided ourselves into groups of eight and the groups then stood by to board the Zodiac rubber rafts that would ferry us ashore, we knew that the "moment of truth" was fast approaching.

Feeling a bit like doomed sailors en route to Davy Jones' locker, we climbed down a gangplank and jumped aboard our rafts for the brief ride to shore. There we would enjoy a guided tour of the native wildlife – starting with such impressive creatures as the leopard seal (aka the "shark of the Antarctic"). Our pre-race sightseeing itinerary also included elephant seals, Weddell seals and Adelie penguins (along with their cousins, the Chinstrap and Gentoo penguins). And of course, we mustn't forget the dive-bombing skuas – ugly, kamikaze-like gulls famous for their territorial aggressiveness. They prey on baby and injured penguins, and they've also been known to attack humans who are unfortunate enough to impinge on their space. Trust me: You don't want to mess with a diving skua, or with its slashing and merciless beak.

Since the number of passengers on each of the two boats was small, and because everyone was in very good shape, we were able to make numerous landings each day on the mainland. Generally, those making the trek to the Antarctic are bird-watchers or seniors who can afford the heavy tariff imposed on them by the cruise ships. But ours was a group of high-energy individuals who wanted to do it all and not miss anything. As soon as the announcement for disembarkation was made over the public address system, everyone quickly retrieved their gear, cameras and life jackets and lined up in orderly fashion for the trip ashore. Once there, however, your return time was uncertain . . . since it depended on how much time each one of these hardy visitors wished to spend on terra firma.

What outlandish beings are these? Erect as men, but hardly as symmetrical, they stand all round the rock like sculptured caryatides, supporting the next range of eaves above. . . And truly neither fish, flesh, nor fowl is the penguin; as an edible, pertaining neither to Carnival nor Lent; without exception the most ambiguous and least lovely creature yet discovered by man. Though dabbling in all three elements, and indeed possessing some rudimental claims to all, the penguin is at home in none. On land it stumps; afloat it sculls; in the air it flops. As if ashamed of her failure, Nature keeps this ungainly child hidden away at the ends of the earth.

– Herman Melville, *The Encantadas,* 1854

One day the tour included a fascinating visit to a penguin rookery. I'd seen penguins in zoos before, of course, and I'd also watched more than a few of them do their thing on this particular trip. But never had I seen an estimated 750,000 chinstrap penguins hanging out in the same neighborhood. As we approached the rookery, we were assaulted by the nauseating odor of penguin guano, otherwise known as "poop." The smell was overwhelming, even vomit-inducing, but somehow we gradually became inured to the aroma (not to mention the continual uproar caused by almost one million penguins having a "private conversation" among themselves).

It was a remarkable scene, and the first thing we noticed was how *busy* these strange-looking birds were. While some marched in file toward the ocean, others were constantly hopping out of the water to return to the rookery. At the center of all this activity, however, there loomed a strange tableau that will live with me forever.

It was a cruel and painful-looking display in which a single bloody penguin – surrounded by a mob that included thousands of his kin – stood alone and erect. Above the obviously dying bird, the voracious skuas were circling and biding their time. They were waiting for the unfortunate penguin to keel over, after which they would dive toward and then devour the carcass.

It was a painful scenario to watch. You could tell that as long as the penguin was able to stand upright, it would be safe from the winged marauders. After that, the slaughter would surely begin. Penguins mate for life, and they're monogamous (although it's beyond me how they can tell one from another!) . . . and soon our injured friend was joined by his or her partner for the death watch.

What was happening here? When we asked our naturalist guide, we learned that it was likely the penguin had come out on the wrong end of a spat with a seal. And now the poor bird's fate was sealed. (Pun intended!) It would make for an interesting (albeit gory) story to report that we witnessed the kill – but the truth is that neither Diane nor I wanted to observe the butchery, so we got out of there as quickly as we could. Suffice it to say that the expected outcome inevitably took place – as the hungry skuas closed in for a scene that probably should have been written by Jack London, the author of *The Call of the Wild* and other novels about the savagery of life on the frozen tundra.

One other memorable excursion was to Deception Island, an atoll-like speck of land that featured smooth water in a protected bay. Those of us who felt hardy (and idiotic) enough to make the attempt were advised to wear a bathing suit under our clothing . . . since we'd be visiting the perfect spot for an Antarctic swim! How could we ever pass up a chance like this? Off came the clothing and into the 30-degree water we dove. Then we ran for the beach and the blessed warmth of our discarded clothes. Okay, I don't deny that this was less like a "swim" than a "dunk" – but hey, at least we gave it a shot!

Marathon Day. Thom had left our ship during our first pass near the Uruguayan base from which the race was to begin. Since there were no road markers and it was impossible to drive a vehicle with an odometer on this terrain, his only means of measuring the course consisted of running it each day – and then using his normal times as his sole metric for estimating distances. Thom is an excellent runner and can cover about ten miles per hour . . . so he figured that each 30 minutes of running would constitute five miles. Wrong! What he failed to take into account was the degree of difficulty involved in negotiating this incredibly harsh landscape. As a result, he probably extended the length of the course by about eight tenths of a mile, making it at least 27 miles long instead of the required 26.2.

Regardless of the actual length of the layout, however, we were going to have to run it. Fortunately for all of us, we awoke that morning to beautiful, sunny skies . . . and a temperature that was hovering at around 25 degrees. This would have been balmy weather, if we'd been running in the Maine wintertime – but of course, our endurance test was taking place in the middle of the Antarctic *summer*. I can only imagine what winter would have been like!

As the start of the race drew closer, I wasn't feeling particularly nervous . . . although I *did* make three bathroom runs the night before. (I used the community bathroom in order to let Diane sleep.) Tossing and turning, I dozed off and on . . . and then crawled out of my shelf-covered nest at 5:15 a.m. As I joined the other runners, yawning and stretching, I could see that our normally boisterous group appeared to be subdued and full of a new level of seriousness they had never displayed before.

Evidently, I wasn't the only one suffering from a bad case of nerves. After a light breakfast consisting solely of toast and tea, Thom (who'd returned to the ship after three days of shore-mapping our itinerary) delivered a rousing speech to his jittery troops. I'll quote a few passages directly, since they were an accurate harbinger of some enormously challenging moments to come.

"Ladies and gentlemen, today is very special. You will be partaking in the first sporting event ever held on the Antarctic Continent. If any of you harbored romantic thoughts about running on a glacier, forget it. This is a very tough course. You will be running two loops. The footing will be bad. When you are not running through boulder fields or climbing the glacier, you will be in mud. The going will be slow and you have the option of stopping after one loop and getting credit for having run a half-marathon, if you so choose. Watch for the little red plastic trail markers to guide you through and up and off the glacier and along the course.

"Remember that nature is your master in Antarctica and she cannot be conquered. You must engage her on her terms and be prepared for a grueling challenge. Also remember, this is not a chance to try to destroy yourself. Forget about running a sub 2:06:00 and many of you can also forget about running under five hours. Go the distance and look good in the finish-line photo! Otherwise you will be left for the skuas. I cannot believe that some of you are worried about winning your age category. Someone will poison your borscht if they discover that attitude. And don't pee on the ice; it stays yellow forever, since there are no bacteria and nothing decays. Remember, you must complete the marathon in under 6-1/2 hours as the course will be closed at that time.

"Oh, one more thing: the course is a bit longer than a standard marathon."

Immediately after Thom's reality check, we all returned to our rooms to collect our gear and board the Zodiacs for the short trip to shore. For me, this step meant an interesting twist to the adventure . . . a twist that had actually begun before we left Maine, when MCCP made a call on my behalf to our state's famed sport-clothing outfitters, L.L.Bean. MCCP was hoping that Bean might outfit me for the Antarctic run in return for some publicity – a proposal that struck me as rather comical, since Bean needed PR from Ken Volk like an Eskimo needs a truckload of fresh ice!

Quite frankly, I was a little surprised when LL. Bean actually "bit" on the proposal, at least a little, by agreeing to offer me a discount and also to provide me with a personal shopper who would guide me through the outfitting process. For just over $2000, Diane and I were able to purchase Gore-Tex outfits, leather hiking boots and green-rubber fisherman's boots (which we wore most of the time because of the great comfort they provided). The Bean-Volk Antarctica package also included gloves, hats, thermal socks, binoculars, long underwear, plastic water bottles, two backpacks, several stocking hats and some scarves – along with some nifty-looking sunglasses that were guaranteed to filter out the sun's harmful ultraviolet rays.

Looking at all of this stuff, you'd have thought we were heading off to someplace that was cold! Of course, the custom-tailored running shoes with cleats (a Bart Hersey special) would be an additional expense – as well as a huge tactical mistake. But who knew? After all, this was Antarctica . . . who *wouldn't* have assumed that this marathon would be run on packed snow? And who could have known, in advance, that the event would actually unfold on ice, snow, rocks, puddles and mud?

Like most outsiders, I'd always pictured Antarctica as an immense sheet of glittering ice, several miles deep and several thousand miles across. Wrong again, Volk!

As soon as we landed, almost everyone but yours truly made one last run for the bathrooms, and the line soon extended out of the building. At that particular moment, I felt no urgent need. But as we approached the line Thom had drawn in the dirt as his starting point, the urge to relieve myself intensified. Along with the impulse came an instant replay of Thom's warning about "not urinating while on the course." With his admonition ringing in my ears, I scurried off to the Men's Room. The line had disappeared by now, and I darted inside, eager to "take care of business" and get back to the starting line – where Diane was positioned with her camera.

You can imagine how I felt – I was in mid-stream, of course – as the sound of a gunshot suddenly cut through the air.

They were off . . . and *I* was still in the middle of answering nature's call!

Frantic to get back to the starting line, I set the Antarctic record for both dribbling *and* high-speed zipping. Then I turned and scuttled back toward the starting line, where Diane was hollering at the top of her lungs for me to "get going." Feeling thoroughly sheepish, I lurched across the line and took off. I had started last – *dead* last – among the contingent of 105 runners.

Lumbering along, head down and teeth bared, I hustled to the shoreline and began needling my way across a stretch of rugged boulders and sharply pointed stones.

At this point (with six marathons down and one to go), the last thing I needed was a sprained ankle. My sole priority on this day was to finish the race – and thus also finish my global quest. And if accomplishing that meant walking or crawling on my knees, so be it. So, like Tiny Tim tiptoeing through the tulips, I gingerly negotiated my way across the shoreline and onto the 1.5-mile-long Collins Glacier.

Thom had warned us to disabuse ourselves of any romantic notions we might have about running on a glacier – and he was right on. Up I slogged, while alternating between a surface composed of solid ice and one made of slickly melted snow. The previous winter had been one of the warmest on record, which meant that the permafrost had melted everywhere – and my shoes were now sinking deeply into the runny snow. What a disaster! I'd never imagined, of course, that I might one day *want* to run on solid ice . . . but that day was now here. Is there any doubt that solid ice would have been preferable to watching my shoes sink into mush on every step?

By the time most of the runners had reached the halfway point on the glacier, they were gratefully following Thom's advice . . . which meant that they were now alternating running with walking,

and that they'd continue to do so for the balance of the glacier trek. Do I have to point out that I fully supported their wise decision-making? Let me state for the record right now, please: I've run hills before, but running one and a half miles up a slowly melting glacier was *way* beyond my pay grade.

Somehow, I was still hanging in there, however. And by this time, I'd actually managed to catch up to a few of the tail-end marathoners. Once at the summit – *how the hell did I get here?* – I was finally able to take a breath . . . and then look back at the breathtaking expanse of ice and water below. In the near distance, I could see our ship anchored in the calm waters of Admiralty Bay and awaiting our return. That was encouraging, but my shoes and socks weren't – they were soaking wet as I made my way downhill and onto what appeared to be solid land. . . .

Another misconception! On the next stretch of terrain, which the marathon researchers had defined as "roads," it was virtually impossible to maintain your balance. That's because the surface now consisted almost entirely of slippery rocks and glistening mud. As I staggered across this landscape of treacherous Silly Putty, I kept hearing a "giant sucking sound." It was undoubtedly the same deeply unnerving sound that 1992 and 1996 presidential candidate H. Ross Perot had so famously described, in a comical effort to characterize the impact of the controversial North American Free Trade Agreement, aka "NAFTA," on the U.S. economy!

Yes, that ghastly slurping sound was emanating from my own two feet – as they scrabbled for purchase on some of the slipperiest rocks in the history of rock-dom!

The horror! My right shoe had been sucked completely off my foot by now, and it was mired forlornly in a mud puddle. Unfortunately for me, my momentum had then carried me on past the lost shoe . . . requiring me to remove my already soaked sock and then stagger back through the swamp muck in an effort to retrieve the lost footwear. Was this really happening to Kenneth Volk of the Volk Packaging Corporation? Hopping about frantically, I eventually managed to scrape the mud from my insulted foot. Then, after a pathetic attempt to dry off the offended extremity, I wobbled across the rocky terrain and stumbled into a three-mile stretch of iron-hard boulders that seemed to bruise my poor dogs on every other step.

Can you believe that this delightful game of "shoe sucking" was to be repeated four more times during the hellish hours that lay ahead? It's true. But the footwear nightmare had only begun; all too soon, the sticky mud and the sloppy-wet socks would seem like a minor irritant, as a series of much more threatening obstacles presented themselves one after the next.

Forward, march! Since my first priority was to accomplish my goal of achieving an "L.T." (or "Live Through"), I thought about nothing now except survival. Groaning with anxiety, I hopped and threaded my way from boulder to boulder. Meanwhile, my mind was racing with dreadful images of a twisted or broken ankle that would require a call to the "Meat Wagon" (in this case an all-terrain vehicle that had been requisitioned for the purpose).

Like a terrified mountain goat with a malfunctioning sense of balance, I clawed my way across the stony terrain. To make matters even worse, I soon realized that the mud between the rocks was the *same* mud that had earlier sucked the shoe right off my foot.

By taking one step at a time and placing one foot in front of the other, I finally reached the base at the nine-mile mark: the Chinese station which they call "The Great Wall." To reach this base, we had to climb the steepest hill on the route . . . and by the time I got there, I was truly ready for a nap! The Chinese were lined up outside, and they were happily offering us tea and even cigarettes. (Just what I needed – a tobacco-induced asthma attack!)

For those of us running in the marathon, the endless event had become a slow-motion crawl through an icy version of Dante's Inferno. But that wasn't the case for the scientific researchers on the four national bases we passed that day. For these hard-working scientists, the event was simply an excuse to take it easy – as if the marathon were a national holiday. We were an amusing diversion for these isolated, far-from-home workers . . . and their attitude reminded me of a hilarious episode involving my brother, Douglas, who had once been sent by his accounting firm to take inventory at Bath Iron Works, a Maine shipyard that specialized in building missile cruisers.

Each morning, the fiercely dedicated young accountant would head down to the docks, where he would count the cruisers and then proclaim: "They're all here. The count is two." In the same fashion, I could just picture these Antarctica researchers departing their "igloos" each morning, then studying the vast expanse of ice facing them and echoing Doug's cry: "The ice is still here!" Not that I blamed them, really. I mean, what the hell else is there to do when every day is the same – with no rain or snow -- and with the same predetermined amount of light or darkness each day?

As we trekked past the bases and waved to the laughing idlers, it was easy to see that many of these residents regarded us as wackos. The Chinese were particularly amused by us, and although their English vocabularies were limited, they pushed them to the max in order to describe our colorful antics: "Crazy Americans! These Americans crazy!" How right they were! And we were getting crazier by the minute, too. Example: All four of the bases had set up souvenir shops, and some of the runners actually stopped to shop for gifts! But not this guy. Already burdened with a camera, extra socks, mittens, a face mask and a headband, all I needed was a pile of useless trinkets to make my load totally unmanageable. I'm sure you'll understand when I tell you that I passed on the "gift shop opportunity."

We had been warned that the skuas were prone to attacking humans as they went about their daily search for food, and I wasn't immune. About a mile after I bypassed the Chinese Station, one of these disgusting birds began hovering over my head, and then diving past it. Nearly panicked, I waved my arms frantically in an effort to scare him off. But no luck. Why was this ugly dive-bomber picking on me? Did he think I was a penguin? Okay, I'll admit that I wasn't running much *faster* than a penguin . . . so maybe the skua could be forgiven for his nasty aggressiveness? Whatever. Thankfully, the brute soon gave up on me as a source of nourishment, and I continued on past the Russian and Chilean bases and back to the halfway point in the race – our original starting point.

In order to approach what had been our original starting line, I first had to get across a puddle that was at least 20 feet long and 20 feet wide. Then it would be up a small but steep, 100-yard hill and back down to begin the second half of the ordeal. By this point, I was beginning to feel like I'd entered a steeplechase race – but as the horse rather than the rider! Crossing the puddle, I very carefully hopped from one rock to the next . . . but about halfway across, it became apparent that I wouldn't be able to escape without either falling directly into the water or emerging with totally soaked shoes.

So I said, "To hell with it," and jumped directly into the water. I knew Diane was waiting for me with dry socks and shoes, and at this point, all I wanted to do was get up that hill. And I did, to thunderous applause. One slight problem, however: The applause wasn't for me, but for Harry Johnson, a 39-year-old insurance salesman from Anchorage, Alaska, who had just *finished* the marathon. Oh, well. The good news for me was that I now knew exactly how much time it took me to complete a *half*-marathon: 3:14:06. Harry's time, meanwhile, was almost an hour slower than his usual marathon time (due to the outrageous running conditions). Yet he had still finished 45 minutes ahead of the nearest pursuer!

As I crossed the line just behind Harry (he'd beaten me to breaking the tape), I jokingly asked one of the race directors if I'd finished second. He took me seriously and congratulated me on "a great race." But since my name wasn't Rosie Ruiz – the infamous Boston Marathon "winner" who'd ridden the subway through much of her "victorious" race (she'd even accepted the honorary laurel wreath, before her deception was brought to light) – I knew I still had 13.1 miles ahead of me.

Let's face it: I was dead last and I was going to *remain* dead last. Harry had possessed the great good sense to dress lightly for the event (tank top and shorts) . . . but if I'd been able to run that fast, I would have dressed lightly, too. Instead, I was grossly *over*-dressed and felt weighed down by the layers of clothing I carried on my back. Fearing hypothermia, I had donned a long underwear top, a Gore-Tex jacket and pants, a stocking hat and a tee shirt – along with my lead-weight sneakers and mittens. Swamped beneath this huge load of accoutrements, I was far too encumbered to run a successful marathon.

Diane met me at the hut maintained by the Uruguayans, and I quickly changed my shoes and socks in order to launch my second assault on the Collins Glacier. After a couple of goodbye kisses and Diane's heartfelt suggestion that I "be careful," off I went down the hill and across the rock-strewn beach toward the glacier. There was nobody in sight, either in front of me or behind me, as I took my first halting steps onto the ice. As I looked back over the seashore, I could make out our ship still anchored peacefully and awaiting our return. Oh, blessed vessel, I moaned inwardly, how long before I can return to you? I was exhausted, of course – but I also felt exhilarated at the thought of having only 13 miles left to run.

And then it happened.

Like the proverbial "kiss of death," a new threat arrived to plunge everything into jeopardy – and within a few seconds I was lost in an "Antarctic Whiteout." Suddenly, I couldn't even see where I was running. Hey, I couldn't even see our ship in the harbor! I couldn't even see the water! I had no idea if I was running uphill or downhill, and I quickly lost all sense of equilibrium. I told myself, "Just don't panic. This will soon blow over." But panic was very near, and it was grinning sadistically at me.

Lost in the whirling snow, I tried to stay calm. I knew that if I were to panic, I'd waste valuable energy – and that my chances of getting off this glacier alive would be greatly diminished. During a brief respite from the blinding ocean of white, I looked down the hill . . . and to my amazement, I spotted another struggling runner. Apparently, I wasn't in last place after all!

Not panicking is an easy concept to understand, but it's *not* so easy to achieve. Hoping for encouragement, I hollered to the phantom behind me (I'll simply refer to him as "Mr. X," and you'll soon see why preserving his anonymity is important here). Then I stopped running altogether and waited in place for him to catch up to me. He did so, and he was obviously as happy to see me as I was to see *him*. Actually, I think I might have been even *happier* than he was, because he was a very thin, undernourished-looking guy. Why was I so pleased? Here's my thought: Although I don't know much about biology, I *did* know enough at that point to understand that if you had to spend a night on a glacier, your fat (the fancy term is "adipose tissue") could help you survive.

Let's face it: fat is fuel, and I had plenty of fat to burn for body heat. But this skinny guy didn't. He clearly needed me (although the thought of hugging him all night in order to keep him warm didn't have a lot of appeal) . . . and that was surely why he seemed so overjoyed to be in my presence now.

Look, I know I'm digressing a bit here . . . but I want you to understand that I'm not exaggerating when I describe my "panic on the glacier." How bad was it? Okay: I'm going to tell you right up front, and without any shame, that when I first looked at the new arrival in the middle of that Antarctic Whiteout, a terrible thought crossed my mind. It was a thought that had been triggered by a best-selling book (*Alive: The Story of the Andes Survivors*, by Piers Paul Read, 1975) in which the still-living victims of a ghastly airplane crash had been reduced to eating one another in order to survive their ordeal.

Are you beginning to catch my drift? I'm not proud of this . . . but the honest fact is that when I came upon "Mr. X" on that howling, snow-blasted glacier, I told myself: *If we're stranded here, he'll die first and I'll eat him!*

How's *that* for raging, roaring, out of control panic?

You can imagine the mixed feelings I endured, as Mr. X and I battled the elements in a world where we understood that "all we had was each other."

Moving slowly forward now, side by side, we could catch an occasional glimpse of the terrain ahead. And in one of those briefly clear moments, I spotted some bamboo poles sticking up out of the ice. I'm not a botanist any more than I'm a biologist, but I felt fairly certain that bamboo isn't endemic to the South Pole – a fact that motivated me to follow the poles, since they had to be route guides. Wrong again, Volk! The poles actually led Mr. X and me higher up the glacier and to the right as we faced it. (And we later learned that the marathon route was low and to our left!) But since there were no other visible markings out there, we felt pretty confident that we were finally back on track and headed in the right direction.

On we went, with the blindly uninformed leading the blindly uninformed. Each time we located a pole, we would rush to it and then start looking for our next marker in the ice. At one point, we *also* spotted the one-mile marker, so we felt overwhelmingly confident that we were on the right track. However . . . the original markers had led us on a 1.5-mile trek across the glacier, and we were pretty sure after awhile that we'd covered a lot more than 1.5 miles. Not good!

We had no other alternative, however, so we plodded on. And on. And on. As we staggered along, we also observed what appeared to be lightning bolt-shaped holes in the surface of the glacier. Were those *crevasses*? With my panic surging again, I made sure to stay far away from them. But my meticulous caution could not prevent the inescapable.

On two separate occasions the ice gave way entirely beneath my feet and I plunged chest-deep into a "mini-crevasse." I don't remember exactly how I felt as I toppled into these mini-abysses . . . but I do recall that I didn't look down. As I was falling, my first instinct was to spread my arms and try to stop the fall. Fortunately, this did the trick – and on both occasions the farthest I interred myself in the ice was "only" to the depth of my shoulders. With help from Mr. X, I was able to extricate myself and we continued on. I was utterly terrified by now, but at least I was erect and moving.

As it turned out, I was actually quite lucky – because another runner (an ultra-marathoner from Montreal) had gone through the same experience . . . and had actually been forced to drop out of the race as a result. As a matter of fact, several of the 21 runners who failed to finish wound up being ordered by the race doctor to quit at the 13.1-mile mark. (I'm just glad she never examined me!)

Another runner dropped out voluntarily, after falling into a stream while descending the glacier on his second pass and then beginning to shiver uncontrollably. Later he told an interviewer: "When someone asked me, 'Are you okay?' I said, 'I'm not going to make it.' On contemplation, I decided it was more important to continue living than to finish this marathon. I know hypothermia when I see it."

In the end, I feel sure that I was one of the lucky ones. And I'm very grateful for that, believe me. Even at the height of the glacier whiteout, my good fortune continued. In my life and in my marathon-running, I feel that I've been blessed, and that nothing has ever happened to me that didn't eventually turn out for the best.

For me, that journey through the howling snow was a time to meditate on Diane, on our three children and on our two grandchildren. I couldn't imagine not ever seeing them again, and I couldn't bear to think of them not knowing what had happened to me, should I never be found. But I also knew for certain that I didn't want to die on this miserable "ice cube with a thyroid condition." No way! Tears clouded my eyes as I thought of how close I'd come to having completed the Seven Continent Run – and of all those kids at MCCP who were struggling daily to remain alive. *No,* I told myself as the shrieking snow whipped into my eyes and left me half-blind on that mountain of ice: *I've never quit on anything in my life, and I'm not going to quit now!*

In the interest of full disclosure, I must admit that Mr. X was exactly right in suggesting that the correct route called for traveling lower on the glacier and to the left. Ironically enough, I'd watched another runner taking that route before the whiteout . . . but I'd seen no markings to confirm the accuracy of that approach, so I'd assumed *he* was the one who was lost! In the end, "Mr. Boy Scout Dropout" had relied on bamboo, and poor Mr. X had relied on *him.* Truly, we were a case of the blind leading the blind.

Once you leave her populated bases behind, the Antarctic can be eerily silent. In our entire time on the continent, we didn't see or hear a single plane. But then we suddenly picked up the roaring sound of engine noise in the distance. It was one of Thom's race assistants speeding toward us on his All-Terrain Vehicle, or ATV. (This stalwart performer shall also remain anonymous, however, and for good reason.) What a welcome sound that roaring ATV was to the ears of the two struggling men on the snowy glacier!

Why were we so ardently welcoming this motorized visitor? It was simple: When Mr. X and I failed to show up at a scheduled water station, our absence had been noticed, and a search party had been dispatched to find us. Meanwhile, Diane was frozen with terror, and understandably so – since she had seen Mr. X and me heading up the glacier as she watched from her post at the Uruguayan Base . . . and she could tell we were following an incorrect route. At that moment, she didn't realize how serious our mistake would be – but when we didn't show up as expected at the next stop, she became concerned. And her anxiety was well placed, because soon after that, she heard several race personnel talking over their Walkie-Talkies about two runners who were missing.

She later told me that this wasn't the first time she'd gone into "panic mode" due to my not showing up at a particular spot when expected. But her fear at this moment was extreme. And that's an important point, because most people think it's easy to be a marathon spectator, and it *isn't.* Trust me: When your spouse gets into difficulty and you can't help – that's a truly terrible feeling. Actually, I'm not really sure which is worse: being the spouse or the one in trouble. But I know *Diane* is sure – and I'll bet that she would check the box marked "spouse" every time.

Thankfully for all of us, however, tragedy was averted. And when our rescuer finally reached us, our relief was immense . . . even though he proceeded to ask us the two dumbest questions that would be asked during our entire trip.

Dumb Question No. 1: "What the hell are you guys doing out here?"

Dumb Question No. 2: "Don't you know the marathon route is down *there*?"

Of course we did our best to explain to him that we'd been following the bamboo poles, since they were all we'd had to rely on. He responded by informing us of the fact that he'd removed the actual route-markers in the mistaken belief that all of the runners had passed by.

Forget about eating "Mr. X!" Now I wanted to eat *this* guy – or maybe just drop him into one of those jagged crevasses we'd seen along the way. His next question, almost as stupid as his first two, then emerged: "Do you want to hop on and I'll drive you back to the course?"

No thanks, I said. While Mr. X was quite willing to avail himself of this taxi service, I was adamant that I was going to walk and run the entire 26.2 miles . . . and that whenever I finally managed to reach the finish line, at least my time would be an *official* time. I had no interest in being disqualified. With that point clearly settled, we followed the ATV as he led us back on course, and we were soon on our way down the back side of the glacier and back onto "Boulder Road."

Before I could begin celebrating, however, I was startled to hear our "guide" explain that Thom wanted to close the course after six and a half hours, just as he had stated in his remarks of that morning. Knowing full well that it was now impossible to meet his time requirements (I'd just squandered an entire hour being "lost," after all), I told him in no uncertain terms that this wasn't going to happen. I think my exact words were, "You pulled the f_ _ _ing markers! There's no way I'm going to stop!"

And on I went. Now that we were heading in the right direction, I felt the best I'd felt during the entire run. The end was in sight! I think my adrenaline kicked in at this point. I was running well by now, but regrettably, I can't say the same for Mr. X. The poor guy was hurting, and hurting bad. He was suffering from a severe case of blisters (he'd tried in vain to ease the discomfort with the application of moleskin to his feet at the halfway point), and he was also dragging with exhaustion. I felt some empathy for him . . . and since my chance at being the outright winner of this race had long since passed, I wasn't concerned about time. When Mr. X couldn't run any longer and wanted to walk for a bit, I joined him and we walked together in the spirit of true comrades. And why not? I knew how hard he had trained, just like the rest of us, and I wanted him to be able to finish what he had started. The poor guy was having difficulty not only on the slightest upward incline, but even on level ground and when going downhill.

Interesting, huh? In the end, instead of "eating" my companion, I slowed down and tried to *help* him.

Bleary with fatigue, we lurched forward. And since we were the last two runners out on the course, we were being followed by our "guide" all the way. At one point I overheard him radioing Thom back at the Uruguayan base that we were making progress, but that it was "very slow." Thom was obviously feeling nervous as the long day waned, and he told the driver to tell us to "get moving or I'll take them off the course." He had no idea, of course, that I was doing my best to encourage Mr. X, or that my speed was in fact being dictated by how Mr. X was feeling at any particular moment. When he ran, I ran. When he walked, I walked.

At one point about a mile or so from China Station, Mr. X looked at me and asked: "What do you say to the idea of our turning around here?" Our "guide" had temporarily left us and it would have been very easy to accept his suggestion that we sidestep the steepest hill on the course. But I gave him an incredulous look and turned him down flat. No cheating allowed! When I saw the look of rage cross his face, I knew he wasn't a "happy camper."

After what felt like an eternity, we approached the hill to the Chinese Station. Mr. X tried again, this time suggesting that we hitch a ride on the ATV to the top. I looked at him like he'd just dropped in from the moon. But he was serious. Responding, I managed to convince him that we could make it if he could walk up the hill, which he eventually accomplished. Only four and half miles to go!

As we turned around and began the run down from China Station, I saw that Mr. X wasn't even able to run downhill. He was totally spent, so I kept up a continuous stream of chatter in an effort to take his mind off his fatigue. And I was about two or three paces ahead of him when I suddenly discovered that I was talking to myself! Looking back, I saw him sitting on a rock with his head between his legs. He couldn't move another inch.

Before I could tend to Mr. X, however, my ATV "friend" approached me with the news that the course was about to be closed. I'm not known for having an abundance of patience, so in no uncertain terms I yelled at him: "You cannot do this to me. You caused my delay and I am only trying to help him finish!" His reply was, "Don't argue with me. Just get going. Thom wants everyone off the course before dark."

My last vision of Mr. X was of his being carted away in a semi-prone position by the Meat Wagon, en route to emergency nourishment and restorative fluids.

As tired as I was, I ran like I'd never run before – since I was deathly afraid of being pulled off the course and equally afraid of taking a wrong turn. Three miles to go. Two miles to go. One foot in front of the other in my patented "survival shuffle." Then the sign, "2K to Artigas." Home! Another few steps and victory would be mine!

As I approached what had been a puddle just below the start/finish line on my first go-round, I realized that I was facing a veritable lake. All of the previous runners had softened up what little mud or dirt existed there, and the rocks were now completely submerged. But I could see Diane just above and waving to me. What a wonderful sight! Was I going to try and tiptoe my way through this frigid lagoon? Hell, no! Gritting my teeth, I plowed straight ahead, through water up to my shins, moving as quickly as I could and up the hill to the finish line.

Finis!

My time was 7:37:38, well over the original 6.5-hour time limit Thom had imposed. But as I later learned, he had extended his limit to eight hours to accommodate me. That gesture was certainly appreciated, and it wonderfully illustrates why he's the preeminent marathon tour operator in the United States. Of the 105 original starters in the race, 84 finished and only four of those broke the four-hour mark. Fully 39 percent didn't manage to finish within six hours.

The bottom line was that I hadn't done too badly – especially considering the fact that I'd been lost for the better part of an hour and had also used up a lot of time in helping Mr. X. Describing the hugs and kisses and tears that flooded from both Diane and me can't begin to describe the joy, the awe, and the sense of gratitude we both felt for what we had just accomplished.

Please note, Dear Reader, that in that last sentence I used the pronoun "we" and not "I." The Seven Continent Marathon had been a team effort put together by Diane, my children, and my grandchildren. Not for nothing had I worn the photos of my two grandchildren at the time, Dylan and Mariah, pinned to my singlet!

Finishing those difficult runs – and especially the run in frozen Antarctica – would have been totally impossible without their unwavering support and love.

After disengaging from our embrace, I looked around and wasn't surprised to find the area deserted. Everyone had long ago returned to our ship to begin the celebration. But a lone cameraman remained, and now he asked if he could interview me for the video documentary he was making on the marathon. (I said "yes," of course, but I felt a bit like the last guy drafted into the National Football League. Nobody remembers the next-to-last guy . . . but if you happen to be the final player taken, look out!)

As the interview was being conducted, I heard a round of applause coming from the crest of the hill and, lo and behold, there appeared Mr. X, running full-tilt to the finish line. Diane told me that the look on my face was one of sheer and utter amazement. As he crossed the line, he approached me and said, "Well, it looks like I came in last." Knowing that he'd cheated (he might as well have taken the "Antarctic Subway," like some southern version of the unscrupulous Rosie Ruiz), I was really upset with him. But I managed to keep my feelings in check, and I held my tongue.

I didn't understand exactly what had just happened – but I *did* know for certain that I had run 26.2 miles and I had finished in last place.

In an effort to find out what had just transpired, I approached the Meat Wagon driver and asked for an explanation. "Damnedest thing," he replied. "We got him to the nearest aid station, filled him with fluids and tried to warm him up. Then we loaded him onto the vehicle for the ride back here. As we approached the pond below he yelled to us that he wanted to get out so we stopped and let him off. He tried to get through the water but was unable to do so, so we drove in and loaded him back on the ATV. Then, when we got to the bottom of the hill, he again wanted off so he could run up the hill to the finish. So we let him off."

The more I thought about this unbelievable turn of events, the more aggravated I became. I stewed on it overnight, and then the first thing the next morning, I knocked on Thom Gilligan's door and asked for a private conversation. He was as perplexed as I, and he asked me for my thoughts. "What do you think I should do? He paid his money and says he finished the race. Does it make a difference?" he asked.

I thought for a minute. I knew that Mr. X had worked hard to be able to compete, and I certainly didn't wish him ill. He was a nice guy and I liked and cared for him. However, riding and running are two different animals, and nowhere in the "marathon handbook" is it mentioned that hitching a ride for any portion of a race is permissible.

I felt very sorry for Thom and the position he'd been put into, so I offered him this suggestion: "Since I was really the last 'official' finisher, why don't we just swap places and he can take my time and I'll take his? That way he can have his name among the finishers and the integrity of the race won't be compromised. The race is not an Olympic Qualifier, so who really cares?" Thom was trying to play Solomon and satisfy everyone concerned, and so he was happy to accept my compromise.

But the incident wasn't over yet. Some of our fellow passengers later found out (not from me, of course) about what had happened out there on the course, and they were understandably upset. I didn't learn this until I received a personal letter from Mr. X a month later. In it he wrote, and I quote from his letter verbatim: "I know and you know that I encountered severe problems at the Chilean [my recollection is that it was at the *Chinese* station – but this doesn't affect the meaning of the letter] on the second loop and sought assistance which included medical aid (glucose and water) and about a 2km ride in a vehicle to the outskirts of the Artigas base. After crossing the finish line (and Ken, you finished ahead of me), I asked Dave (one of the tour assistants) if the vehicle assist would have any affect on my status as a marathon 'finisher.' He said, no, and I received a Finisher's Certificate like the other marathoners.

"I chose not to mention the 'irregular finish' to the other folks on the ship, but evidently the word got out. Initially, I was shown on the Finisher's Sheet as 'last place,' but later it was changed to 'second to the last,' and you were put in the last spot because you, indeed, **finished** [the boldface type was his] the race last. I have no problem with that and I commend you for this distinction. When people asked me how I did, I said I 'finished last.' Since no one ever said anything to me to the contrary, I never felt that it was necessary or significant to make a full or technically correct explanation. Unfortunately, it bothered George and he told me (twice) after returning home that it bothered a lot of other folks, too. So, I must ask, how do you feel about this 'issue?' Personally, I am trying to enjoy the 'high' of having gone to the Antarctic, having participated in its first marathon, and having had a lot of fun and great memories to boot.

"As you will recall, there were times during the second loop when I considered 'going back' but you pushed and encouraged me and I am forever grateful that you did. We stayed together most of the way and the enclosed pictures document this incredible feat. Thank you so much for your support. If you have some comments on this subject, please feel free to let me know; if not, I will consider the subject as a 'non-issue.'"

Mr. X later explained to me in a personal conversation that he had "finished" the race, but that he had not "completed" it. I guess if you care to deal in semantics, then he's technically correct. But the bottom line here is that I *do* know who came in last. I also know that his letter to me fully justified my staying with him – since it was clearly "the right thing to do." And looking back at the entire sequence of events, I now agree with him that it's a "non-issue." Case closed. I finished last. There were no "official" finishers behind me. Period.

Diane hopped (I wasn't hopping, however; I *hobbled*) onto the last Zodiac back to the ship, and I had great difficulty making my way up the gangplank. With the exception of Cairo, this race made me the sorest of all. My left leg was hurting as much as it had hurt during my earlier case of plantar fasciitis – but I assumed that the pain I felt was simply a case of "marathon fatigue" and would prove to be temporary.

After three transoceanic calls to our children and a long hot shower, I visited the lady doctor on board for my pre-scheduled massage. I was so late in returning that she assumed I'd forgotten. This was to be the first massage I had ever received while totally naked – but at that point I didn't care if it was televised on NBC for worldwide distribution!

After the rubdown, I was too spent to get back onto another Zodiac for the evening celebration at the Uruguayan Station . . . but I'm told that they put on a great Mardi Gras party at the helicopter pad. Another party missed – but that bed sure felt good!

As the ship made its way north to Ushuaia through the Drake Passage and past Cape Horn, we were blessed with calm seas. Since ships are forbidden to approach within a few miles of the Cape, the captain radioed that he required a "bearing check" for his instruments. When this measure is requested, safety regulations assure that it cannot be denied. Thanks to this clever strategy, he was able to steer us quite close to land and thus provide us with a beautiful view of the Cape.

On our second day out I was summoned to the deck, along with three other runners, for an interview that would be part of the ongoing documentary. While I was the only one of the four who'd made it his explicit goal to run a marathon on all seven continents, the other three had also accomplished the feat. But I felt no disappointment whatsoever in sharing my accomplishment with this group – one of whom, Wally Herman, had already run 432 marathons in 69 different countries and all 50 states. He was ranked second in the world for total marathons and I was proud to be in his company.

Wally is a very quiet guy who walked with a cane but runs like a 25-year-old. (As I mentioned earlier, however, I suspect that the cane was merely a prop.) Wally was laconic in the extreme, and getting even a couple of words out of him was an accomplishment. During the interview, he appeared to be chewing on something that I assumed was gum. When the interviewer asked, "Wally, how cold was it out there?" he looked the questioner straight in the eye, then reached in his mouth to remove whatever he'd been chewing. It turned out to be a tiny rubber o-ring. Wally held it up for the camera, then piped: "How cold was it? It was so cold that my penis could have fit through this tiny o-ring without touching the sides! That's how cold it was."

Coming from a guy as taciturn as Wally, the shock value was enormous, and I nearly fell over laughing. Needless to say, that exquisite comment didn't make the final cut for the documentary.

Thom, ever the businessman, has in recent years created an "industry" for runners wishing to run on all seven continents. He calls this very interesting enterprise "Seven Continent Fever." There are now more than 200 runners who've met the challenge and you can find them listed as a group at the marathontours.com website. I feel very proud of the small part I played in helping to create this organization – and I only wish I'd copyrighted the name myself!

As the ship steamed north toward civilization, I limped around on my sore foot while Diane and I availed ourselves of the ship's gift shop and Thom's own offerings. He had monogrammed various articles of clothing, and we bought them all: 26 tee shirts, a polypro top, eight sweaters, two jackets, two pullovers, five hats and two fanny packs. We also snapped up several items that carried the ship's monogram.

Soon it was land-ho and time to bid goodbye to our fellow passengers. Some chose to remain in Argentina for another tour, but Diane and I flew directly from Ushuaia to Buenos Aires and then to our condo in Boynton Beach, Florida.

Some moderate running is always good after a marathon, but I was in no shape to run even for five minutes. The left foot still throbbed constantly, and I was soon knocking again on the door of Orthopedic Associates in Portland, in search of yet another consult. Bill Heinz, the foot specialist, took a long hard look and came up with the following diagnosis: "Ken comes in for evaluation of new problems. He states that in early February he ran a marathon in Antarctica. He did not run for approximately one month afterwards because of problems with bronchitis [Did I mention that? Oh well, just one more aggravation!] and soreness.

"One week ago he attempted to run and had pain in his left anterior distal one-third tibia. He states it hurt him at the start of the run and got progressively worse as he tried to run through it. He is also complaining of some swelling in his distal leg [What the hell leg is *that*?] He denies any numbness or tingling and has already had a series of physical therapy sessions. . . ."

Bill ordered a series of x-rays which showed no abnormalities, but he knew me well enough after his previous experience with me to know that my pain threshold was high. Clearly, there was something wrong. In order to detect the problem, he ordered a bone scan and asked me to avoid any impact activities until we could reach a finding. Two days later he called with the results, as follows:

"I called Ken with the report of his bone scan. I reviewed the films and feel that the tibia uptake does represent a stress fracture. The other hot spots revealed in the scan are probably related to degenerative changes [this was the first time I'd ever been called a "degenerate!"]. I suggest that Ken go into a short-leg bivalve walking cast because of his limping and pain with walking. He understands that he is to wear this cast for most of the time and remove it only for bathing." (At least I was an "experienced walking cast wearer," after my Cairo struggles with my lame foot – and that was quite an accomplishment, don't you think?) One month later I revisited Dr. Heinz and he allowed me to remove the cast but warned me to avoid running for another six weeks. I could, however, play golf, bike and swim. I enjoyed myself as best I could with those three pastimes, and in June I was finally cleared to resume my running.

By now I had returned to my primary job of selling corrugated boxes, and I'm happy to say that I experienced very little letdown, if any, after my quest had been completed.

After all the injuries I'd endured, I felt that it would be wise to put my marathon running to bed and merely enjoy a little ten-miler now and then. Diane agreed enthusiastically. She'd just about had it with my endless running and my endless visits to doctors. Our children joined her in this, and on the day when I finally announced that I was done, they all proclaimed together: "He's done! He's done running! At long last!"

I was mighty happy, as well. *Now all I have to do,* I told myself, *is pray that they never find the Lost Continent of Atlantis!*

Yes, my running days were over forever – or so it seemed.

And then one day early in 1996, Thom Gilligan called with an offer he said I couldn't refuse . . . an offer to participate in one last "running hurrah" by signing on as a participant in the Boston Marathon's upcoming 100th Anniversary. As Thom kindly pointed out, I had no chance of qualifying for the event, based on my previous marathon times. Yet he also felt that because of my having run the Seven Continents, I surely deserved one of the "official entry" numbers he'd been given to hand out to runners, as the director of the official travel agency for the race. That gesture was very nice of him, and also very much appreciated.

One more run? One more chance at long-distance fame and glory?

Thom knew me very, very well. How could I tell this man no?

"Honey," I was soon yelling in the direction of the longsuffering Diane, "do you happen to know where I put my running shoes?"

Boston Marathon

THE EIGHTH CONTINENT
APRIL 16, 1996

After returning to civilization from Antarctica, I had no intention of running another marathon, and there were several reasons for this. The training was too grueling, for one thing, and I knew that the event was taking too much of a toll on my body. I certainly didn't need any more broken legs or plantar fasciitis in my life! And what about the huge amounts of *time* required for conditioning and preparation? No . . . I had vowed that Diane and the kids would "get their Dad back," and I could tell they were very pleased as a result.

Let's be honest: At this point, after so much struggle and exhaustion out there on the marathon trail, my heart simply wasn't in it anymore.

Convinced that my running days were over, I didn't pay much attention when my marathon buddies started talking about competing in Boston's upcoming 100th-anniversary event . . . or when they started filling out applications that would allow them to participate in the lottery for official entry-numbers. Of course, the demand for these precious numbers was huge . . . and most of the plodders in Portland (some of them were almost as slow as I was!)

had little hope of making the field, if they didn't get really lucky during the lottery. Making the crowded field in Boston was so difficult, in fact, that some of them were even talking about completing the advance training and then running from the back of the pack as "bandits" without official entry status. (The "bandits" are individuals who have no formal standing in the race and whose time is never recorded.)

In my view, however, such obsessive dedication to making the Boston Marathon seemed a bit silly. Try as I might, I'd never been able to understand why anyone would be willing to put in all that effort – merely in order to run behind 36,748 other runners, and without any hope of receiving a certificate or other verification. Why not just pick a nice day and run the route on your own?

Oh, well. As always, I kept my thoughts to myself. Let my pals bust a gut if they wanted; I had no interest in putting myself through a torturous training regimen for nothing. Instead, I enjoyed a leisurely run now and then – while they kept up a brutal training regimen in preparation for the big day. My goal at this point was simply to get some mild exercise occasionally, and I felt no guilt at all about "taking the day off" from running whenever I felt like it.

And then Thom Gilligan called. As the Official Travel Agency of the Boston Marathon, Thom's organization had been provided with entry numbers to dole out to clients. And he was nice enough to think of me – even though he pretty much knew that my marathon days were in the past. Still, as we talked, I felt a flicker of interest somewhere deep inside. This wasn't just *any* marathon, I reminded myself; this was the *Boston* Marathon. This was the signature event, the granddaddy of them all . . . and I had to admit that the world-famous run from Hopkinton to Boston had a certain appeal. In addition, running in Boston would bring me back to my happy childhood days of watching the race with my Mom and Dad on Patriots Day.

It was a tempting prospect, to say the least. But Boston was hardly the only place where you could exhaust yourself in a 26-mile endurance test. There are marathons taking place all over the world, from one week to the next, and some of them are highly regarded indeed. Take the New York City Marathon, for instance. Was there any doubt that the Big Apple event held a certain magnetic charm – a distinctively unique cachet – among long-distance runners all across America? The originator of the NYC run, the late Fred Lebow, had established it as an international gem . . . by helping to design a marathon route that meandered through every borough of New York City.

The popularity of the New York race was also enhanced by the major-league prize money that was handed out each year to elite runners from all over the world. Quite understandably, New Yorkers tend to think of their event as the "ultimate marathon." (But then, New Yorkers think of *everything* that takes place in their city as "the ultimate.") If you're from New England, however, and you grew up watching runners struggle from Hopkinton to the heart of Boston's downtown for no prize money at all – but just for the sheer love of running and competing – how can you help but favor the Massachusetts event over the NYC version?

The more I thought about that one word – *Boston, Boston* – the more I felt its magical power, its hypnotic grip on so many of us who love the challenge of long-distance running.

Remember, also, that Thom Gilligan had just made me the kind of "offer you can't refuse" – the offer of a guaranteed entry number in the event, so that if I did decide to take part, it would be as an official, on-the-record competitor.

In the end, my resistance crumbled like a child's sand castle in the face of the incoming tide.

And so it was with some trepidation that I returned home on the evening of Thom's call. Gathering my nerve, I took a deep breath – and then broke the news to Diane that she was about to endure another three months of pure hell, starting in January of

1996. Amazed and a bit alarmed at first, she quickly reverted to her usual form . . . and I wasn't at all surprised when she offered her total and unequivocal support. That was nothing new, really; whether she was agreeing to uproot herself and our infant son in order to move with me to Maine in 1968 . . . or quickly joining me in some harebrained scheme that at first glance seemed doomed to failure . . . Diane's loyalty and love and support never wavered.

With this wonderful woman at my side, I knew I could handle another 26-mile blaster – regardless of my advancing years and my increasingly brittle bones!

Once we'd agreed that I would make the attempt, we jumped on the phone to Judd and Debbie and Allison and Drew and asked them to make plane reservations that would allow them to attend the race in Boston. (Our middle son, Derek, and his wife, Amy, lived in Maine – so they wouldn't need an airplane ride in order to join us.)

All three of them wished me well . . . and then asked me the same question they'd been asking me with increasing urgency in recent years: "Dad, are you sure you're in your *right mind*?"

It was time to begin the struggle again.

Early in January – in the very teeth of another icy Maine winter – I began training in earnest. Perhaps "earnest" isn't the correct word, however, because I now felt that the pressure was off. For one thing, I was no longer involved in raising money for MCCP. I'd kept my word when I promised that my pre-Antarctic solicitation would be the last time I ever called anyone for donations. And now, with my fundraising complete, it didn't really matter whether I finished the marathon or not. I wasn't worried about anything, really, and that was a new, exhilarating feeling. This time, I wasn't going to sweat the weather, the dangers of dehydration, or the risk of injury. If I could simply run this race without breaking anything, I'd consider it a huge success. Yes, my attitude was healthy, and my spirits were soaring: "Jimmy crack corn and I don't care!"

My new outlook was relaxed and easygoing – but Diane knew me too well, and she wasn't convinced. She listened to me talking about my "laid back" approach for a while . . . and then just shook her head. "You aren't going to worry about *finishing*?" she asked. "Oh, yeah, sure! Ken, once you commit yourself to something, that's it – and if you've committed to running the Boston Marathon, there's no *way* you're not going to finish that race!"

I had plenty of company during the training, since a number of friends had been lucky in the lottery. Of course, I had to pretend that I, too, had drawn a "lucky entry number" . . . since Thom had asked me not to reveal the fact that he'd provided me with an entry permit, based on my successful Seven Continents odyssey. I was happy to oblige, of course, since I knew it would have created a problem for him if other clients learned of his generosity to me. (After so many years, however, I'm sure he won't mind if I thank him for his kindness now!)

Looking back, I'm pleased to report that my training was mostly uneventful. My weight had remained at just over 200 pounds, so as a by-now-savvy marathoner, I knew I couldn't expect an impressive time, but I didn't really care. Enjoying myself was my primary goal, and having my entire family with me along the route was a prime motivation. Our three children had been with me at my first marathon and now the family had been increased by two wives, a future son-in-law and two grandchildren. The three months passed quickly, and this time I actually took pleasure in a lot of the training. (Actually, I was sort of hoping that the excellent physical conditioning of my running partners would rub off on me as if by osmosis!)

Diane and I had booked a room at the Four Seasons Hotel, located on the Boston Common and in close proximity to the bus departure points for Hopkinton and the start of the race at noon on Patriots Day. The family was to arrive from Maine early in the morning via a van I had rented for the day. Since public transportation along the route was notoriously inadequate, I asked one of the

Volk Packaging salesmen who lived in the Boston area (and who was familiar with the route and the side streets) to be their driver. That way they wouldn't have to worry about parking, and he could simply drop them off at various points along the way, based upon my estimated times of arrival.

I usually run at a steady pace, which made it easy to work out a plan that would allow them to intercept me every five miles or so.

I awoke early the morning of the race, in order to be on the first bus leaving Boston. Getting up early was no problem, and for good reason: No matter how much I told myself that I really didn't care, my nerves were jangling and the pre-marathon butterflies were doing loop-the-loops through my midsection. So I quietly left Diane sleeping, around 5:00 a.m., and walked across the Common to board that first bus. And it was a good thing I *did* get there early – since some of the buses later broke down on the way out of Boston, and to this day I don't know if those unlucky passengers made it on time for the start of the race.

Once in Hopkinton, a pretty little town south of Boston, I and my fellow passengers were deposited in a field behind the high school. We were also instructed not to leave the area. The race organizers wanted everyone together in one spot, which turned out to be a frozen football field. I'd had the foresight to bring along some reading material and an old towel to sit on, but as the light frost melted and the mobs of runners moved restlessly back and forth, the field became a morass of sticky mud. Fortunately I found a plastic soda container on which to sit, and I was soon the envy of my neighbors. But after about two hours of sitting and waiting, I grew restive and decided to violate the "rule" and head to downtown Hopkinton.

No cars were allowed in the general area, but I soon came upon a bus that was just starting up and asked if I could hitch a ride into town. Luckily, the driver was a nice guy and I was soon strolling around in beautiful downtown Hopkinton, where at 10 a.m. I was scheduled to do a television interview with Mike Lynch, the principal sportscaster on WCVB, Channel 5, the CBS TV affiliate in Boston. My brother Roger had called to alert him that I'd be running and had told him about my Seven Continent adventure. Since Mike was from our hometown, Swampscott, and his dad had been my high school basketball coach, he was happy to conduct the interview.

Just before the appointed time, I signaled him that I'd arrived and was soon outfitted with earphones and given a microphone for what was supposed to be a two-minute interview. It hardly seemed worth the effort . . . but at least I was out of the mud on that football field! I still had about two hours to kill before the start of the race, so I located a small coffee shop for a bite to eat and the use of a bathroom before heading back to join the massive crowd of racers.

Seeding for the race was based on two factors, the first and most important of which was the number you'd been given, based on the personal running time history listed on your application. The second factor was the number of the bus on which you'd ridden out to the starting point. In my case, I wound up being seeded far back, due to my past running times. But I also wound up in the front row of my section, based on the colored band I'd been given as a passenger on bus number one.

At precisely noon, a gun went off somewhere (I was so far back I never heard it), and the race began. Each official runner had been provided with a magnetic chip to be attached to his or her shoe. The chip accomplished two things: First, it prevented another "Rosie Ruiz incident," since the device registered each time it passed a prearranged (but randomly chosen) point on the route; and second, it recorded exactly when the runner crossed the starting line. With 25,000-30,000 runners participating, it took me almost 30 minutes to reach that point. Thanks to the chip, however, each runner's time could be calculated with pinpoint accuracy, since the device knew how to subtract the minutes that had been spent moving toward the starting line.

The Boston Marathon is a very pretty run. The first mile presents the participants with the steepest hill on the course, as it dips about 130 feet. It's also interesting to note that whereas most people instantly think of "Heartbreak Hill" when somebody mentions the Marathon, the actual course of the entire endurance run is *downhill.* The route begins 410 feet above sea level and drops to about ten feet at the finish. But this promising statistic does *not* mean that the Boston run is a "piece of cake." Make no mistake: 26.2 miles is still a major grind.

Still, you can't deny that the layout is quite pleasing to the eye. Mile by mile, the route wends its way through the rural bedroom towns of Boston, with their stately New England homes and their beautiful front porches nicely punctuating the bucolic landscape. During the first five miles, I stopped and started frequently – but not because I was tired. At the Boston Marathon, remember, the huge number of runners causes frequent traffic jams, since the country roads simply can't accommodate all those pounding feet. After a few miles, however, the field began to stretch out, and I was soon able to establish my own pace and feel comfortable in my stride.

It wasn't long before I arrived in Framingham and my first visit with the family. They'd been awaiting my arrival with some anticipation . . . and as they later explained, their thoughts were ranging from "Will we miss him as he goes by?" to "Is he okay, or has the course begun to take its toll?" They needn't have fretted, though, because I was easy to spot – since I was doing the unique "Penguin Stride" I'd mastered in the wilds of Antarctica.

As you can easily imagine, the sudden vision of Diane and our offspring happily waving their hand-made signs lit me up like Fenway Park for a night game . . . and I became even more animated when I stopped briefly to chat with them and heard them expressing a powerful interest in becoming marathoners themselves!

Most Boston Marathon runners will tell you that the halfway point of the race is a highlight: the runner can now begin the countdown to the finish. More importantly, though, this landmark is also the home of Wellesley College. Wellesley is a fabulous institution of higher learning . . . and the student body consists entirely of nubile young ladies with smiles powerful enough to knock down a pro heavyweight. On Marathon Day, hundreds of these youthful beauties interrupt their studies and gather along the route to cheer the runners on. The result is the fabled "scream tunnel" – a wonderfully perfumed assemblage of high-spirited young girls who wave and leap about furiously – and any male runner who doesn't get a 10,000-watt battery charge out of their antics is a runner who needs a check of his testosterone!

At the "Scream Tunnel"
Wellesley, Massachusetts

Is there any joy like it? But a word to the wise: Before you reach the Scream Tunnel at Wellesley, you must pass through a troublesome subdivision known as Wellesley Hills. Please note: There's a reason why they call it that . . . instead of something like "Wellesley Flats" or "Wellesley Plains." This section of rolling hills was the first of its kind that I'd faced, and it left me begging for oxygen on every gasp. But the torture was soon ended, and as I entered downtown Wellesley I was buoyed by the screaming ladies and quickly forgot about the hills I'd just left behind.

In addition, two of my Portland friends and fellow runners – Bill Davenny and Sandy Utterstrom – had driven down to cheer me on. Greeting them was a total upper, and it boosted my spirits nicely for the approaching and inevitable struggle known as "Heartbreak Hill."

This legendary rise is an aptly named, two-mile series of hills that make their appearance at the worst possible place – right at the 19-mile mark, where most runners must begin to confront that ugly frontier zone of exhaustion and paralysis known as "The Wall." And it was here, as I staggered through a miasma of numbing fatigue, that my wise children began to change their minds about someday running marathons. Please understand: When they had greeted me at Mile 5, I'd seemed cheerful and energetic; but now, as I fought my way up Heartbreak Hill (they told me this later), I seemed to have stepped directly out of that 1968 film classic, *Night of the Living Dead*.

Stricken, they looked at me in horror, and I could imagine what was going through their minds: *Maybe I need to rethink that marathon plan for awhile, before I fully commit to it?*

I could hardly blame them, of course. At this point, I was dragging myself desperately through my patented "survival shuffle," and I'm sure they were asking each other if they should call for an ambulance. And I should also note for the record, right here, that not one of them ever *did* run a marathon, after greeting me on Heartbreak Hill! (I'd like to take credit for their intelligence in this matter, of course, but it's obvious that *those* genes had to have come from their mom.)

Somehow, I kept on moving. But the Hill was clearly taking its fearsome toll, and this fact became evident whenever I stopped running in order to use one of the "Port-a-Potties" scattered along the route, or to gab for a bit with Diane and the kids. The problem was that once I stopped, I had great difficulty convincing my legs to move again without severe pain in my iliotibial bands (the flat ligaments that descend from the side of the hip to the knee). Of course, I knew the cure for this problem was rest . . . a fact which greatly comforted me and also allowed me to continue the run – since I knew a great deal of "rest" would be available to me in the days ahead.

Diane and the family were waiting for me as I topped the last of the "Heartbreak" hills in Newton, and they were certainly a welcome sight. I later learned that there was actually a loud band of Japanese kettle drummers stationed at this point – but I wasn't aware of seeing or hearing them until much later, when I got a look at a videotape of the race. (Nobody believed me, after the marathon, when I explained that I'd been so preoccupied with my struggle to finish that I never even *heard* the din of those pounding drums!)

On we went to Coolidge Corner, the location of Boston College, and also the beginning of the Commonwealth Avenue stretch that runs to the finish line. As I passed through Kenmore Square, I couldn't help but think back on my childhood, when the happiest and most exciting day of the year was always Marathon Day. For a moment, it all came back to me, as my sneakers rose and fell on the pavement . . . those long-ago days with my beloved Mother and Father, days when we cheered for the Red Sox at Fenway and then hurried down to Kenmore Square to watch the runners cross the finish line at the annual Boston Marathon.

For a moment, I lived it all again: my vanished youth, and the love I had felt (and still feel!) for my wonderful family, and the joyful thrill of listening to the roaring crowd as the runners one by one crossed the magic line and entered the pages of history.

Yes, I had come full circle in my life, and now it was time to sit back and enjoy *our* accomplishment – since without the love and encouragement of Diane and the kids, none of this would have been even remotely possible.

Finis. The longest runs of my life were over now, and it was time to sit back and smell the roses.

I finished in 5:21:40 and in 34,085th place (ahead of 1,663 other runners) but who cares about that? I had achieved my final "L.T!"

I've always felt that I'm one of the luckiest guys in the world, and I'm very grateful for that. Thank you for reading this memoir. I hope you enjoyed it!

Thanksgiving 2004 in Maine
Back row: Dylan, Diane, Ken, Mariah, Serena
Front row: Lily, Emily, Zachary, Max, Amanda, Brian, Ethan

Epilogue - 2010

Writing this book has been a great adventure, and I'm very happy that I finally managed to get it done.

But it sure wasn't easy! As a matter of fact, the process took me more than 14 years. Some background: The germ of the idea that led to *Don't Look Back* was actually born in the mid-1990s, not long after I staggered to the finish line in my final 26-miler, at Boston in 1996. But until quite recently, I lacked the urgency – and the discipline – to sit down and put the words on paper.

Fortunately, however, I had decided (who knows why?) back about ten years ago that I should sit down and prepare an outline that would describe the key events in each of the marathons I had completed at various points around the globe. Once that chore was accomplished, I left the chapter outlines sitting on my computer for more than a decade.

Once in a great while, I'd take a quick look at them and tell myself: "Yes, this summer (or maybe winter? Next spring?) will surely be the time to write the memoir!"

The actual "time" never came, of course. That is, it didn't come until I was diagnosed with melanoma – in May 2010 – and quickly returned from Florida to Maine to be operated on at the famed Dana Farber Cancer Institute in Boston.

To be honest, the diagnosis hit me like a bolt from the blue. I had visited my dermatologist about a week prior to her shocking phone call . . . and in the course of her routine examination I had casually mentioned that I'd noticed what appeared to me to be a small, black-colored blood blister on my chest. When she asked me about it, I told her that to the best of my recollection, it had only been visible for about a month. Right after examining it, and without hesitation, she announced: "We have to biopsy that!"

Then I showed her something on my right shin – and got the same response. In the end, she performed three excisions for biopsies and I left her office feeling carefree and totally unconcerned.

But I soon received the phone call that would change my life.

On the Friday before Diane and I were to leave Florida for a three-week jaunt back to Maine – with golf games scheduled in Indiana, Kentucky, Illinois and New York (okay, I realize that driving from Florida to Maine via Indiana isn't exactly the most direct route, but you gotta go where the *golf* courses are, right?) – I got some very disturbing news on my cell.

The caller was my faithful dermatologist, Dr. Shauna Kranendonk, and she had placed the call herself. As soon as I heard her voice, my antennae went up . . . since I knew she would have asked one of her *staffers* to deliver the news about the biopsy, if that news had been good.

I gripped the phone hard and waited. "The biopsy on your upper lip was nothing," she said calmly. These words were followed by a brief silence. Then: "And the biopsy on your shin showed that it was squamous cell cancer [the second-most lethal form of the disease]. I'd like you to come over to the office so I can freeze it."

More silence. Fearing what was to come, I uttered one word: "And?"

"The biopsy on your chest is melanoma."

My first instinctive response was to blurt at the lady-like physician: "Shit!"

Then, recovering a bit, I asked what my next step was and she told me that I needed to see a surgeon as soon as possible. She also said she was pretty certain that it had been caught in time and that its thickness (the key test in determining the likelihood that skin cancer has spread to the lymph nodes) was only .65 centimeters.

I nodded. A 1.0 reading would signal the danger point, she explained, while also ensuring that the surgery would be more invasive and debilitating. If the nodes were involved, I would be forced to undergo radiation and chemotherapy, all the while knowing that although these two treatments could steer me into a remission, the prognosis would be highly uncertain. Once the lymph nodes are involved, the specialist pointed out, tiny cancer cells that had not been destroyed might very well end up floating around in my bloodstream, where they could trigger a new attack at any time.

I hung up and sat down. Then I clenched my jaw. If this meant a fight, then so be it. The following Monday morning, Diane and I were in an oncology surgeon's office for an examination and to schedule my surgery. But when the oncology surgeon couldn't coordinate his schedule with that of a plastic surgeon he wanted to include, he told me that we'd have to wait at least two weeks to operate.

Extremely distraught, Diane and I returned to our Florida home and placed a call to my brother. Roger Volk is a terrific tax accountant, and representing physicians is a major part of his practice. He doesn't do audits, and he doesn't do normal accounting – he just does *taxes*. (As a matter of fact, the two of us had been in the income tax business together in the 1960s . . . before I sold out to him so that I could move to Maine and help my father launch Volk Packaging Corporation.)

Luckily for me, having Roger as a brother is like having one's own "Concierge Doctor" as a member of the family. Roger knows doctors everywhere and has never failed to secure appointments on short notice for anyone in difficulty. And I was certainly "in difficulty." In addition, my fine brother has a heart of gold and loves to help anyone in need.

After hearing me complain that I couldn't be operated on for at least two weeks, Roger's response was typical: "That's ridiculous! I'll call you right back." Within ten minutes, he was back on the line – and recommending that I call a friend named Kim at the Dana Farber Cancer Center at eight o'clock the following morning. Kim would be happy to schedule an appointment for me, said Roger, and she would make sure that it took place *pronto*.

Thank you, Roger! Promptly at eight the next morning, I was speaking with the very efficient Kim. And two hours later, Diane and I had already packed our car and were on our way directly to Maine to meet with a surgeon at Dana Farber. (Goodbye, three-week golf trip.) We made it home in two days, and all the while my stomach was tied up in knots. I didn't know much about melanoma, except for one key fact: people often *died* from it. It's not that I was afraid of dying, mind you. What I feared was not seeing my grandchildren grow up and become young adults. That was something I didn't want to miss.

The following week – after my initial appointments with my new oncology surgeon, Dr. Anna Russell, and my new oncology dermatologist, Dr. Andrew Worshniak – I presented myself at the surgical center at Brigham and Women's Hospital in Boston, ardently hoping to rid myself of this miserable affliction. To my great relief, the surgery went quickly and very well – and the pathology report confirmed Dr. Kranendonk's and Dr. Russell's evaluations.

I was "cancer free," with no further treatments indicated. All that remained was a four-inch scar below my right nipple: a small price to pay for a wonderful outcome.

As you may have guessed by now, I kicked off this Epilogue with a story about surviving cancer for a very logical reason: That scary diagnosis is what gave me the impetus to write this memoir and not procrastinate any longer. Since that attention-getting phone call, I've come to realize that life is not only very short, but also very precious. If I wanted to have my grandchildren and then *their* offspring ever know what I'd accomplished as a super-slow runner and a passionate fundraiser for sick children, I knew that I would have to get off my *tuchas* (that's Yiddish for *hindquarters*) and start writing. So this tome is for them – and for anyone else with the stick-to-it-iveness to read my entire opus!

A lot has transpired in the 14 years since I slogged through the 100th Boston Marathon in 1996, and all of it is good. First and foremost, as mentioned in previous chapters, I should note that early on I ran my marathons with a photo of my first grandchild, Dylan Volk, on my singlet. Then his sister, Mariah, was born in 1994 – so I then had two grandchildren who could provide inspiration and momentum on my runs.

Today our three children are all happily married and settled in their lives and have provided Diane and me with untold happiness. Judd, our oldest, married Debbie Fishman, whom he met while both were students at the University of Pennsylvania, and they now have three children: Ethan, Brian and Amanda. They live in Great Neck, New York. Judd is in the mortgage business and Debbie runs her company, More Than Paper, out of their home. (She does most of her business over the Internet.) Our second child, Derek, married his high school sweetheart, Amy Murchison, after their freshman year at the University of Georgia and they now have four children: Dylan, Mariah, Lilly and Serena. (Derek and my brother Douglas currently own and operate the company I started with my

Dad, Volk Packaging Corporation.)

Up until 2010, Derek's wife Amy was pretty much a stay at home mom (with four children, that's a full-time job), but in 2010 she ran for and won a seat in the Maine House of Representatives. Her victory took place in the Scarborough, Maine district, and she defeated an incumbent Democrat in the process. Meanwhile, our "baby" – the delightful Allison – graduated from the University of Pennsylvania and then settled in the Washington, D.C. area, where she met and fell in love with Drew Isaacman. They currently live in San Diego with their three children – Emily (who was born on my birthday), Max and Zachary. Drew owns a business which refinishes teak furniture and decks in southern California and Allison is involved very heavily in community projects with the kids' school . . . in addition to having completed a 60-mile walk over three days during each of the past two years, in order to benefit breast cancer awareness.

Having 10 grandchildren is simply wonderful. We have enough for a five-on-five basketball game and also enough to field a baseball team with a Designated Hitter (in the event we should find ourselves playing in the American League!). If we play National League-style (with no DH), then we have a *substitute* in case anybody pulls a hamstring. Their current ages range from six to 19, and the last three were born within six months of each other. Diane and I get a great deal of joy out of seeing them interact with each other. It's like having three chipmunks in the house!

I have been "officially retired" from Volk Packaging for the past three years and I'm loving retirement more every day. The company has had its ups and downs, like most other companies during these troubled times, but it's now on very solid footing and doing well under the aegis of Douglas and Derek. 9/11 was a disaster for U.S. industry nation-wide, and Volk was no exception. For a while there, I must admit that we were on "life-support" . . . but with lots of hard work and dedication from everyone involved in the company, we survived the most traumatic event in United States' history.

These days I act as a Volk Packaging "Goodwill Ambassador" when I return home each summer, and I make personal visits to customers that Derek and his sales force target for me. I love being back out on the road and I always look forward to my calls. It's wonderful having no direct responsibility and when customers sometimes say to me, "I have an order for you," my response is always: "Don't give me an order, I'll just screw it up! I'll have someone call you." And then it's off to the next account. What a life!

Diane and I continue to meet with our SPOOC friends on an annual basis. Only one of the couples still skis, however, so we're free to stay at appealing resorts that don't feature snow. We usually get together somewhere out west, since that means easier travel for most of the crew. And we like the fact that traveling to California means we can *also* visit Allison, Drew, Emily, Max and Zachary. These annual reunions are lots of fun . . . but time marches on, and we've been saddened in recent years to have lost three of our male members: Bobby Kohlmann (the founder of the group), Jim Nelson from Wisconsin and Jerry Hardison from Dallas. We miss them and think of them often, even as we contemplate our own mortality.

When each of our three children graduated college, I'd wanted to take them on a "one-on-one" jaunt to celebrate. But their love-lives – and my marathon journeys – got in the way and I wasn't able to make it happen. No harm done, however: Instead of the one-on-ones, Diane and I took each of the three (along with their spouses) to destinations of their choice. With Judd and Debbie, we enjoyed a golf trip to Scotland and were able to play each of the courses on the British Open Rota. In hindsight, that wasn't really fair to Debbie, since she didn't play golf – but she was a good sport and walked the courses with us as we played. Nor did she utter a single complaint. I'm sure she would have enjoyed hanging out in some other exotic locale . . . but she was a real "trooper," as they say.

Our trip with Derek and Amy was also a blast. Since Amy had

never been to Europe, we traveled to the French countryside and eventually wound up in Paris for the French Open Tennis Tournament. We began our visit by flying into Brussels . . . and our first day overseas found us dining on Belgian waffles for breakfast. Lunch took place in England (we boarded the Eurostar train under the English Channel on a whim) and consisted of traditional fish n' chips. By dinnertime, though, we were back in France – and settling down to a typically Gallic repast of roast duckling drenched in half a dozen savory sauces. Three meals...three countries.

Allison and Drew, meanwhile, opted for a more adventurous trip, so we flew to Costa Rica for a week of rafting, hiking and zip-lining. (Diane flunked this last exercise, however, and nearly wiped out our two guides, who were required to stand atop platforms and catch her before she crashed head-on into nearby trees!)

In the year 2000 Diane and I moved from our home in Boynton Beach to a golf community, Ibis, in West Palm Beach, Florida. This is a younger, more up-scale community with three different Jack Nicklaus Golf Courses and some terrific players with whom I enjoy hitting the links. Had I not purchased a membership when I did, I think we'd still be in Boynton Beach, since 9/11 was so disruptive to my company. Let's face it: I probably wouldn't have had the guts to take on a new house. But the whole thing has worked out wonderfully, and we love being in the Palm Beach area. Each year at Thanksgiving the entire family migrates to Florida and we celebrate that wonderful time together. The adults stay in a local hotel and we eagerly welcome any and all of the grandchildren who want to stay with us.

Also in the year 2000 I became a Panelist for Golf Digest, the leading golf publication in the country. A Panelist's job is to visit top courses throughout the nation and the world, and to rate them for possible inclusion in the prestigious list of "Top 100" golf courses in the United States. It's a non-paying position, but then again, almost any Panelist would pay *them* for the privilege of doing these ratings. Diane and I often make it a point to plan our trips around visits to world-class golf courses. To get the job done, all I have to do is call the club and identify myself as a Golf Digest Panelist – and then I'm usually welcomed with open arms. In most cases, they also allow Diane to accompany me . . . so it's a fabulous opportunity to play the greatest courses in the country, both public and private, with Diane at my side. And this adventure has certainly has shown us how the "other half" lives. Thanks to my Panelist position, I have now played more than 500 different courses in my lifetime.

After Dylan was born in 1991, I reconstructed my "golf life" and secured bag tags from each of the courses I had played to that point. My intention was to give him these tags as a remembrance of where his grandfather had played golf. I thought I'd collect them for the first-born offspring of each of our children – but now I'm going to need *six* tags per course, since three of the younger kids have also requested them. (All I ask is that they keep one set per family together as complete.) To tell you the truth, however, at this age they couldn't care less about them – and the tags sit forlornly in their boxes, without anyone having the faintest idea of what to do with them. And each time I bring in the next round of fresh tags, they humor me and roll their eyes, and I can easily tell what they're thinking: "What in the world are we ever going to do with Papa?"

In recent years, I've been a participant in a father/son golf tournament held annually at the Winchester Country Club in Winchester, Massachusetts. My Dad and I began playing in this tournament together in 1950, and I now play with both Judd and Derek – along with any of the male grandchildren who might be on hand (and not away at camp or elsewhere). What a thrill it is to tee it up with a grandson! Judd's son, Ethan, and I even won "Low Gross" in our division in 2008. And Judd once holed out a four wood from 224 yards on their par-three 11th: a hole-in-one! Lately I've been dreaming of playing seven rounds (with Judd, Derek and the five grandsons) in the three days – a feat that would set a record for the tournament . . . but with summer camp and other activities also on the schedule, the most I've been able to play is five rounds. Still, that's not too bad for a septuagenarian!

For my 70th birthday, Diane presented me with an unusual gift: a ten-day excursion spent chasing tornados in the Midwest. I've always been fascinated by this magnificent force of nature, so I headed to Oklahoma City to meet with 16 other inveterate cyclone-chasers at the height of the tornado season in May. We then spent 10 days chasing the mighty storms. Of course there's no guarantee that you'll ever actually *spot* a tornado . . . but I got lucky and caught sight of a real beauty as it hit land and headed right toward us. When our tour leader shouted, "Everyone in the car; we're in extreme danger!" we hot-footed it out of harm's way with not much room to spare. As I checked "Tornado Chasing" off my Bucket List, I was suddenly reminded of the bungee-jumping I'd done in Australia – and it was good to know that I was still having fun by acting like a total maniac!

In 2008 we finally cut the cord and sold our home in Portland (after 39 years). Then we moved into a condominium in Cumberland Foreside, Maine. I fought like the devil against the idea of buying another "residence" – I wanted to rent – but Diane persisted and I must admit now that she was correct. We've enjoyed "condo living" more than I ever thought we would. We also continue to maintain our Lake House on Sebago Lake in Raymond, Maine. These days we can go from condo to lake in less than an hour, and we use the waterfront home every summer. Our children and grandchildren all have wonderful memories of days spent at the lake . . . but no one enjoys the setting more than Diane and I, as we watch the grandkids learn to water ski, swim and hit golf balls into the lake from my improvised driving platform. It's a truly special place for us all.

Another enjoyable tradition is celebrating birthdays and anniversaries with our extended family – a real treasure. In 2010 we even hosted a 100th birthday party for my father. The fact that he'd been gone for 14 years was immaterial. Almost all of the Ben and Charlotte Volk extended family members were there, with the exception of a few who were away at camp or had other commitments. We also plan on celebrating my mother's 100th in 2013. She'll surely be there with us in spirit!

The years since I ran the global marathons have been very good to Diane and me. But no one can escape the shadows cast by mortality, and it was painful for both of us to lose our parents. My Dad passed away in 1996, after fighting a courageous battle with esophageal cancer. My mother, Charlotte, followed in 2005. I like to imagine that she died "because she wanted to" . . . since her quality of life wasn't very good before her passing. Indeed, she had told me more than once that she planned on "going to be with Ben" after the birth of her granddaughter's (Melissa's) baby. And she kept her word: She was gone only six weeks later. Yes, the will to live (or die) is very powerful.

Diane's Dad, Max, passed away peacefully as the result of a heart condition, in 2000. He was a very special guy who always had a smile for everyone and *didn't* have a mean bone in his entire body. His departure was followed by the death of Diane's mother, Natalie, in 2007, also from a heart ailment. It was a painful time for both Diane and me, and we had to face up to a sobering fact: As the oldest members of our respective families, we are now the "Old Guard."

Having visited all seven continents of the world, where do we go now? What could ever top the Antarctic? In the ensuing years, Diane and I have taken trips to Costa Rica, the Dominican Republic, the Galapagos Islands, Russia, and numerous European countries. All of these latter journeys have included stops in Paris to see Diane's French family and enjoy yet another steak dinner at L'Entrecote. In addition, Diane made a commitment to each of our grandchildren that we would take them to Europe when they reached the age of 15. Sounded like a good plan at the time, right? That is, until Allison brought us back to Earth by announcing: "You know, Mom, you're not getting any younger and by waiting until the kids are 15, you may not be around!" So now the age has been lowered to 11-13 and we take them two at a time. As it stands right now, we're two trips down (Dylan/Mariah and Lilly/Emily), with three to go.

Thus far, each trip has been to London and Paris, with our second trip adding a stop at the French Riviera. I know the grandchildren have a great time on these adventures . . . but I also suspect that Diane and I have an even better time!

As an aside to the previous paragraph, I should mention that one evening Diane and I were out to dinner with Serena, who was six at the time. She was busily coloring on her placemat when Diane casually said: "You know, Serena, we just took your sister to Europe and in five years we'll take you, too."

Serena never looked up from her coloring as she calmly responded: "Oh, no! You'll be dead by then!" Hey, you just gotta love those kids!

So here I am, nearing the age of 73, and I can tell you this much: life is good! I have been blessed with a spectacular wife who's been with me for 47 years, along with three children and their spouses and 10 grandchildren. All are healthy, so for what more could I ever ask? I've beaten cancer, and everything that has ever happened to me has turned out for the best.

I thank you, dear reader, for taking the time to look through this memoir.

I hope I've given you a few laughs and that you came away with the thought that when you truly believe the glass is half-full, anything is possible!

Au revoir!

– **Ken Volk**, Portland, Maine
2010

Thanksgiving in Florida 2010
Back row: Drew, Allison, Dylan, Ethan, Ken, Diane, Judd, Debbie, Mariah, Amy, Derek
Front row: Emily, Zachary, Max, Amanda, Serena, Lilly, Brian

Acknowledgements

First and foremost, I would like to thank my wife of 47 years, Diane, for her loving support. Diane was my "editor before the editor," as she read and made many suggestions for this memoir. She has been my rock during all these years and has provided me with love and support in every endeavor of our life together. In addition to being a sound foundation to our family, she has been the perfect wife and mother. I love her dearly.

And to my children, Judd, Derek and Allison and their respective spouses, whom Diane and I consider and love as our own, Debbie, Amy and Drew: thank you for your constant support and encouragement, and also for giving us the new loves of our lives, our ten grandchildren – Dylan, Mariah, Ethan, Lilly, Emily, Brian, Max, Serena, Amanda and Zachary. In addition to supplying us with a baseball team (including even a "designated hitter!"), you've given us enough grandchildren for a five-on-five basketball game! Nothing brings Diane and me greater pleasure than spending time with them.

To my running buddies: Thank you, because I couldn't have completed my quest without your help. I hereby salute my "short-run" team of Bob Delaney, Tracey Mezzanotte and Bob Rodman – along with my "long-run" team of Bill Davenny, Al Mack and the late Kim Konieczny, who passed away tragically at the age of 33.

Guys, I thank you from the bottom of my heart. You never left me alone on those cold, early morning runs! And to Thom Gilligan, the owner of Marathon Tours, who made the Antarctic marathon doable: many thanks. I can't believe how naïve I was to think I could just travel to the Antarctic, get off the boat, and then run 26.2 miles by my lonesome! Thom put together a great trip and I was happy to give him the germ of the idea to create the Seven Continents Fever Club for marathon runners.

To my brother and business partner, Douglas, and to my son and business partner, Derek, I thank you for never begrudging me the time off from work that I took to achieve the Seven Continent run. This adventure required a lot of time away from the office (and even when I was at work, I wasn't always terribly productive, due to fatigue) . . . but never did I feel that you resented my time away. Thank you.

To my late parents, Ben and Charlotte Volk, I just wish you were here to enjoy my book. I miss you to this day. Thank you for being such wonderful parents and role models.

To my editor, Tom Nugent, who pared down more than a few of my more long-winded phrases in order to help make this memoir more readable, my sincere thanks. You have been so easy to work with, and you quickly realized just what it was that I wanted to impart to the reader . . . and what I wanted to leave behind for my children, grandchildren and future generations as a permanent memory of Ken and Diane Volk.

To the Maine Childrens Cancer Program: I am so happy to see that your organization is thriving and prospering and continuing to provide for Maine children afflicted with this horrible disease. I like to think I've had some small part in your success.

And finally, to repeat what I've said more than once in this book: I consider myself the luckiest guy on earth. Thank you, dear reader, for taking the time to read my memoir!